PENGUIN BOOKS

THE WRETCHED OF THE EARTH

Born in 1925 in Martinique, Frantz Fanon studied medicine in France and later specialized in psychiatry. When he was twenty-seven he published his first book. He was assigned to a hospital in Algeria during the rising against the French. His experiences and observations there led him to throw in his lot with the 'rebels' and he became one of their most articulate spokesmen. This and another book, *L'An V de la Révolution Algérienne*, were written at that time.

Fanon did not live to see peace restored to an autonomous Algeria. In 1961 it was discovered that he was suffering from leukaemia; commitments to work forbade him leaving until it was too late to cure him. He was taken to Washington in late 1961 and died there in December of that year at the age of thirty-six. After his death a compilation of his theoretical writing was gathered together in a volume entitled *The Revolutionary Thought of Frantz Fanon*, and *Black Skins, White Masks* was published in England in 1967.

Frantz Fanon

THE WRETCHED OF
THE EARTH

PREFACE BY

JEAN-PAUL SARTRE

TRANSLATED BY

CONSTANCE FARRINGTON

PENGUIN BOOKS

Penguin Books Ltd, Harmondsworth, Middlesex, England
Penguin Books Australia Ltd, Ringwood, Victoria, Australia
Penguin Books (N.Z.) Ltd, 182–190 Wairau Road, Auckland 10, New Zealand

—

Les damnés de la terre first published in France
by François Maspéro éditeur 1961
First published in Great Britain by
Macgibbon & Kee 1965
Published in Penguin Books 1967
Reprinted 1969, 1970, 1972, 1973, 1974, 1976

—

Copyright © *Présence Africaine*, 1963

—

Made and printed in Great Britain
by Richard Clay (The Chaucer Press), Ltd,
Bungay, Suffolk
Set in Monotype Plantin

Contents

Preface

NOT so very long ago, the earth numbered two thousand million inhabitants: five hundred million men, and one thousand five hundred million natives. The former had the Word; the others had the use of it. Between the two there were hired kinglets, overlords and a bourgeoisie, sham from beginning to end, which served as go-betweens. In the colonies the truth stood naked, but the citizens of the mother country preferred it with clothes on: the native had to love them, something in the way mothers are loved. The European *élite* undertook to manufacture a native *élite*. They picked out promising adolescents; they branded them, as with a red-hot iron, with the principles of western culture; they stuffed their mouths full with high-sounding phrases, grand glutinous words that stuck to the teeth. After a short stay in the mother country they were sent home, whitewashed. These walking lies had nothing left to say to their brothers; they only echoed. From Paris, from London, from Amsterdam we would utter the words 'Parthenon! Brotherhood!' and somewhere in Africa or Asia lips would open '. . . thenon! . . . therhood!' It was the golden age.

It came to an end; the mouths opened by themselves; the yellow and black voices still spoke of our humanism but only to reproach us with our inhumanity. We listened without displeasure to these polite statements of resentment, at first with proud amazement. What? They are able to talk by themselves? Just look at what we have made of them! We did not doubt but that they would accept our ideals, since they accused us of not being faithful to them. Then, indeed, Europe could believe in her mission; she had hellenized the Asians; she had created a new breed, the Graeco-Latin Negroes. We might add, quite between ourselves, as men of the world: 'After all, let them bawl their heads off, it relieves their feelings; dogs that bark don't bite.'

A new generation came on the scene, which changed the issue. With unbelievable patience, its writers and poets tried to explain to us that our values and the true facts of their lives did not hang together, and that they could neither reject them completely nor yet assimilate them. By and large, what they were saying was this: 'You are making us into monstrosities; your humanism claims we are at one with the rest of humanity but your racist methods set us apart.' Very much at our ease, we listened to them all; colonial administrators are not paid to read Hegel, and for that matter they do not read much of him, but they do not need a philosopher to tell them that uneasy consciences are caught up in their own contradictions. They will not get anywhere; so, let us perpetuate their discomfort; nothing will come of it but talk. If they were, the experts told us, asking for anything at all precise in their wailing, it would be integration. Of course, there is no question of granting that; the system, which depends on over-exploitation, as you know, would be ruined. But it's enough to hold the carrot in front of their noses, they'll gallop all right. As to a revolt, we need not worry at all; what native in his senses would go off to massacre the fair sons of Europe simply to become European as they are? In short, we encouraged these disconsolate spirits and thought it not a bad idea for once to award the Prix Goncourt to a Negro. That was before '39.

1961. Listen: 'Let us waste no time in sterile litanies and nauseating mimicry. Leave this Europe where they are never done talking of Man, yet murder men everywhere they find them, at the corner of every one of their own streets, in all the corners of the globe. For centuries they have stifled almost the whole of humanity in the name of a so-called spiritual experience.' The tone is new. Who dares to speak thus? It is an African, a man from the Third World, an ex-'native'. He adds: 'Europe now lives at such a mad, reckless pace that she is running headlong into the abyss; we would do well to keep away from it.' In other words, she's done for. A truth which is not pleasant to state but of which we are all convinced, are we not, fellow-Europeans, in the marrow of our bones?

We must however make one reservation. When a Frenchman, for example, says to other Frenchmen 'The country is done for' – which has happened, I should think, almost every day since 1930 – it is emotional talk; burning with love and fury, the speaker includes himself with his fellow-countrymen. And then, usually, he adds 'Unless . . .' His meaning is clear; no more mistakes must be made; if his instructions are not carried out to the letter, then and only then will the country go to pieces. In short, it is a threat followed by a piece of advice and these remarks are so much the less shocking in that they spring from a national intersubjectivity. But on the contrary when Fanon says of Europe that she is rushing to her doom, far from sounding the alarm he is merely setting out a diagnosis. This doctor neither claims that she is a hopeless case – miracles have been known to exist – nor does he give her the means to cure herself. He certifies that she is dying, on external evidence, founded on symptoms that he can observe. As to curing her, no; he has other things to think about; he does not give a damn whether she lives or dies. Because of this, his book is scandalous. And if you murmur, jokingly embarrassed, 'He has it in for us!' the true nature of the scandal escapes you; for Fanon has nothing in for you at all; his work – red-hot for some – in what concerns you is as cold as ice; he speaks of you often, never to you. The black Goncourts and the yellow Nobels are finished; the days of colonized laureats are over. An ex-native, French-speaking, bends that language to new requirements, makes use of it, and speaks to the colonized only: 'Natives of all under-developed countries, unite!' What a downfall! For the fathers, we alone were the speakers; the sons no longer even consider us as valid intermediaries: we are the objects of their speeches. Of course, Fanon mentions in passing our well-known crimes: Sétif, Hanoï, Madagascar: but he does not waste his time in condemning them; he uses them. If he demonstrates the tactics of colonialism, the complex play of relations which unite and oppose the colonists to the people of the mother country, it is for his brothers; his aim is to teach them to beat us at our own game.

In short, the Third World finds *itself* and speaks to *itself* through his voice. We know that it is not a homogeneous world; we know too that enslaved peoples are still to be found there, together with some who have achieved a simulacrum of phoney independence, others who are still fighting to attain sovereignty and others again who have obtained complete freedom but who live under the constant menace of imperialist aggression. These

differences are born of colonial history, in other words of
oppression. Here, the mother country is satisfied to keep some
feudal rulers in her pay; there, dividing and ruling she has
created a native bourgeoisie, sham from beginning to end;
elsewhere she has played a double game: the colony is planted
with settlers and exploited at the same time. Thus Europe has
multiplied divisions and opposing groups, has fashioned classes
and sometimes even racial prejudices, and has endeavoured by
every means to bring about and intensify the stratification of
colonized societies. Fanon hides nothing: in order to fight
against us the former colony must fight against itself: or, rather,
the two struggles form part of a whole. In the heat of battle, all
internal barriers break down; the puppet bourgeoisie of
businessmen and shopkeepers, the urban proletariat, which is
always in a privileged position, the *lumpen-proletariat* of the
shanty towns – all fall into line with the stand made by the rural
masses, that veritable reservoir of a national revolutionary
army; for in those countries where colonialism has deliberately
held up development, the peasantry, when it rises, quickly stands
out as the revolutionary class. For it knows naked oppression,
and suffers far more from it than the workers in the towns, and
in order not to die of hunger, it demands no less than a complete
demolishing of all existing structures. In order to triumph, the
national revolution must be socialist; if its career is cut short,
if the native bourgeoisie takes over power, the new State, in
spite of its formal sovereignty, remains in the hands of the
imperialists. The example of Katanga illustrates this quite well.
Thus the unity of the Third World is not yet achieved. It is a
work in progress, which begins by the union, in each country,
after independence as before, of the whole of the colonized
people under the command of the peasant class. This is what
Fanon explains to his brothers in Africa, Asia and Latin
America: we must achieve revolutionary socialism all together
everywhere, or else one by one we will be defeated by our former
masters. He hides nothing, neither weaknesses, nor discords,
nor mystification. Here, the movement gets off to a bad start;
there, after a striking initial success it loses momentum; elsewhere it has come to a standstill, and if it is to start again, the
peasants must throw their bourgeoisie overboard. The reader is

sternly put on his guard against the most dangerous will o' the wisps: the cult of the leader and of personalities, Western culture, and what is equally to be feared, the withdrawal into the twilight of past African culture. For the only true culture is that of the Revolution; that is to say, it is constantly in the making. Fanon speaks out loud; we Europeans can hear him, as the fact that you hold this book in your hand proves; is he not then afraid that the colonial powers may take advantage of his sincerity?

No; he fears nothing. Our methods are out-of-date; they can sometimes delay emancipation, but not stop it. And do not think that we can change our ways; neo-colonialism, that idle dream of mother countries, is a lot of hot air; the 'Third Forces' don't exist, or if they do they are only the tin-pot bourgeoisies that colonialism has already placed in the saddle. Our Machiavellian-ism has little purchase on this wide-awake world that has run our falsehoods to earth one after the other. The settler has only recourse to one thing: brute force, when he can command it; the native has only one choice, between servitude or supremacy. What does Fanon care whether you read his work or not? It is to his brothers that he denounces our old tricks, and he is sure we have no more up our sleeves. It is to them he says: 'Europe has laid her hands on our continents, and we must slash at her fingers till she lets go. It's a good moment; nothing can happen at Bizerta, at Elizabethville or in the Algerian *bled* * that the whole world does not hear about. The rival blocks take opposite sides, and hold each other in check; let us take advantage of this paralysis, let us burst into history, forcing it by our invasion into universality for the first time. Let us start fighting; and if we've no other arms, the waiting knife's enough.'

Europeans, you must open this book and enter into it. After a few steps in the darkness you will see strangers gathered around a fire; come close, and listen, for they are talking of the destiny they will mete out to your trading-centres and to the hired soldiers who defend them. They will see you, perhaps, but they will go on talking among themselves, without even lowering their voices. This indifference strikes home: their fathers, shadowy creatures, *your* creatures, were but dead souls; you it

* Up-country in North Africa (*translator*).

was who allowed them glimpses of light, to you only did they dare speak, and you did not bother to reply to such zombies. Their sons ignore you; a fire warms them and sheds light around them, and you have not lit it. Now, at a respectful distance, it is you who will feel furtive, nightbound and perished with cold. Turn and turn about; in these shadows from whence a new dawn will break, it is you who are the zombies.

In this case, you will say, let's throw away this book. Why read it if it is not written for us? For two reasons; the first is that Fanon explains you to his brothers and shows them the mechanism by which we are estranged from ourselves; take advantage of this, and get to know yourselves seen in the light of truth, objectively. Our victims know us by their scars and by their chains, and it is this that makes their evidence irrefutable. It is enough that they show us what we have made of them for us to realize what we have made of ourselves. But is it any use? Yes, for Europe is at death's door. But, you will say, we live in the mother country, and we disapprove of her excesses. It is true, you are not settlers, but you are no better. For the pioneers belonged to you; you sent them overseas, and it was you they enriched. You warned them that if they shed too much blood you would disown them, or say you did, in something of the same way as any state maintains abroad a mob of agitators, *agents provocateurs* and spies whom it disowns when they are caught. You, who are so liberal and so humane, who have such an exaggerated adoration of culture that it verges on affectation, you pretend to forget that you own colonies and that in them men are massacred in your name. Fanon reveals to his comrades – above all to some of them who are rather too Westernized – the solidarity of the people of the mother country and of their representatives in the colonies. Have the courage to read this book, for in the first place it will make you ashamed, and shame, as Marx said, is a revolutionary sentiment. You see, I, too, am incapable of ridding myself of subjective illusions; I, too, say to you: 'All is lost, unless . . . ' As a European, I steal the enemy's book, and out of it I fashion a remedy for Europe. Make the most of it.

And here is the second reason: if you set aside Sorel's fascist utterances, you will find that Fanon is the first since Engels to bring the processes of history into the clear light of day. Moreover, you need not think that hot-headedness or an unhappy childhood have given him some uncommon taste for violence; he acts as the interpreter of the situation, that's all. But this is enough to enable him to constitute, step by step, the dialectic which liberal hypocrisy hides from you and which is as much responsible for our existence as for his.

During the last century, the middle classes looked on the workers as covetous creatures, made lawless by their greedy desires; but they took care to include these great brutes in our own species, or at least they considered that they were free men – that is to say, free to sell their labour. In France, as in England, humanism claimed to be universal.

In the case of forced labour, it is quite the contrary. There is no contract; moreover, there must be intimidation and thus oppression grows. Our soldiers overseas, rejecting the universalism of the mother country, apply the 'numerus clausus' to the human race: since none may enslave, rob or kill his fellowman without committing a crime, they lay down the principle that the native is not one of our fellow-men. Our striking-power has been given the mission of changing this abstract certainty into reality: the order is given to reduce the inhabitants of the annexed country to the level of superior monkeys in order to justify the settler's treatment of them as beasts of burden. Violence in the colonies does not only have for its aim the keeping of these enslaved men at arm's length; it seeks to dehumanize them. Everything will be done to wipe out their traditions, to substitute our language for theirs and to destroy their culture without giving them ours. Sheer physical fatigue will stupefy them. Starved and ill, if they have any spirit left, fear will finish the job; guns are levelled at the peasant; civilians come to take over his land and force him by dint of flogging to till the land for them. If he shows fight, the soldiers fire and he's a dead man; if he gives in, he degrades himself and he is no longer a man at all; shame and fear will split up his character and make his inmost self fall to pieces. The business is conducted with flying colours and by experts: the 'psychological services' weren't established yesterday; nor was brain-washing. And yet, in spite of all these efforts, their ends are nowhere achieved:

neither in the Congo, where Negroes' hands were cut off, nor in Angola, where until very recently malcontents' lips were pierced in order to shut them with padlocks. I do not say that it is impossible to change a man into an animal: I simply say that you won't get there without weakening him considerably. Blows will never suffice; you have to push the starvation further, and that's the trouble with slavery.

For when you domesticate a member of our own species, you reduce his output, and however little you may give him, a farmyard man finishes by costing more than he brings in. For this reason the settlers are obliged to stop the breaking-in half-way; the result, neither man nor animal, is the native. Beaten, under-nourished, ill, terrified – but only up to a certain point – he has, whether he's black, yellow or white, always the same traits of character: he's a sly-boots, a lazybones and a thief, who lives on nothing, and who understands only violence.

Poor settler; here is his contradiction naked, shorn of its trappings. He ought to kill those he plunders, as they say djinns do. Now, this is not possible, because he must exploit them as well. Because he can't carry massacre on to genocide, and slavery to animal-like degradation, he loses control, the machine goes into reverse, and a relentless logic leads him on to decolonization.

But it does not happen immediately. At first the European's reign continues. He has already lost the battle, but this is not obvious; he does not yet know that the natives are only half-native; to hear him talk, it would seem that he ill-treats them in order to destroy or to repress the evil that they have rooted in them; and after three generations their pernicious instincts will reappear no more. What instincts does he mean? The instincts that urge slaves on to massacre their master? Can he not here recognize his own cruelty turned against himself? In the savagery of these oppressed peasants, does he not find his own settler's savagery, which they have absorbed through every pore and for which there is no cure? The reason is simple; this imperious being, crazed by his absolute power and by the fear of losing it, no longer remembers clearly that he was once a man; he takes himself for a horsewhip or a gun; he has come to believe that the domestication of the 'inferior races' will come about by the conditioning of their reflexes. But in this he leaves out of account the human memory and the ineffaceable marks left upon it; and then, above all there is something which perhaps he has never known: we only become what we are by the radical and deep-seated refusal of that which others have made of us. Three generations did we say? Hardly has the second generation opened their eyes than from then on they've seen their fathers being flogged. In psychiatric terms, they are 'traumatized', for life. But these constantly renewed aggressions, far from bringing them to submission, thrust them into an unbearable contradiction which the European will pay for sooner or later. After that, when it is their turn to be broken in, when they are taught what shame and hunger and pain are, all that is stirred up in them is a volcanic fury whose force is equal to that of the pressure put upon them. You said they understand nothing but violence? Of course; first, the only violence is the settler's; but soon they will make it their own; that is to say, the same violence is thrown back upon us as when our reflection comes forward to meet us when we go towards a mirror.

Make no mistake about it; by this mad fury, by this bitterness and spleen, by their ever-present desire to kill us, by the permanent tensing of powerful muscles which are afraid to relax, they have become men: men *because of* the settler, who wants to make beasts of burden of them – because of him, and against him. Hatred, blind hatred which is as yet an abstraction, is their only wealth; the Master calls it forth because he seeks to reduce them to animals, but he fails to break it down because his interests stop him half-way. Thus the 'half-natives' are still humans, through the power and the weakness of the oppressor which is transformed within them into a stubborn refusal of the animal condition. We realize what follows; they're lazy: of course – it's a form of sabotage. They're sly and thieving; just imagine! But their petty thefts mark the beginning of a resistance which is still unorganized. That is not enough; there are those among them who assert themselves by throwing themselves barehanded against the guns; these are their heroes. Others make men of themselves by murdering Europeans, and these are shot down; brigands or martyrs, their agony exalts the terrified masses.

Yes, terrified; at this fresh stage, colonial aggression turns inward in a current of terror among the natives. By this I do not only mean the fear that they experience when faced with our inexhaustible means of repression but also that which their own fury produces in them. They are cornered between our guns pointed at them and those terrifying compulsions, those desires for murder which spring from the depth of their spirits and which they do not always recognize; for at first it is not *their* violence, it is ours, which turns back on itself and rends them; and the first action of these oppressed creatures is to bury deep down that hidden anger which their and our moralities condemn and which is however only the last refuge of their humanity. Read Fanon: you will learn how, in the period of their helplessness, their mad impulse to murder is the expression of the natives' collective unconscious.

If this suppressed fury fails to find an outlet, it turns in a vacuum and devastates the oppressed creatures themselves. In order to free themselves they even massacre each other. The different tribes fight between themselves since they cannot face the real enemy – and you can count on colonial policy to keep up their rivalries; the man who raises his knife against his brother thinks that he has destroyed once and for all the detested image of their common degradation, even though these expiatory victims don't quench their thirst for blood. They can only stop themselves from marching against the machine-guns by doing our work for us; of their own accord they will speed up the dehumanization that they reject. Under the amused eye of the settler, they will take the greatest precautions against their own kind by setting up supernatural barriers, at times reviving old and terrible myths, at others binding themselves by scrupulous rites. It is in this way that an obsessed person flees from his deepest needs – by binding himself to certain observances which require his attention at every turn. They dance; that keeps them busy; it relaxes their painfully contracted muscles; and then the dance mimes secretly, often without their knowing, the refusal they cannot utter and the murders they dare not commit. In certain districts they make use of that last resort – possession by spirits. Formerly this was a religious experience in all its simplicity, a certain communion of the faithful with sacred things; now they make of it a weapon against humiliation and despair; Mumbo-Jumbo and all the idols of the tribe come down among them, rule over their violence and waste it in trances until it is exhausted. At the same time these high-placed personages protect them; in other words the colonized people protect themselves against colonial estrangement by going one better in religious estrangement, with the unique result that finally they add the two estrangements together and each reinforces the other. Thus in certain psychoses the hallucinated person, tired of always being insulted by his demon, one fine day starts hearing the voice of an angel who pays him compliments; but the jeers don't stop for all that; only from then on, they alternate with congratulations. This is a defence, but it is also the end of the story; the self is disassociated, and the patient heads for madness. Let us add, for certain other carefully selected unfortunates, that other witchery of which I have already spoken: Western culture. If I were them, you may say, I'd prefer my mumbo-jumbo to their Acropolis. Very good: you've grasped the situation. But not altogether, because you *aren't* them – or not yet. Otherwise you would know that they can't choose; they must have both. Two worlds: that makes two bewitchings; they dance all night and at dawn they crowd into the churches to hear mass; each day the split widens. Our enemy betrays his brothers and becomes our accomplice; his brothers do the same thing. The status of 'native' is a nervous condition introduced and maintained by the settler among colonized people *with their consent*.

Laying claim to and denying the human condition at the same time: the contradiction is explosive. For that matter it does explode, you know as well as I do; and we are living at the moment when the match is put to the fuse. When the rising birthrate brings wider famine in its wake, when these newcomers have life to fear rather more than death, the torrent of violence sweeps away all barriers. In Algeria and Angola, Europeans are massacred at sight. It is the moment of the boomerang; it is the third phase of violence; it comes back on us, it strikes us, and we do not realize any more than we did the other times that it's we that have launched it. The 'liberals' are stupefied; they admit that we were not polite enough to the natives, that it would have been wiser and fairer to allow them certain rights in so far as this was possible; they ask nothing better than to admit them in batches and without sponsors to that very exclusive club, our species; and now this barbarous, mad outburst doesn't spare them any more than the bad settlers. The Left at home is embarrassed; they know the true situation of the natives, the merciless oppression they are submitted to; they do not condemn their revolt, knowing full well that we have done everything to provoke it. But, all the same, they think to themselves, there *are* limits; these guerrillas should be bent on showing that they are chivalrous; that would be the best way of showing they are men. Sometimes the Left scolds them ... 'You're going too far; we won't support you any more.' The natives don't give a damn about their support; for all the good it does them they might as well stuff it up their backsides. Once their war began, they saw this hard truth: that every single one of us has made his bit, has got something out of them; they don't need to call anyone to witness; they'll grant favoured treatment to no one.

There is one duty to be done, one end to achieve: to thrust out colonialism by *every* means in their power. The more far-seeing among us will be, in the last resort, ready to admit this duty and this end; but we cannot help seeing in this ordeal by force the altogether inhuman means that these less-than-men make use of to win the concession of a charter of humanity. Accord it to them at once, then, and let them endeavour by peaceful undertakings to deserve it. Our worthiest souls contain racial prejudice.

They would do well to read Fanon; for he shows clearly that this irrepressible violence is neither sound and fury, nor the resurrection of savage instincts, nor even the effect of resentment: it is man re-creating himself. I think we understood this truth at one time, but we have forgotten it – that no gentleness can efface the marks of violence; only violence itself can destroy them. The native cures himself of colonial neurosis by thrusting out the settler through force of arms. When his rage boils over, he rediscovers his lost innocence and he comes to know himself in that he himself creates his self. Far removed from his war, we consider it as a triumph of barbarism; but of its own volition it achieves, slowly but surely, the emancipation of the rebel, for bit by bit it destroys in him and around him the colonial gloom. Once begun, it is a war that gives no quarter. You may fear or be feared; that is to say, abandon yourself to the disassociations of a sham existence or conquer your birthright of unity. When the peasant takes a gun in his hands, the old myths grow dim and the prohibitions are one by one forgotten. The rebel's weapon is the proof of his humanity. For in the first days of the revolt you must kill: to shoot down a European is to kill two birds with one stone, to destroy an oppressor and the man he oppresses at the same time: there remain a dead man, and a free man; the survivor, for the first time, feels a *national* soil under his foot. At this moment the Nation does not shrink from him; wherever he goes, wherever he may be, she is; she follows, and is never lost to view, for she is one with his liberty. But, after the first surprise, the colonial army strikes; and then all must unite or be slaughtered. Tribal dissensions weaken and tend to disappear; in the first place because they endanger the Revolution, but for the more profound reason that they served no other purpose before than to divert violence against false foes. When they remain – as in the Congo – it's because they are kept up by the agents of colonialism. The Nation marches forward; for each of her children she is to be found wherever his brothers are fighting. Their feeling for each other is the reverse of the hatred they feel for you; they are brothers inasmuch as each of them has killed and may at any moment have to kill again. Fanon shows his readers the limits of 'spontaneity' and the need for and dangers of 'organization'. But however great may be the task at each turning of the way the revolutionary consciousness deepens. The last complexes flee away; no one need come to us talking of the 'dependency' complex of an A.L.N. soldier.*

With his blinkers off, the peasant takes account of his real needs; before they were enough to kill him, but he tried to ignore them; now he sees them as infinitely great requirements. In this violence which springs from the people, which enables them to hold out for five years – for eight years as the Algerians have done – the military, political and social necessities cannot be separated. The war, by merely setting the question of command and responsibility, institutes new structures which will become the first institutions of peace. Here, then, is man even now established in new traditions, the future children of a horrible present; here then we see him legitimized by a law which will

* National Army of Liberation in Algeria (*translator*).

be born or is born each day under fire: once the last settler is killed, shipped home or assimilated, the minority breed disappears, to be replaced by socialism. And that's not enough; the rebel does not stop there; for you can be quite sure that he is not risking his skin to find himself at the level of a former inhabitant of the old mother country. Look how patient he is! Perhaps he dreams of another Dien Bien Phu, but don't think he's really counting on it; he's a beggar fighting, in his poverty, against rich men powerfully armed. While he is waiting for decisive victories, or even without expecting them at all, he tires out his adversaries until they are sick of him.

It will not be without fearful losses; the colonial army becomes ferocious; the country is marked out, there are mopping-up operations, transfers of population, reprisal expeditions, and they massacre women and children. He knows this; this new man begins his life as a man at the end of it; he considers himself as a potential corpse. He will be killed; not only does he accept this risk, he's sure of it. This potential dead man has lost his wife and his children; he has seen so many dying men that he prefers victory to survival; others, not he, will have the fruits of victory; he is too weary of it all. But this weariness of the heart is the root of an unbelievable courage. We find our humanity on this side of death and despair; he finds it beyond torture and death. We have sown the wind; he is the whirlwind. The child of violence, at every moment he draws from it his humanity. We were men at his expense, he makes himself man at ours: a different man; of higher quality.

Here Fanon stops. He has shown the way forward: he is the spokesman of those who are fighting and he has called for union, that is to say the unity of the African continent against all dissensions and all particularisms. He has gained his end. If he had wished to describe in all its details the historical phenomenon of decolonization he would have to have spoken of us; this is not at all his intention. But, when we have closed the book, the argument continues within us, in spite of its author; for we feel the strength of the peoples in revolt and we answer by force. Thus there is a fresh moment of violence; and this time we ourselves are involved, for by its nature this violence is changing us, accordingly as the 'half-native' is changed. Everyone of us must think for himself – always provided that he thinks at all; for in Europe today, stunned as she is by the blows received by France, Belgium or England, even to allow your mind to be diverted, however slightly, is as good as being the accomplice in crime of colonialism. This book has not the slightest need of a preface, all the less because it is not addressed to us. Yet I have written one, in order to bring the argument to its conclusion; for we in Europe too are being decolonized: that is to say that the settler which is in every one of us is being savagely rooted out. Let us look at ourselves, if we can bear to, and see what is becoming of us. First, we must face that unexpected revelation, the strip-tease of our humanism. There you can see it, quite naked, and it's not a pretty sight. It was nothing but an ideology of lies, a perfect justification for pillage; its honeyed words, its affectation of sensibility were only alibis for our aggressions. A fine sight they are too, the believers in non-violence, saying that they are neither executioners nor victims. Very well then; if you're not victims when the government which you've voted for, when the army in which your younger brothers are serving without hesitation or remorse have undertaken race murder, you are, without a shadow of doubt, executioners. And if you chose to be victims and to risk being put in prison for a day or two, you are simply choosing to pull your irons out of the fire. But you will not be able to pull them out; they'll have to stay there till the end. Try to understand this at any rate: if violence began this very evening and if exploitation and oppression had never existed on the earth, perhaps the slogans of non-violence might end the quarrel. But if the whole regime, even your non-violent ideas, are conditioned by a thousand-year-old oppression, your passivity serves only to place you in the ranks of the oppressors.

You know well enough that we are exploiters. You know too that we have laid hands on first the gold and metals, then the petroleum of the 'new continents', and that we have brought them back to the old countries. This was not without excellent results, as witness our palaces, our cathedrals and our great industrial cities; and then when there was the threat of a slump, the colonial markets were there to soften the blow or to divert it. Crammed with riches, Europe accorded the human status *de jure* to its inhabitants. With us, to be a man is to be an accom-

plice of colonialism, since all of us without exception have pro-
fited by colonial exploitation. This fat, pale continent ends by
falling into what Fanon rightly calls narcissism. Cocteau became irritated with Paris – 'that city which talks about itself
the whole time'. Is Europe any different? And that super-
European monstrosity, North America? Chatter, chatter:
liberty, equality, fraternity, love, honour, patriotism and what
have you. All this did not prevent us from making anti-racial
speeches about dirty niggers, dirty Jews and dirty Arabs.
High-minded people, liberal or just soft-hearted, protest that
they were shocked by such inconsistency; but they were either
mistaken or dishonest, for with us there is nothing more consistent than a racist humanism since the European has only
been able to become a man through creating slaves and monsters.
While there was a native population somewhere this imposture
was not shown up; in the notion of the human race we found an
abstract assumption of universality which served as cover for
the most realistic practices. On the other side of the ocean there
was a race of less-than-humans who, thanks to us, might reach
our status a thousand years hence, perhaps; in short, we mistook
the *élite* for the genus. Today, the native populations reveal
their true nature, and at the same time our exclusive 'club'
reveals its weakness – that it's neither more nor less than a
minority. Worse than that: since the others become men in
name against us, it seems that we are the enemies of mankind;
the *élite* shows itself in its true colours – it is nothing more than
a gang. Our precious sets of values begin to moult; on closer
scrutiny you won't see one that isn't stained with blood. If you
are looking for an example, remember these fine words: 'How
generous France is!' Us, generous? What about Sétif, then?
And those eight years of ferocious war which have cost the lives
of over a million Algerians? And the tortures?

But let it be understood that nobody reproaches us with
having been false to such-and-such a mission – for the very good
reason that we had no mission at all. It is generosity itself that's
in question; this fine melodious word has only one meaning:
the granting of a statutory charter. For the folk across the water,
new men, freed men, no one has the power nor the right to give
anything to anybody; for each of them has every right, and the

right to everything. And when one day our human kind becomes full-grown, it will not define itself as the sum total of the whole world's inhabitants, but as the infinite unity of their mutual needs. Here I stop; you will have no trouble in finishing the job; all you have to do is to look our aristocratic virtues straight in the face, for the first and last time. They are cracking up; how could they survive the aristocracy of underlings who brought them into being? A few years ago, a bourgeois colonialist commentator found only this to say in defence of the West: 'We aren't angels. But we, at least, feel some remorse.' What a confession! Formerly our continent was buoyed up by other means: the Parthenon, Chartres, the Rights of Man or the swastika. Now we know what these are worth; and the only chance of our being saved from shipwreck is the very Christian sentiment of guilt. You can see it's the end; Europe is springing leaks everywhere. What then has happened? It simply is that in the past we made history and now it is being made of us. The ratio of forces has been inverted; decolonization has begun; all that our hired soldiers can do is to delay its completion.

The old 'mother countries' have still to go the whole hog; they still have to engage their entire forces in a battle which is lost before it has begun. At the end of the adventure we again find that colonial brutality which was Bugeaud's* doubtful glory; but though it has been multiplied ten-fold, it's still not enough. The national service units are sent to Algeria, and they remain there seven years with no result. Violence has changed its direction. When we were victorious we practised it without its seeming to alter us; it broke down the others, but for us men our humanism remained intact. United by their profits, the peoples of the mother countries baptized their commonwealth of crimes, calling them fraternity and love; today violence, blocked everywhere, comes back on us through our soldiers, comes inside and takes possession of us. Involution starts; the native re-creates himself, and we, settlers and Europeans, ultras and liberals, we break up. Rage and fear are already blatant; they show themselves openly in the nigger-hunts in Algiers. Now, which

* Thomas-Robert Bugeaud de la Piconnerie (1784–1849), Duke of Islay, Marshall of France. Famous for military exploits in the conquest of Algeria, he was appointed Governor of Algeria in 1840 (*translator*).

side are the savages on? Where is barbarism? Nothing is missing, not even the tom-toms; the motor-horns beat out '*Al-gér-ie fran-çaise*' while the Europeans burn Moslems alive. Fanon reminds us that not so very long ago, a congress of psychiatrists was distressed by the criminal propensities of the native population. 'Those people kill each other,' they said, 'that isn't normal. The Algerian's cortex must be under-developed.' In central Africa, others have established that 'the African makes very little use of his frontal lobes'. These learned men would do well today to follow up their investigations in Europe, and particularly with regard to the French. For we, too, during the last few years, must be victims of 'frontal sluggishness' since our patriots do quite a bit of assassinating of their fellow-countrymen and if they're not at home, they blow up their house and their *concierge*. This is only a beginning; civil war is forecast for the autumn, or for the spring of next year. Yet our lobes seem to be in perfect condition; is it not rather the case that, since we cannot crush the natives, violence comes back on its tracks, accumulates in the very depths of our nature and seeks a way out? The union of the Algerian people causes the disunion of the French people; throughout the whole territory of the ex-mother-country, the tribes are dancing their war-dances. The terror has left Africa, and is settling here; for quite obviously there are certain furious beings who want to make us pay with our own blood for the shame of having been beaten by the native. Then too, there are the others, all the others who are equally guilty (for after Bizerta, after the lynchings of September, who among them came out into the streets to shout 'We've had enough'?) but less spectacular – the liberals, and the toughs of the tender Left.

The fever is mounting amongst them too, and resentment at the same time. And they certainly have the wind up! They hide their rage in myths and complicated rites; in order to stave off the day of reckoning and the need for decision they have put at the head of our affairs a Grand Magician whose business it is to keep us all in the dark at all costs. Nothing is being done; violence, proclaimed by some, disowned by others, turns in a vacuum; one day it bursts out at Metz, the next at Bordeaux; it's here, there and everywhere, like in a game of hunt the slipper.

It's our turn to tread the path, step by step, which leads down to native level. But to become natives altogether, our soil must be occupied by a formerly colonized people and we must starve of hunger. This won't happen; for it's a discredited colonialism which is taking hold on us; this is the senile, arrogant master who will straddle us; here he comes, our mumbo-jumbo.

And when you have read Fanon's last chapter, you will be convinced that it would be better for you to be a native at the uttermost depths of his misery than to be a former settler. It is not right for a police official to be obliged to torture for ten hours a day; at that rate, his nerves will fall to bits, unless the torturers are forbidden in their own interests to work overtime. When it is desirable that the morality of the Nation and the Army should be protected by the rigours of the law, it is not right that the former should systematically demoralize the latter, nor that a country with a Republican tradition should confide hundreds and thousands of its young folk to the care of *putschist* officers. It is not right, my fellow-countrymen, you who know very well all the crimes committed in our name, it's not at all right that you do not breathe a word about them to anyone, not even to your own soul, for fear of having to stand in judgement on yourself. I am willing to believe that at the beginning you did not realize what was happening; later, you doubted whether such things could be true; but now you know, and still you hold your tongues. Eight years of silence; what degradation! And your silence is all of no avail; today, the blinding sun of torture is at its zenith; it lights up the whole country. Under that merciless glare, there is not a laugh that does not ring false, not a face that is not painted to hide fear or anger, not a single action that does not betray our disgust, and our complicity. It is enough today for two French people to meet together for there to be a dead man between them. One dead man did I say? In other days France was the name of a country. We should take care that in 1961 it does not become the name of a nervous disease.

Will we recover? Yes. For violence, like Achilles' lance, can heal the wounds that it has inflicted. Today, we are bound hand and foot, humiliated and sick with fear; we cannot fall lower. Happily this is not yet enough for the colonialist aristocracy; it cannot complete its delaying mission in Algeria until it has first finished colonizing the French. Every day we retreat in front of the battle, but you may be sure that we will not avoid it; the killers need it; they'll go for us and hit out blindly to left and right.

Thus the day of magicians and fetishes will end; you will have to fight, or rot in concentration camps. This is the end of the dialectic; you condemn this war but do not yet dare to declare yourselves to be on the side of the Algerian fighters; never fear, you can count on the settlers and the hired soldiers; they'll make you take the plunge. Then, perhaps, when your back is to the wall, you will let loose at last that new violence which is raised up in you by old, oft-repeated crimes. But, as they say, that's another story: the history of mankind. The time is drawing near, I am sure, when we will join the ranks of those who make it.

                                                        Jean-Paul Sartre

1. Concerning Violence

NATIONAL liberation, national renaissance, the restoration of nationhood to the people, commonwealth: whatever may be the headings used or the new formulas introduced, decolonization is always a violent phenomenon. At whatever level we study it – relationships between individuals, new names for sports clubs, the human admixture at cocktail parties, in the police, on the directing boards of national or private banks – decolonization is quite simply the replacing of a certain 'species' of men by another 'species' of men. Without any period of transition, there is a total, complete and absolute substitution. It is true that we could equally well stress the rise of a new nation, the setting up of a new state, its diplomatic relations, and its economic and political trends. But we have precisely chosen to speak of that kind of *tabula rasa* which characterizes at the outset all decolonization. Its unusual importance is that it constitutes, from the very first day, the minimum demands of the colonized. To tell the truth, the proof of success lies in a whole social structure being changed from the bottom up. The extraordinary importance of this change is that it is willed, called for, demanded. The need for this change exists in its crude state, impetuous and compelling, in the consciousness and in the lives of the men and women who are colonized. But the possibility of this change is equally experienced in the form of a terrifying future in the consciousness of another 'species' of men and women: the colonizers.

Decolonization, which sets out to change the order of the world, is, obviously, a programme of complete disorder. But it cannot come as a result of magical practices, nor of a natural shock, nor of a friendly understanding. Decolonization, as we know, is a historical process: that is to say that it cannot be understood, it cannot become intelligible nor clear to itself except in the exact measure that we can discern the movements which give it historical form and content. Decolonization is the meeting of two forces, opposed to each other by their very nature, which in fact owe their originality to that sort of substantification which results from and is nourished by the situation in the colonies. Their first encounter was marked by violence and their existence together – that is to say the exploitation of the native by the settler – was carried on by dint of a great array of bayonets and cannon. The settler and the native are old acquaintances. In fact, the settler is right when he speaks of knowing 'them' well. For it is the settler who has brought the native into existence and who perpetuates his existence. The settler owes the fact of his very existence, that is to say his property, to the colonial system.

Decolonization never takes place unnoticed, for it influences individuals and modifies them fundamentally. It transforms spectators crushed with their inessentiality into privileged actors, with the grandiose glare of history's floodlights upon them. It brings a natural rhythm into existence, introduced by new men, and with it a new language and a new humanity. Decolonization is the veritable creation of new men. But this creation owes nothing of its legitimacy to any supernatural power; the 'thing' which has been colonized becomes man during the same process by which it frees itself.

In decolonization, there is therefore the need of a complete calling in question of the colonial situation. If we wish to describe it precisely, we might find it in the well-known words: 'The last shall be first and the first last.' Decolonization is the putting into practice of this sentence. That is why, if we try to describe it, all decolonization is successful.

The naked truth of decolonization evokes for us the searing bullets and bloodstained knives which emanate from it. For if the last shall be first, this will only come to pass after a murderous and decisive struggle between the two protagonists. That affirmed intention to place the last at the head of things, and to make them climb at a pace (too quickly, some say) the well-known steps which characterize an organized society, can only triumph if we use all means to turn the scale, including, of course, that of violence.

You do not turn any society, however primitive it may be, upside-down with such a programme if you are not decided from the very beginning, that is to say from the actual formulation of that programme, to overcome all the obstacles that you will come across in so doing. The native who decides to put the programme into practice, and to become its moving force, is ready for violence at all times. From birth it is clear to him that this narrow world, strewn with prohibitions, can only be called in question by absolute violence.

The colonial world is a world divided into compartments. It is probably unnecessary to recall the existence of native quarters and European quarters, of schools for natives and schools for Europeans; in the same way we need not recall Apartheid in South Africa. Yet, if we examine closely this system of compartments, we will at least be able to reveal the lines of force it implies. This approach to the colonial world, its ordering and its geographical lay-out will allow us to mark out the lines on which a decolonized society will be reorganized.

The colonial world is a world cut in two. The dividing line, the frontiers are shown by barracks and police stations. In the colonies it is the policeman and the soldier who are the official, instituted go-betweens, the spokesmen of the settler and his rule of oppression. In capitalist societies the educational system, whether lay or clerical, the structure of moral reflexes handed down from father to son, the exemplary honesty of workers who are given a medal after fifty years of good and loyal service, and the affection which springs from harmonious relations and good behaviour – all these aesthetic expressions of respect for the established order serve to create around the exploited person an atmosphere of submission and of inhibition which lightens the task of policing considerably. In the capitalist countries a multitude of moral teachers, counsellors and 'bewilderers' separate the exploited from those in power. In the colonial countries, on the contrary, the policeman and the soldier, by their immediate presence and their frequent and direct action maintain contact with the native and advise him by means of rifle-butts and napalm not to budge. It is obvious here that the agents of government speak the language of pure force. The intermediary does not lighten the oppression, nor seek to hide the domination; he shows them up and puts them into practice with the clear conscience of an upholder of the peace; yet he is the bringer of violence into the home and into the mind of the native.

The zone where the natives live is not complementary to the zone inhabited by the settlers. The two zones are opposed, but not in the service of a higher unity. Obedient to the rules of pure Aristotelian logic, they both follow the principle of reciprocal exclusivity. No conciliation is possible, for of the two terms, one is superfluous. The settler's town is a strongly-built town, all made of stone and steel. It is a brightly-lit town; the streets are covered with asphalt, and the garbage-cans swallow all the leavings, unseen, unknown and hardly thought about. The settler's feet are never visible, except perhaps in the sea; but there you're never close enough to see them. His feet are protected by strong shoes although the streets of his town are clean and even, with no holes or stones. The settler's town is a well-fed town, an easygoing town; its belly is always full of good things. The settler's town is a town of white people, of foreigners.

The town belonging to the colonized people, or at least the native town, the Negro village, the medina, the reservation, is a place of ill fame, peopled by men of evil repute. They are born there, it matters little where or how; they die there, it matters not where, nor how. It is a world without spaciousness; men live there on top of each other, and their huts are built one on top of the other. The native town is a hungry town, starved of bread, of meat, of shoes, of coal, of light. The native town is a crouching village, a town on its knees, a town wallowing in the mire. It is a town of niggers and dirty arabs. The look that the native turns on the settler's town is a look of lust, a look of envy; it expresses his dreams of possession – all manner of possession: to sit at the settler's table, to sleep in the settler's bed, with his wife if possible. The colonized man is an envious man. And this the settler knows very well; when their glances meet he ascertains bitterly, always on the defensive 'They want to take our place'. It is true, for there is no native who does not dream at least once a day of setting himself up in the settler's place.

This world divided into compartments, this world cut in two is inhabited by two different species. The originality of the colonial context is that economic reality, inequality and the immense difference of ways of life never come to mask the human realities. When you examine at close quarters the colonial context, it is evident that what parcels out the world is to begin with the fact of belonging to or not belonging to a given race, a given species. In the colonies the economic substructure is also a superstructure. The cause is the consequence; you are rich because you are white, you are white because you are rich. This is why Marxist analysis should always be slightly stretched every time we have to do with the colonial problem.

Everything up to and including the very nature of pre-capitalist society, so well explained by Marx, must here be thought out again. The serf is in essence different from the knight, but a reference to divine right is necessary to legitimize this statutory difference. In the colonies, the foreigner coming from another country imposed his rule by means of guns and machines. In defiance of his successful transplantation, in spite of his appropriation, the settler still remains a foreigner. It is neither the act of owning factories, nor estates, nor a bank balance which distinguishes the governing classes. The governing race is first and foremost those who come from elsewhere, those who are unlike the original inhabitants, 'the others'.

The violence which has ruled over the ordering of the colonial world, which has ceaselessly drummed the rhythm for the destruction of native social forms and broken up without reserve the systems of reference of the economy, the customs of dress and external life, that same violence will be claimed and taken over by the native at the moment when, deciding to embody history in his own person, he surges into the forbidden quarters. To wreck the colonial world is henceforward a mental picture of action which is very clear, very easy to understand and which may be assumed by each one of the individuals which constitute the colonized people. To break up the colonial world does not mean that after the frontiers have been abolished lines of communication will be set up between the two zones. The destruction of the colonial world is no more and no less than the abolition of one zone, its burial in the depths of the earth or its expulsion from the country.

The natives' challenge to the colonial world is not a rational confrontation of points of view. It is not a treatise on the universal, but the untidy affirmation of an original idea propounded as an absolute. The colonial world is a Manichaean world. It is not enough for the settler to delimit physically, that is to say with the help of the army and the police force, the place of the native. As if to show the totalitarian character of colonial exploitation the settler paints the native as a sort of quintessence of evil.* Native society is not simply described as a society lacking in values. It is not enough for the colonist to affirm that those values have disappeared from, or still better never existed in, the colonial world. The native is declared insensible to ethics; he represents not only the absence of values, but also the negation of values. He is, let us dare to admit, the enemy of values, and in this sense he is the absolute evil. He is the corrosive element, destroying all that comes near him; he is the deforming element, disfiguring all that has to do with beauty or morality; he is the depository of maleficent powers, the unconscious and irretrievable instrument of blind forces. Monsieur Meyer could thus state seriously in the French National Assembly that the Republic must not be prostituted by allowing the Algerian people to become part of it. All values, in fact, are irrevocably poisoned and diseased as soon as they are allowed in contact with the colonized race. The customs of the colonized people, their traditions, their myths – above all, their myths – are the very sign of that poverty of spirit and of their constitutional depravity. That is why we must put the D.D.T. which destroys parasites, the bearers of disease, on the same level as the Christian religion which wages war on embryonic heresies and instincts, and on evil as yet unborn. The recession of yellow fever and the advance of evangelization form part of the same balance-sheet. But the triumphant *communiqués* from the missions are in fact a source of information concerning the implantation of foreign influences in the core of the colonized people. I speak of the Christian religion, and no one need be astonished. The Church in the colonies is the white people's Church, the foreigner's Church. She does not call the native to God's ways but to the ways of the white man, of the master, of the oppressor. And as we know, in this matter many are called but few chosen.

At times this Manichaeism goes to its logical conclusion and dehumanizes the native, or to speak plainly it turns him into an animal. In fact, the terms the settler uses when he mentions the

---

* We have demonstrated the mechanism of this Manichaean world in *Peau noire, masques blancs*, Éditions du Seuil.

native are zoological terms. He speaks of the yellow man's reptilian motions, of the stink of the native quarter, of breeding swarms, of foulness, of spawn, of gesticulations. When the settler seeks to describe the native fully in exact terms he constantly refers to the bestiary. The European rarely hits on a picturesque style; but the native, who knows what is in the mind of the settler, guesses at once what he is thinking of. Those hordes of vital statistics, those hysterical masses, those faces bereft of all humanity, those distended bodies which are like nothing on earth, that mob without beginning or end, those children who seem to belong to nobody, that laziness stretched out in the sun, that vegetative rhythm of life – all this forms part of the colonial vocabulary. General de Gaulle speaks of 'the yellow multitudes' and François Mauriac of the black, brown and yellow masses which soon will be unleashed. The native knows all this, and laughs to himself every time he spots an allusion to the animal world in the other's words. For he knows that he is not an animal; and it is precisely at the moment he realizes his humanity that he begins to sharpen the weapons with which he will secure its victory.

As soon as the native begins to pull on his moorings, and to cause anxiety to the settler, he is handed over to well-meaning souls who in cultural congresses point out to him the specificity and wealth of Western values. But every time Western values are mentioned they produce in the native a sort of stiffening or muscular lock-jaw. During the period of decolonization, the native's reason is appealed to. He is offered definite values, he is told frequently that decolonization need not mean regression, and that he must put his trust in qualities which are well-tried, solid and highly esteemed. But it so happens that when the native hears a speech about Western culture he pulls out his knife – or at least he makes sure it is within reach. The violence with which the supremacy of white values is affirmed and the aggressiveness which has permeated the victory of these values over the ways of life and of thought of the native mean that, in revenge, the native laughs in mockery when Western values are mentioned in front of him. In the colonial context the settler only ends his work of breaking in the native when the latter admits loudly and intelligibly the supremacy of the white

man's values. In the period of decolonization, the colonized
masses mock at these very values, insult them and vomit them
up.

This phenomenon is ordinarily masked because, during the
period of decolonization, certain colonized intellectuals have begun a dialogue with the bourgeoisie of the colonialist country. During this phase, the indigenous population is discerned only as an
indistinct mass. The few native personalities whom the colonialist
bourgeois have come to know here and there have not sufficient
influence on that immediate discernment to give rise to nuances.
On the other hand, during the period of liberation, the colonialist
bourgeoisie looks feverishly for contacts with the *élite*, and it is
with these *élite* that the familiar dialogue concerning values is
carried on. The colonialist bourgeoisie, when it realizes that it is
impossible for it to maintain its domination over the colonial
countries, decides to carry out a rear-guard action with regard
to culture, values, techniques and so on. Now what we must
never forget is that the immense majority of colonized people is
oblivious of these problems. For a colonized people the most
essential value, because the most concrete, is first and foremost
the land: the land which will bring them bread and, above all,
dignity. But this dignity has nothing to do with the dignity of
the human individual: for that human individual has never heard
tell of it. All that the native has seen in his country is that they
can freely arrest him, beat him, starve him: and no professor of
ethics, no priest has ever come to be beaten in his place, nor to
share their bread with him. As far as the native is concerned,
morality is very concrete; it is to silence the settler's defiance, to
break his flaunting violence – in a word, to put him out of the
picture. The well-known principle that all men are equal will
be illustrated in the colonies from the moment that the native
claims that he is the equal of the settler. One step more, and he is
ready to fight to be more than the settler. In fact, he has already
decided to eject him and to take his place; as we see it, it is a
whole material and moral universe which is breaking up. The
intellectual who for his part has followed the colonialist with regard to the universal abstract will fight in order that the settler
and the native may live together in peace in a new world. But the
thing he does not see, precisely because he is permeated by

colonialism and all its ways of thinking, is that the settler, from the moment that the colonial context disappears, has no longer any interest in remaining or in coexisting. It is not by chance that, even before any negotiation* between the Algerian and French governments has taken place, the European minority which calls itself 'liberal' has already made its position clear: it demands nothing more nor less than twofold citizenship. By setting themselves apart in an abstract manner, the liberals try to force the settler into taking a very concrete jump into the unknown. Let us admit it, the settler knows perfectly well that no phraseology can be a substitute for reality.

Thus the native discovers that his life, his breath, his beating heart are the same as those of the settler. He finds out that the settler's skin is not of any more value than a native's skin; and it must be said that this discovery shakes the world in a very necessary manner. All the new, revolutionary assurance of the native stems from it. For if, in fact, my life is worth as much as the settler's, his glance no longers shrivels me up nor freezes me, and his voice no longer turns me into stone. I am no longer on tenterhooks in his presence; in fact, I don't give a damn for him. Not only does his presence no longer trouble me, but I am already preparing such efficient ambushes for him that soon there will be no way out but that of flight.

We have said that the colonial context is characterized by the dichotomy which it imposes upon the whole people. Decolonization unifies that people by the radical decision to remove from it its heterogeneity, and by unifying it on a national, sometimes a racial basis. We know the fierce words of the Senegalese patriots, referring to the manoeuvres of their president, Senghor: 'We have demanded that the higher posts should be given to Africans; and now Senghor is Africanizing the Europeans.' That is to say that the native can see clearly and immediately if decolonization has come to pass or no, for his minimum demands are simply that the last shall be first.

But the native intellectual brings variants to this petition, and, in fact, he seems to have good reasons: higher civil servants, technicians, specialists – all seem to be needed. Now, the ordinary native interprets these unfair promotions as so many acts of

* Fanon is writing in 1961 (*translator*).

sabotage, and he is often heard to declare: 'It wasn't worth while, then, our becoming independent. . . .'

In the colonial countries where a real struggle for freedom has taken place, where the blood of the people has flowed and where the length of the period of armed warfare has favoured the backward surge of intellectuals towards bases grounded in the people, we can observe a genuine eradication of the superstructure built by these intellectuals from the bourgeois colonialist environment. The colonialist bourgeoisie, in its narcissistic dialogue, expounded by the members of its universities, had in fact deeply implanted in the minds of the colonized intellectual that the essential qualities remain eternal in spite of all the blunders men may make: the essential qualities of the West, of course. The native intellectual accepted the cogency of these ideas, and deep down in his brain you could always find a vigilant sentinel ready to defend the Graeco-Latin pedestal. Now it so happens that during the struggle for liberation, at the moment that the native intellectual comes into touch again with his people, this artificial sentinel is turned into dust. All the Mediterranean values – the triumph of the human individual, of clarity and of beauty – become lifeless, colourless knick-knacks. All those speeches seem like collections of dead words; those values which seemed to uplift the soul are revealed as worthless, simply because they have nothing to do with the concrete conflict in which the people is engaged.

Individualism is the first to disappear. The native intellectual had learnt from his masters that the individual ought to express himself fully. The colonialist bourgeoisie had hammered into the native's mind the idea of a society of individuals where each person shuts himself up in his own subjectivity, and whose only wealth is individual thought. Now the native who has the opportunity to return to the people during the struggle for freedom will discover the falseness of this theory. The very forms of organization of the struggle will suggest to him a different vocabulary. Brother, sister, friend – these are words outlawed by the colonialist bourgeoisie, because for them my brother is my purse, my friend is part of my scheme for getting on. The native intellectual takes part, in a sort of *auto-da-fé*, in the destruction of all his idols: egoism, recrimination that springs from pride, and the childish stupidity of those who always want to have the last word. Such a colonized intellectual, dusted over by colonial culture, will in the same way discover the substance of village assemblies, the cohesion of people's committees, and the extraordinary fruitfulness of local meetings and groupments. Henceforward, the interest of one will be the interests of all, for in concrete fact *everyone* will be discovered by the troops, *everyone* will be massacred – or *everyone* will be saved. The motto 'look out for yourself', the atheist's method of salvation, is in this context forbidden.

Self-criticism has been much talked about of late, but few people realize that it is an African institution. Whether in the *djemaas** of Northern Africa or in the meetings of Western Africa, tradition demands that the quarrels which occur in a village should be settled in public. It is communal self-criticism, of course, and with a note of humour, because everybody is relaxed, and because in the last resort we all want the same things. But the more the intellectual imbibes the atmosphere of the people, the more completely he abandons the habits of calculation, of unwonted silence, of mental reservations, and shakes off the spirit of concealment. And it is true that already at that level we can say that the community triumphs, and that it spreads its own light and its own reason.

But it so happens sometimes that decolonization occurs in areas which have not been sufficiently shaken by the struggle for liberation, and there may be found those same know-all, smart, wily intellectuals. We find intact in them the manners and forms of thought picked up during their association with the colonialist bourgeoisie. Spoilt children of yesterday's colonialism and of today's national governments, they organize the loot of whatever national resources exist. Without pity, they use today's national distress as a means of getting on through scheming and legal robbery, by import–export combines, limited liability companies gambling on the stock-exchange, or unfair promotion. They are insistent in their demands for the nationalization of commerce, that is to say the reservation of markets and advantageous bargains for nationals only. As far as doctrine is concerned, they proclaim the pressing necessity of nationalizing the robbery of

* Village assemblies (*translator*).

the nation. In this arid phase of national life, the so-called period of austerity, the success of their depredations is swift to call forth the violence and anger of the people. For this same people, poverty-stricken yet independent, comes very quickly to possess a social conscience in the African and international context of today; and this the petty individualists will quickly learn.

In order to assimilate and to experience the oppressor's culture, the native has had to leave certain of his intellectual possessions in pawn. These pledges include his adoption of the forms of thought of the colonialist bourgeoisie. This is very noticeable in the inaptitude of the native intellectual to carry on a two-sided discussion; for he cannot eliminate himself when confronted with an object or an idea. On the other hand, when once he begins to militate among the people he is struck with wonder and amazement; he is literally disarmed by their good faith and honesty. The danger that will haunt him continually is that of becoming the uncritical mouthpiece of the masses; he becomes a kind of yes-man who nods assent at every word coming from the people, which he interprets as considered judgements. Now, the *fellah*, the unemployed man, the starving native do not lay a claim to the truth; they do not *say* that they represent the truth, for they *are* the truth.

Objectively, the intellectual behaves in this phase like a common opportunist. In fact he has not stopped manoeuvring. There is never any question of his being either rejected or welcomed by the people. What they ask is simply that all resources should be pooled. The inclusion of the native intellectual in the upward surge of the masses will in this case be differentiated by a curious cult of detail. That is not to say that the people are hostile to analysis; on the contrary, they like having things explained to them, they are glad to understand a line of argument and they like to see where they are going. But at the beginning of his association with the people the native intellectual over-stresses details and thereby comes to forget that the defeat of colonialism is the real object of the struggle. Carried away by the multitudinous aspects of the fight, he tends to concentrate on local tasks, performed with enthusiasm but almost always too solemnly. He fails to see the whole of the movement all the time. He introduces the idea of special disciplines, of specialized functions, of departments within the terrible stone crusher, the fierce mixing machine which a popular revolution is. He is occupied in action on a particular front, and it so happens that he loses sight of the unity of the movement. Thus, if a local defeat is inflicted, he may well be drawn into doubt, and from thence to despair. The people, on the other hand, take their stand from the start on the broad and inclusive positions of *Bread and the land*: how can we obtain the land, and bread to eat? And this obstinate point of view of the masses, which may seem shrunken and limited, is in the end the most worthwhile and the most efficient mode of procedure.

The problem of truth ought also to be considered. In every age, among the people, truth is the property of the national cause. No absolute verity, no discourse on the purity of the soul can shake this position. The native replies to the living lie of the colonial situation by an equal falsehood. His dealings with his fellow-nationals are open; they are strained and incomprehensible with regard to the settlers. Truth is that which hurries on the break-up of the colonialist regime; it is that which promotes the emergence of the nation; it is all that protects the natives, and ruins the foreigners. In this colonialist context there is no truthful behaviour: and the good is quite simply that which is evil for 'them'.

Thus we see that the primary Manichaeism which governed colonial society is preserved intact during the period of decolonization; that is to say that the settler never ceases to be the enemy, the opponent, the foe that must be overthrown. The oppressor, in his own sphere, starts the process, a process of domination, of exploitation and of pillage, and in the other sphere the coiled, plundered creature which is the native provides fodder for the process as best he can, the process which moves uninterruptedly from the banks of the colonial territory to the palaces and the docks of the mother country. In this becalmed zone the sea has a smooth surface, the palm-tree stirs gently in the breeze, the waves lap against the pebbles and raw materials are ceaselessly transported, justifying the presence of the settler: and all the while the native, bent double, more dead than alive, exists interminably in an unchanging dream. The settler makes history; his life is an epoch, an Odyssey. He is the absolute beginning: 'This land was created by us'; he is the unceasing cause: 'If we leave, all is lost, and the country will go back to the Middle Ages.' Over against him torpid creatures, wasted by fevers, obsessed by ancestral customs, form an almost inorganic background for the innovating dynamism of colonial mercantilism.

The settler makes history and is conscious of making it. And because he constantly refers to the history of his mother country, he clearly indicates that he himself is the extension of that mother country. Thus the history which he writes is not the history of the country which he plunders but the history of his own nation in regard to all that she skims off, all that she violates and starves.

The immobility to which the native is condemned can only be called in question if the native decides to put an end to the history of colonization – the history of pillage – and to bring into existence the history of the nation – the history of decolonization.

A world divided into compartments, a motionless, Manichaeistic world, a world of statues: the statue of the general who carried out the conquest, the statue of the engineer who built the bridge; a world which is sure of itself, which crushes with its stones the backs flayed by whips: this is the colonial world. The native is a being hemmed in; apartheid is simply one form of the division into compartments of the colonial world. The first thing which the native learns is to stay in his place, and not to go beyond certain limits. This is why the dreams of the native are always of muscular prowess; his dreams are of action and of aggression. I dream I am jumping, swimming, running, climbing; I dream that I burst out laughing, that I span a river in one stride, or that I am followed by a flood of motor-cars which never catch up with me. During the period of colonization, the native never stops achieving his freedom from nine in the evening until six in the morning.

The colonized man will first manifest this aggressiveness which has been deposited in his bones against his own people. This is the period when the niggers beat each other up, and the police and magistrates do not know which way to turn when faced with the astonishing waves of crime in North Africa. We shall see later how this phenomenon should be judged.* When the native is confronted with the colonial order of things, he finds he is in a state of permanent tension. The settler's world is a hostile world, which spurns the native, but at the same time it is a world of which he is envious. We have seen that the native never ceases to dream of putting himself in the place of the settler – not of becoming the settler but of substituting himself for the settler. This hostile world, ponderous and aggressive because it fends off the colonized masses with all the harshness it is capable of, represents not merely a hell from which the swiftest flight possible is desirable, but also a paradise close at hand which is guarded by terrible watchdogs.

The native is always on the alert, for since he can only make out with difficulty the many symbols of the colonial world, he is never sure whether or not he has crossed the frontier. Confronted with a world ruled by the settler, the native is always presumed guilty. But the native's guilt is never a guilt which he accepts; it is rather a kind of curse, a sort of sword of Damocles, for, in his innermost spirit, the native admits no accusation. He is overpowered but not tamed; he is treated as an inferior but he is not convinced of his inferiority. He is patiently waiting until the settler is off his guard to fly at him. The native's muscles are always tensed. You can't say that he is terrorized, or even apprehensive. He is in fact ready at a moment's notice to exchange the role of the quarry for that of the hunter. The native is an oppressed person whose permanent dream is to become the persecutor. The symbols of social order – the police, the bugle-calls in the barracks, military parades and the waving flags – are at one and the same time inhibitory and stimulating: for they do not convey the message 'Don't dare to budge'; rather, they cry out 'Get ready to attack.' And, in fact, if the native had any tendency to fall asleep and to forget, the settler's *hauteur* and the settler's anxiety to test the strength of the colonial system would remind him at every turn that the great show-down cannot be put off indefinitely. That impulse to take the settler's place implies a tonicity of muscles the whole time; and in fact we know that in certain emotional conditions the presence of an obstacle accentuates the tendency towards motion.

* See Chapter 5: Colonial War and Mental Disorders.

The settler–native relationship is a mass relationship. The settler pits brute force against the weight of numbers. He is an exhibitionist. His preoccupation with security makes him remind the native out loud that there he alone is master. The settler keeps alive in the native an anger which he deprives of outlet; the native is trapped in the tight links of the chains of colonialism. But we have seen that inwardly the settler can only achieve a pseudo-petrification. The native's muscular tension finds outlet regularly in bloodthirsty explosions – in tribal warfare, in feuds between septs and in quarrels between individuals.

Where individuals are concerned, a positive negation of common sense is evident. While the settler or the policeman has the right the live-long day to strike the native, to insult him and to make him crawl to them, you will see the native reaching for his knife at the slightest hostile or aggressive glance cast on him by another native; for the last resort of the native is to defend his personality *vis-à-vis* his brother. Tribal feuds only serve to perpetuate old grudges deep buried in the memory. By throwing himself with all his force into the vendetta, the native tries to persuade himself that colonialism does not exist, that everything is going on as before, that history continues. Here on the level of communal organizations we clearly discern the well-known behaviour patterns of avoidance. It is as if plunging into a fraternal blood-bath allowed them to ignore the obstacle, and to put off till later the choice, nevertheless inevitable, which opens up the question of armed resistance to colonialism. Thus collective auto-destruction in a very concrete form is one of the ways in which the native's muscular tension is set free. All these patterns of conduct are those of the death reflex when faced with danger, a suicidal behaviour which proves to the settler (whose existence and domination is by them all the more justified) that these men are not reasonable human beings. In the same way the native manages to by-pass the settler. A belief in fatality removes all blame from the oppressor; the cause of misfortunes and of poverty is attributed to God; He is Fate. In this way the individual accepts the disintegration ordained by God, bows down before the settler and his lot, and by a kind of interior restabilization acquires a stony calm.

Meanwhile, however, life goes on, and the native will strengthen the inhibitions which contain his aggressiveness by drawing on the terrifying myths which are so frequently found in under-developed communities. There are maleficent spirits which inter-vene every time a step is taken in the wrong direction, leopardmen serpent-men, six-legged dogs, zombies – a whole series of tiny animals or giants which create around the native a world of prohibitions, of barriers and of inhibitions far more terrifying than the world of the settler. This magical superstructure which permeates native society fulfils certain well-defined functions in the dynamism of the libido. One of the characteristics of under-developed societies is in fact that the libido is first and foremost the concern of a group, or of the family. The feature of com-munities whereby a man who dreams that he has sexual relations with a woman other than his own must confess it in public and pay a fine in kind or in working days to the injured husband or family is fully described by ethnologists. We may note in passing that this proves that the so-called prehistoric societies attach great importance to the unconscious.

The atmosphere of myth and magic frightens me and so takes on an undoubted reality. By terrifying me, it integrates me in the traditions and the history of my district or of my tribe, and at the same time it reassures me, it gives me a status, as it were an identification paper. In under-developed countries the occult sphere is a sphere belonging to the community which is entirely under magical jurisdiction. By entangling myself in this in-extricable network where actions are repeated with crystalline inevitability, I find the everlasting world which belongs to me, and the perenniality which is thereby affirmed of the world be-longing to us. Believe me, the zombies are more terrifying than the settlers; and in consequence the problem is no longer that of keeping oneself right with the colonial world and its barbed-wire entanglements, but of considering three times before urinating, spitting or going out into the night.

The supernatural, magical powers reveal themselves as essen-tially personal; the settler's powers are infinitely shrunken, stamped with their alien origin. We no longer really need to fight against them since what counts is the frightening enemy created by myths. We perceive that all is settled by a permanent con-frontation on the phantasmic plane.

It has always happened in the struggle for freedom that such a people, formerly lost in an imaginary maze, a prey to unspeakable terrors yet happy to lose themselves in a dreamlike torment, such a people becomes unhinged, reorganizes itself, and in blood and tears gives birth to very real and immediate action. Feeding the *moudjahidines*,* posting sentinels, coming to the help of families which lack the bare necessities, or taking the place of a husband who has been killed or imprisoned: such are the concrete tasks to which the people is called during the struggle for freedom.

In the colonial world, the emotional sensitivity of the native is kept on the surface of his skin like an open sore which flinches from the caustic agent; and the psyche shrinks back, obliterates itself and finds outlet in muscular demonstrations which have caused certain very wise men to say that the native is a hysterical type. This sensitive emotionalism, watched by invisible keepers who are, however, in unbroken contact with the core of the personality, will find its fulfilment through eroticism in the driving forces behind the dissolution of the crisis.

On another level we see the native's emotional sensibility exhausting itself in dances which are more or less ecstatic. This is why any study of the colonial world should take into consideration the phenomena of the dance and of possession. The native's relaxation takes precisely the form of a muscular orgy in which the most acute aggressivity and the most impelling violence are canalized, transformed and conjured away. The circle of the dance is a permissive circle: it protects and permits. At certain times on certain days, men and women come together at a given place, and there, under the solemn eye of the tribe, fling themselves into a seemingly unorganized pantomime, which is in reality extremely systematic, in which by various means – shakes of the head, bending of the spinal column, throwing of the whole body backwards – may be deciphered as in an open book the huge effort of a community to exorcise itself, to liberate itself, to explain itself. There are no limits – inside the circle. The hillock up which you have toiled as if to be nearer to the moon; the river bank down which you slip as if to show the connexion

* Highly-trained soldiers who are completely dedicated to the Moslem cause (*translator*).

between the dance and ablutions, cleansing and purification – these are sacred places. There are no limits – for in reality your purpose in coming together is to allow the accumulated libido, the hampered aggressivity to dissolve as in a volcanic eruption. Symbolical killings, fantastic rites, imaginary mass murders – all must be brought out. The evil humours are undammed, and flow away with a din as of molten lava.

One step further and you are completely possessed. In fact, these are actually organized séances of possession and exorcism; they include vampirism, possession by djinns, by zombies, and by Legba, the famous god of the Voodoo. This disintegrating of the personality, this splitting and dissolution, all this fulfils a primordial function in the organism of the colonial world. When they set out, the men and women were impatient, stamping their feet in a state of nervous excitement; when they return, peace has been restored to the village; it is once more calm and unmoved.

During the struggle for freedom, a marked alienation from these practices is observed. The native's back is to the wall, the knife is at his throat (or, more precisely, the electrode at his genitals): he will have no more call for his fancies. After centuries of unreality, after having wallowed in the most outlandish phantoms, at long last the native, gun in hand, stands face to face with the only forces which contend for his life – the forces of colonialism. And the youth of a colonized country, growing up in an atmosphere of shot and fire, may well make a mock of, and does not hesitate to pour scorn upon the zombies of his ancestors, the horses with two heads, the dead who rise again, and the djinns who rush into your body while you yawn. The native discovers reality and transforms it into the pattern of his customs, into the practice of violence and into his plan for freedom.

We have seen that this same violence, though kept very much on the surface all through the colonial period, yet turns in the void. We have also seen that it is canalized by the emotional outlets of dance and possession by spirits; we have seen how it is exhausted in fratricidal combats. Now the problem is to lay hold of this violence which is changing direction. When formerly it was appeased by myths and exercised its talents in finding fresh ways of committing mass suicide, now new conditions will make possible a completely new line of action.

Nowadays a theoretical problem of prime importance is being set, on the historical plane as well as on the level of political tactics, by the liberation of the colonies: when can one affirm that the situation is ripe for a movement of national liberation? In what form should it first be manifested? Because the various means whereby decolonization has been carried out have appeared in many different aspects, reason hesitates and refuses to say which is a true decolonization, and which a false. We shall see that for a man who is in the thick of the fight it is an urgent matter to decide on the means and the tactics to employ: that is to say, how to conduct and organize the movement. If this coherence is not present there is only a blind will towards freedom, with the terribly reactionary risks which it entails.

What are the forces which in the colonial period open up new outlets and engender new aims for the violence of colonized peoples? In the first place there are the political parties and the intellectual or commercial *élites*. Now, the characteristic feature of certain political structures is that they proclaim abstract principles but refrain from issuing definite commands. The entire action of these nationalist political parties during the colonial period is action of the electoral type: a string of philosophico-political dissertations on the themes of the rights of peoples to self-determination, the rights of man to freedom from hunger and human dignity, and the unceasing affirmation of the principe: 'One man, one vote.' The national political parties never lay stress upon the necessity of a trial of armed strength, for the good reason that their objective is not the radical overthrowing of the system. Pacifists and legalists, they are in fact partisans of order, the new order – but to the colonialist bourgeoisie they put bluntly enough the demand which to them is the main one: 'Give us more power.' On the specific question of violence, the *élite* are ambiguous. They are violent in their words and reformist in their attitudes. When the nationalist political leaders *say* something, they make quite clear that they do not really *think* it.

This characteristic on the part of the nationalist political

parties should be interpreted in the light both of the make-up of
their leaders and the nature of their followings. The rank-and-
file of a nationalist party is urban. The workers, primary school-
teachers, artisans and small shopkeepers who have begun to
profit – at a discount, to be sure – from the colonial set-up, have
special interests at heart. What this sort of following demands is
the betterment of their particular lot: increased salaries, for example. The dialogue between these political parties and colonialism is never broken off. Improvements are discussed, such as
full electoral representation, the liberty of the Press, and liberty
of association. Reforms are debated. Thus it need not astonish
anyone to notice that a large number of natives are militant
members of the branches of political parties which stem from
the mother country. These natives fight under an abstract
watchword: 'Government by the workers', and they forget that
in their country it should be *nationalist* watchwords which are
first in the field. The native intellectual has clothed his aggressiveness in his barely veiled desire to assimilate himself to the
colonial world. He has used his aggressiveness to serve his own
individual interests.

Thus there is very easily brought into being a kind of class of
affranchised slaves, or slaves who are individually free. What the
intellectual demands is the right to multiply the emancipated,
and the opportunity to organize a genuine class of emancipated
citizens. On the other hand, the mass of the people have no intention of standing by and watching individuals increase their
chances of success. What they demand is not the settler's position
or status, but the settler's place. The immense majority of natives
want the settler's farm. For them, there is no question of entering into competition with the settler. They want to take his
place.

The peasantry is systematically disregarded for the most part
by the propaganda put out by the nationalist parties. And it is
clear that in the colonial countries the peasants alone are revolutionary, for they have nothing to lose and everything to gain. The
starving peasant, outside the class system, is the first among the
exploited to discover that only violence pays. For him there is
no compromise, no possible coming to terms; colonization and
decolonization are simply a question of relative strength. The

exploited man sees that his liberation implies the use of all means, and that of force first and foremost. When in 1956, after the capitulation of Monsieur Guy Mollet to the settlers in Algeria, the *Front de Libération Nationale*, in a famous leaflet, stated that colonialism only loosens its hold when the knife is at its throat, no Algerian really found these terms too violent. The leaflet only expressed what every Algerian felt at heart: colonialism is not a thinking machine, nor a body endowed with reasoning faculties. It is violence in its natural state, and it will only yield when confronted with greater violence.

At the decisive moment, the colonialist bourgeoisie, which up till then has remained inactive, comes into the field. It introduces that new idea which is in proper parlance a creation of the colonial situation: non-violence. In its simplest form this non-violence signifies to the intellectual and economic *élite* of the colonized country that the bourgeoisie has the same interests as them and that it is therefore urgent and indispensable to come to terms for the public good. Non-violence is an attempt to settle the colonial problem around a green baize table, before any regrettable act has been performed or irreparable gesture made, before any blood has been shed. But if the masses, without waiting for the chairs to be arranged around the baize table, listen to their own voice and begin committing outrages and setting fire to buildings, the *élites* and the nationalist bourgeois parties will be seen rushing to the colonialists to exclaim 'This is very serious! We do not know how it will end; we must find a solution – some sort of compromise.'

This idea of compromise is very important in the phenomenon of decolonization, for it is very far from being a simple one. Compromise involves the colonial system and the young nationalist bourgeoisie at one and the same time. The partisans of the colonial system discover that the masses may destroy everything. Blown-up bridges, ravaged farms, repressions and fighting harshly disrupt the economy. Compromise is equally attractive to the nationalist bourgeoisie, who since they are not clearly aware of the possible consequences of the rising storm, are genuinely afraid of being swept away by this huge hurricane and never stop saying to the settlers: 'We are still capable of stopping the slaughter; the masses still have confidence in us; act quickly if you do not want to put everything in jeopardy.' One step more, and the leader of the nationalist party keeps his distance with regard to that violence. He loudly proclaims that he has nothing to do with these Mau-Mau, these terrorists, these throat-slitters. At best, he shuts himself off in a no-man's-land between the terrorists and the settlers and willingly offers his services as go-between; that is to say, that as the settlers cannot discuss terms with these Mau-Mau, he himself will be quite willing to begin negotiations. Thus it is that the rear-guard of the national struggle, that very party of people who have never ceased to be on the other side in the fight, find themselves somersaulted into the van of negotiations and compromise – precisely because that party has taken very good care never to break contact with colonialism.

Before negotiations have been set on foot, the majority of nationalist parties confine themselves for the most part to explaining and excusing this 'savagery'. They do not assert that the people have to use physical force, and it sometimes even happens that they go so far as to condemn, in private, the spectacular deeds which are declared to be hateful by the Press and public opinion in the mother country. The legitimate excuse for this ultra-conservative policy is the desire to see things in an objective light; but this traditional attitude of the native intellectual and of the leaders of the nationalist parties is not, in reality, in the least objective. For in fact they are not at all convinced that this impatient violence of the masses is the most efficient means of defending their own interests. Moreover, there are some individuals who are convinced of the ineffectiveness of violent methods; for them, there is no doubt about it, every attempt to break colonial oppression by force is a hopeless effort, an attempt at suicide, because in the innermost recesses of their brains the settler's tanks and aeroplanes occupy a huge place. When they are told 'Action must be taken', they see bombs raining down on them, armoured cars coming at them on every path, machine-gunning and police action . . . and they sit quiet. They are beaten from the start. There is no need to demonstrate their incapacity to triumph by violent methods; they take it for granted in their everyday life and in their political manoeuvres. They have remained in the same childish position as Engels took up in his famous polemic with that monument of puerility, Monsieur Dühring:

> In the same way that Robinson [Crusoe] was able to obtain a sword, we can just as well suppose that [Man] Friday might appear one fine morning with a loaded revolver in his hand, and from then on the whole relationship of violence is reversed: Man Friday gives the orders and Crusoe is obliged to work. . . . Thus, the revolver triumphs over the sword, and even the most childish believer in axioms will doubtless form the conclusion that violence is not a simple act of will, but needs for its realization certain very concrete preliminary conditions, and in particular the implements of violence; and the more highly-developed of these implements will carry the day against primitive ones. Moreover, the very fact of the ability to produce such weapons signifies that the producer of highly-developed weapons, in everyday speech the arms manufacturer, triumphs over the producer of primitive weapons. To put it briefly, the triumph of violence depends upon the production of armaments, and this in its turn depends on production in general, and thus . . . on economic strength, on the economy of the State, and in the last resort on the material means which that violence commands.*

In fact, the leaders of reform have nothing else to say than: 'With what are you going to fight the settlers? With your knives? Your shot-guns?'

It is true that weapons are important when violence comes into play, since all finally depends on the distribution of these implements. But it so happens that the liberation of colonial countries throws new light on the subject. For example, we have seen that during the Spanish campaign, which was a very genuine colonial war, Napoleon, in spite of an army which reached in the offensives of the spring of 1810 the huge figure of 400,000 men, was forced to retreat. Yet the French army made the whole of Europe tremble by its weapons of war, by the bravery of its soldiers and by the military genius of its leaders. Face to face with the enormous potentials of the Napoleonic troops, the Spaniards, inspired by an unshakeable national ardour, rediscovered the famous methods of guerrilla warfare which, twenty-five years before, the American militia had tried out on

* Engels: *Anti-Dühring*, Part II, Chapter III, Theory of Violence, Éditions Sociales, p. 199.

the English forces. But the native's guerrilla warfare would be of no value as opposed to other means of violence if it did not form a new element in the world-wide process of competition between trusts and monopolies.

In the early days of colonization, a single column could occupy immense stretches of country: the Congo, Nigeria, the Ivory Coast and so on. Today, however, the colonized countries' national struggle crops up in a completely new international situation. Capitalism, in its early days, saw in the colonies a source of raw materials which, once turned into manufactured goods, could be distributed on the European market. After a phase of accumulation of capital, capitalism has today come to modify its conception of the profit-earning capacity of a commercial enterprise. The colonies have become a market. The colonial population is a customer who is ready to buy goods. Consequently, if the garrison has to be perpetually reinforced, if buying and selling slackens off, that is to say if manufactured and finished goods can no longer be exported, there is clear proof that the solution of military force must be set aside. A blind domination founded on slavery is not economically speaking worth while for the bourgeoisie of the mother country. The monopolistic group within this bourgeoisie does not support a government whose policy is solely that of the sword. What the factory-owners and finance magnates of the mother country expect from their government is not that it should decimate the colonial peoples, but that it should safeguard with the help of economic conventions their own 'legitimate interests'.

Thus there exists a sort of detached complicity between capitalism and the violent forces which blaze up in colonial territory. What is more, the native is not alone against the oppressor, for indeed there is also the political and diplomatic support of progressive countries and peoples. But above all there is competition, that pitiless war which financial groups wage upon each other. A Berlin Conference was able to tear Africa into shreds and divide her up between three or four imperial flags. At the moment, the important thing is not whether such-and-such a region in Africa is under French or Belgian sovereignty, but rather that the economic zones are respected. Today, wars of repression are no longer waged against rebel sultans; everything is more elegant, less bloodthirsty; the liquidation of the Castro regime will be quite peaceful. They do all they can to strangle Guinea and they eliminate Mossadegh. Thus the nationalist leader who is frightened of violence is wrong if he imagines that colonialism is going to 'massacre all of us'. The military will of course go on playing with tin soldiers which date from the time of the conquest, but higher finance will soon bring the truth home to them.

This is why reasonable nationalist political parties are asked to set out their claims as clearly as possible, and to seek with their colonialist opposite numbers, calmly and without passion, for a solution which will take the interests of both parties into consideration. We see that if this nationalist reformist tendency which often takes the form of a kind of caricature of trade unionism decides to take action, it will only do so in a highly peaceful fashion, through stoppages of work in the few industries which have been set up in the towns, mass demonstrations to cheer the leaders, and the boycotting of buses or of imported commodities. All these forms of action serve at one and the same time to bring pressure to bear on the forces of colonialism, and to allow the people to work off their energy. This practice of therapy by hibernation, this sleep-cure used on the people, may sometimes be successful; thus out of the conference around the green baize table comes the political selectiveness which enables Monsieur M'ba, the president of the Republic of Gabon to state in all seriousness on his arrival in Paris for an official visit: 'Gabon is independent, but between Gabon and France nothing has changed; everything goes on as before.' In fact, the only change is that Monsieur M'ba is president of the Gabonese Republic and that he is received by the president of the French Republic.

The colonialist bourgeoisie is helped in its work of calming down the natives by the inevitable religion. All those saints who have turned the other cheek, who have forgiven trespasses against them, and who have been spat on and insulted without shrinking are studied and held up as examples. On the other hand, the *élites* of the colonial countries, those slaves set free, when at the head of the movement inevitably end up by producing an ersatz conflict. They use their brothers' slavery to shame the slave-drivers or to provide an ideological policy of quaint humanitarianism for their oppressors' financial competitors. The truth is that they never make any real appeal to the aforesaid slaves; they never mobilize them in concrete terms. On the contrary, at the decisive moment (that is to say, from their point of view the moment of indecision) they brandish the danger of a 'mass mobilization' as the crucial weapon which would bring about as if by magic the 'end of the colonial regime'. Obviously there are to be found at the core of the political parties and among their leaders certain revolutionaries who deliberately turn their backs upon the farce of national independence. But very quickly their questionings, their energy and their anger obstruct the party machine; and these elements are gradually isolated, and then quite simply brushed aside. At this moment, as if there existed a dialectic concomitance, the colonialist police will fall upon them. With no security in the towns, avoided by the militants of their former party and rejected by its leaders, these undesirable firebrands will be stranded in country districts. Then it is that they will realize bewilderedly that the peasant masses catch on to what they have to say immediately, and without delay ask them the question to which they have not yet prepared the answer: 'When do we start?'

This meeting of revolutionaries coming from the towns and country dwellers will be dealt with later on. For the moment we must go back to the political parties, in order to show the nature of their action, which is all the same progressive. In their speeches the political leaders give a name to the nation. In this way the native's demands are given shape.

There is however no definite subject-matter and no political or social programme. There is a vague outline or skeleton, which is nevertheless national in form, what we describe as 'minimum requirements'. The politicians who make speeches and who write in the nationalist newspapers make the people dream dreams. They avoid the actual overthrowing of the State, but in fact they introduce into their readers' or hearers' consciousness the terrible ferment of subversion. The national or tribal language is often used. Here, once again, dreams are encouraged, and the imagination is let loose outside the bounds of the colonial order; and sometimes these politicians speak of 'We Negroes, we Arabs', and these terms which are so profoundly ambivalent take on during the colonial epoch a sacramental signification. The nationalist politicians are playing with fire: for, as an African leader recently warned a group of young intellectuals 'Think well before you speak to the masses, for they flare up quickly.' This is one of the terrible tricks that destiny plays in the colonies.

When a political leader calls a mass meeting, we may say that there is blood in the air. Yet the same leader very often is above all anxious to 'make a show' of force, so that in fact he need not use it. But the agitation which ensues, the coming and going, the listening to speeches, seeing the people assembled in one place, with the police all around, the military demonstrations, arrests, and the deportation of the leaders – all this hubbub makes the people think that the moment has come for them to take action. In these times of instability the political parties multiply their appeals to the left for calm, while on their right they scan the horizon, trying to make out the liberal intentions of colonialism.

In the same way the people make use of certain episodes in the life of the community in order to hold themselves ready and to keep alive their revolutionary zeal. For example, the gangster who holds up the police set on to track him down for days on end, or who dies in single combat after having killed four or five policemen, or who commits suicide in order not to give away his accomplices – these types light the way for the people, form the blueprints for action and become heroes. Obviously, it's a waste of breath to say that such-and-such a hero is a thief, a scoundrel or a reprobate. If the act for which he is prosecuted by the colonial authorities is an act exclusively directed against a colonialist person or colonialist property, the demarcation line is definite and manifest. The process of identification is automatic.

We must also notice in this ripening process the role played by the history of the resistance at the time of the conquest. The great figures of the colonized people are always those who led the national resistance to invasion. Behanzin, Soundiata, Samory, Abdel Kader – all spring again to life with peculiar intensity in the period which comes directly before action. This is the proof that the people are getting ready to begin to go forward again, to put an end to the static period begun by colonization, and to make history.

The uprising of the new nation and the breaking down of colonial structures are the result of two causes: either of a violent struggle of the people in their own right, or of action on the part of surrounding colonized peoples which acts as a brake on the colonial regime in question.

A colonized people is not alone. In spite of all that colonialism can do, its frontiers remain open to new ideas and echoes from the world outside. It discovers that violence is in the atmosphere, that it here and there bursts out, and here and there sweeps away the colonial regime – that same violence which fulfils for the native a role that is not simply informatory, but also operative. The great victory of the Vietnamese people at Dien Bien Phu is no longer, strictly speaking, a Vietnamese victory. Since July 1954, the question which the colonized peoples have asked themselves has been 'What must be done to bring about another Dien Bien Phu? How can we manage it?' Not a single colonized individual could ever again doubt the possibility of a Dien Bien Phu; the only problem was how best to use the forces at their disposal, how to organize them, and when to bring them into action. This encompassing violence does not work upon the colonized people only; it modifies the attitude of the colonialists who become aware of manifold Dien Bien Phus. This is why a veritable panic takes hold of the colonialist governments in turn. Their purpose is to capture the vanguard, to turn the movement of liberation towards the right and to disarm the people: quick, quick, let's decolonize. Decolonize the Congo before it turns into another Algeria. Vote the constitutional framework for all Africa, create the French *Communauté*, renovate that same *Communauté*, but for God's sake let's decolonize quick. . . . And they decolonize at such a rate that they impose independence on Houphouët-Boigny. To the strategy of Dien Bien Phu, defined by the colonized peoples, the colonialist replies by the strategy of encirclement – based on the respect of the sovereignty of States.

But let us return to that atmosphere of violence, that violence which is just under the skin. We have seen that in its process towards maturity many leads are attached to it, to control it and show it the way out. Yet in spite of the metamorphoses which the colonial regime imposes upon it in the way of tribal or regional quarrels, that violence makes its way forward, and the native identifies his enemy and recognizes all his misfortunes, throwing all the exacerbated might of his hate and anger into this new channel. But how do we pass from the atmosphere of violence to violence in action? What makes the lid blow off? There is first of all the fact that this development does not leave the settler's blissful existence intact. The settler who 'understands' the natives is made aware by several straws in the wind showing that something is afoot. 'Good' natives become scarce; silence falls when the oppressor approaches; sometimes looks are black, and attitudes and remarks openly aggressive. The nationalist parties are astir, they hold a great many meetings, the police are increased and reinforcements of soldiers are brought in. The settlers, above all the farmers isolated on their land, are the first to become alarmed. They call for energetic measures.

The authorities do in fact take some spectacular measures. They arrest one or two leaders, they organize military parades and manoeuvres, and air force displays. But the demonstrations and warlike exercises, the smell of gunpowder which now fills the atmosphere, these things do not make the people draw back. Those bayonets and cannonades only serve to reinforce their aggressiveness. The atmosphere becomes dramatic, and everyone wishes to show that he is ready for anything. And it is in these circumstances that the guns go off by themselves, for nerves are jangled, fear reigns and everyone is trigger-happy. A single commonplace incident is enough to start the machine-gunning: Sétif in Algeria, the Central Quarries in Morocco, Moramanga in Madagascar.

The repressions, far from calling a halt to the forward rush of national consciousness, urge it on. Mass slaughter in the colonies at a certain stage of the embryonic development of consciousness increases that consciousness, for the hecatombs are an indication that between oppressors and oppressed everything can be solved by force. It must be remarked here that the political parties have not called for armed insurrection, and have made no preparations for such an insurrection. All these repressive measures, all those actions which are a result of fear are not within the leader's intentions: they are overtaken by events. At this moment, then, colonialism may decide to arrest the nationalist leaders. But today the governments of colonized countries know very well that it is extremely dangerous to deprive the masses of their leaders; for then the people, unbridled, fling themselves into *jacqueries*, mutinies, and 'brutish murders'. The masses give free rein to their 'bloodthirsty instincts' and force colonialism to free their leaders, to whom falls the difficult task of bringing them back to order. The colonized people, who have spontaneously brought their violence to the colossal task of destroying the colonial system, will very soon find themselves with the barren, inert slogan 'Release X or Y'.* Then colonialism will release these men, and hold discussions with them. The time for dancing in the streets has come.

In certain circumstances, the party political machine may remain intact. But as a result of the colonialist repression and of the spontaneous reaction of the people the parties find themselves outdistanced by their militants. The violence of the masses is vigorously pitted against the military forces of the occupying power, and the situation deteriorates and comes to a head. Those leaders who are free remain, therefore, on the touchline. They have suddenly become useless, with their bureaucracy and their reasonable demands; yet we see them, far removed from events, attempting the crowning imposture – that of 'speaking in the name of the silenced nation'. As a general rule, colonialism welcomes this godsend with open arms, transforms these 'blind mouths' into spokesmen, and in two minutes endows them with independence, on condition that they restore order.

So we see that all parties are aware of the power of such violence and that the question is not always to reply to it by a greater violence, but rather to see how to relax the tension.

What is the real nature of this violence? We have seen that it is the intuition of the colonized masses that their liberation must, and can only, be achieved by force. By what spiritual aberration do these men, without technique, starving and enfeebled, confronted with the military and economic might of the occupation, come to believe that violence alone will free them? How can they hope to triumph?

It is because violence (and this is the disgraceful thing) may constitute, in so far as it forms part of its system, the slogan of a

* It may happen that the arrested leader is in fact the authentic mouthpiece of the colonized masses. In this case colonialism will make use of his period of detention to try to launch new leaders.

political party. The leaders may call on the people to enter upon
an armed struggle. This problematical question has to be thought
over. When militarist Germany decides to settle its frontier disputes by force, we are not in the least surprised; but when the
people of Angola, for example, decide to take up arms, when the
Algerian people reject all means which are not violent, these are
proofs that something has happened or is happening at this very
moment. The colonized races, those slaves of modern times, are
impatient. They know that this apparent folly alone can put
them out of reach of colonial oppression. A new type of relations
is established in the world. The under-developed peoples try to
break their chains, and the extraordinary thing is that they succeed. It could be argued that in these days of sputniks it is
ridiculous to die of hunger; but for the colonized masses the
argument is more down-to-earth. The truth is that there is no
colonial power today which is capable of adopting the only form
of contest which has a chance of succeeding, namely, the prolonged establishment of large forces of occupation.

As far as their internal situation is concerned, the colonialist
countries find themselves faced with contradictions in the form
of working-class demands which necessitate the use of their
police forces. As well, in the present international situation, these
countries need their troops to protect their regimes. Finally
there is the well-known myth of liberating movements directed
from Moscow. In the regime's panic-stricken reasoning, this
signifies 'If that goes on, there is a risk that the communists
will turn the troubles to account and infiltrate into these
parts'.

In the native's eagerness, the fact that he openly brandishes
the threat of violence proves that he is conscious of the unusual
character of the contemporary situation and that he means to
profit by it. But, still on the level of immediate experience, the
native, who has seen the modern world penetrate into the further-
most corners of the bush, is most acutely aware of all the things
he does not possess. The masses by a sort of (if we may say so)
childlike process of reasoning convince themselves that they
have been robbed of all these things. That is why in certain
under-developed countries the masses forge ahead very quickly,
and realize two or three years after independence that they have

been frustrated, that 'it wasn't worth while' fighting, and that nothing could really change. In 1789, after the bourgeois revolution, the smallest French peasants benefited substantially from the upheaval. But it is a commonplace to observe and to say that in the majority of cases, for ninety-five per cent of the population of under-developed countries, independence brings no immediate change. The enlightened observer takes note of the existence of a kind of masked discontent, like the smoking ashes of a burnt-down house after the fire has been put out, which still threaten to burst into flames again.

So they say that the natives want to go too quickly. Now, let us never forget that only a very short time ago they complained of their slowness, their laziness and their fatalism. Already we see that violence used in specific ways at the moment of the struggle for freedom does not magically disappear after the ceremony of trooping the national colours. It has all the less reason for disappearing since the reconstruction of the nation continues within the framework of cut-throat competition between capitalism and socialism.

This competition gives an almost universal dimension to even the most localized demands. Every meeting held, every act of repression committed, reverberates in the international arena. The murders of Sharpeville shook public opinion for months. In the newspapers, over the wavelengths and in private conversations Sharpeville has become a symbol. It was through Sharpeville that men and women first became acquainted with the problem of apartheid in South Africa. Moreover, we cannot believe that demagogy alone is the explanation for the sudden interest the big powers show in the petty affairs of under-developed regions. Each *jacquerie*, each act of sedition in the Third World makes up part of a picture framed by the Cold War. Two men are beaten up at Salisbury, and at once the whole of a *bloc* goes into action, talks about those two men, and uses the beating-up incident to bring up the particular problem of Rhodesia, linking it, moreover, with the whole African question and with the whole question of colonized people. The other *bloc*, however, is equally concerned in measuring by the magnitude of the campaign the local weaknesses of its system. Thus the colonized peoples realize that neither clan remains outside local incidents.

They no longer limit themselves to regional horizons, for they have caught on to the fact that they live in an atmosphere of international stress.

When every three months or so we hear that the 6th or the 7th flotilla is moving towards such-and-such a coast; when Khrushchev threatens to come to Castro's help with rockets; when Kennedy decides upon some desperate solution for the Laos question, the colonized person or the newly independent native has the impression that whether he wills it or not he is being carried away in a kind of frantic cavalcade. In fact, he is marching in it already. Let us take, for example, the case of the governments of recently liberated countries. The men at the head of affairs spend two-thirds of their time in watching the approaches and trying to anticipate the dangers which threaten them, and the remaining one-third of their time in working for their country. At the same time, they search for allies. Obedient to the same dialectic, the national parties of opposition leave the paths of parliamentary behaviour. They also look for allies to support them in their ruthless ventures into sedition. The atmosphere of violence, after having coloured all the colonial phase, continues to dominate national life, for as we have already said, the Third World is not cut off from the rest. Quite on the contrary, it is at the middle of the whirlpool. This is why the statesmen of under-developed countries keep up indefinitely the tone of aggressiveness and exasperation in their public speeches which in the normal way ought to have disappeared. Herein, also, may be found the reasons for that lack of politeness so often spoken of in connexion with newly established rulers. But what is less visible is the extreme courtesy of these same rulers in their contacts with their brothers or their comrades. Discourtesy is first and foremost a manner to be used in dealings with the others, with the former colonists who come to observe and to investigate. The 'ex-native' too often gets the impression that these reports are already written. The photos which illustrate the article are simply a proof that one knows what one is talking about, and that one has visited the country. The report intends to verify the evidence: everything's going badly out there since we left. Frequently reporters complain of being badly received, of being forced to work under bad conditions and of being fenced round by indifference or hostility: all this is quite normal. The nationalist leaders know that international opinion is formed solely by the Western Press. Now, when a journalist from the West asks us questions, it is seldom in order to help us. In the Algerian war, for example, even the most liberal of the French reporters never ceased to use ambiguous terms in describing our struggle. When we reproached them for this, they replied in all good faith that they were being objective. For the native, objectivity is always directed against him. We may in the same way come to understand the new tone which swamped international diplomacy at the United Nations General Assembly in September 1960. The representatives of the colonial countries were aggressive and violent, and carried things to extremes, but the colonial peoples did not find that they exaggerated. The radicalism of the African spokesmen brought the abscess to a head and showed up the inadmissible nature of the veto and of the dialogue between the great powers, and above all the tiny role reserved for the Third World.

Diplomacy, as inaugurated by the newly independent peoples, is no longer an affair of nuances, of implications, and of hypnotic passes. For the nation's spokesmen are responsible at one and the same time for safeguarding the unity of the nation, the progress of the masses towards a state of well-being and the right of all peoples to bread and liberty. Thus it is a diplomacy which never stops moving, a diplomacy which leaps ahead, in strange contrast to the motionless, petrified world of colonization. And when Mr Khrushchev brandishes his shoe at the United Nations, or thumps the table with it, there's not a single ex-native, nor any representative of an under-developed country, who laughs. For what Mr Khrushchev shows the colonized countries which are looking on is that he, the moujik, who moreover is the possessor of space-rockets, treats these miserable capitalists in the way that they deserve. In the same way, Castro sitting in military uniform in the United Nations Organization does not scandalize the under-developed countries. What Castro demonstrates is the consciousness he has of the continuing existence of the rule of violence. The astonishing thing is that he did not come into UNO with a machine-gun; but if he had, would anyone have minded? All the *jacqueries* and desperate deeds, all those bands armed with cutlasses or axes find their nationality in the implacable struggle which opposes socialism and capitalism.

In 1945, the 45,000 dead at Sétif could pass unnoticed; in 1947, the 90,000 dead in Madagascar could be the subject of a simple paragraph in the papers; in 1952, the 200,000 victims of the repression in Kenya could meet with relative indifference. This was because the international contradictions were not sufficiently distinct. Already the Korean and Indo-Chinese wars had begun a new phase. But it is above all Budapest and Suez which constitute the decisive moments of this confrontation.

Strengthened by the unconditional support of the socialist countries, the colonized peoples fling themselves with whatever arms they have against the impregnable citadel of colonialism. If this citadel is invulnerable to knives and naked fists, it is no longer so when we decide to take into account the context of the cold war.

In this fresh juncture, the Americans take their role of patron of international capitalism very seriously. Early on, they advise the European countries to decolonize in friendly fashion. Later on, they do not hesitate to proclaim first the respect for and then the support of the principle of 'Africa for the Africans'. The United States is not afraid today of stating officially that they are the defenders of the right of all peoples to self-determination. Mr Mennen Williams's last journey is only the illustration of the consciousness which the Americans have that the Third World ought not to be sacrificed. From then on we understand why the violence of the native is only hopeless if we compare it in the abstract to the military machine of the oppressor. On the other hand, if we situate that violence in the dynamics of the international situation, we see at once that it constitutes a terrible menace for the oppressor. Persistent *jacqueries* and Mau-Mau disturbances unbalance the colony's economic life but do not endanger the mother country. What is more important in the eyes of imperialism is the opportunity for socialist propaganda to infiltrate among the masses and to contaminate them. This is already a serious danger in the cold war; but what would happen to that colony in case of real war, riddled as it is by murderous guerrillas?

Thus capitalism realizes that its military strategy has everything to lose by the outbreak of nationalist wars. Again, within the framework of peaceful coexistence, all colonies are destined to disappear, and in the long run neutralism is destined to be respected by capitalism. What must at all costs be avoided is strategic insecurity: the break-through of enemy doctrine into the masses and the deep-rooted hatred of millions of men. The colonized peoples are very well aware of these imperatives which rule international political life; for this reason even those who thunder denunciations of violence take their decisions and act in terms of this universal violence. Today, peaceful coexistence between the two *blocs* provokes and feeds violence in the colonial countries. Tomorrow, perhaps we shall see the shifting of that violence after the complete liberation of the colonial territories. Perhaps we will see the question of minorities cropping up. Already certain minority groups do not hesitate to preach violent methods for resolving their problems and it is not by chance (so the story runs) that in consequence Negro extremists in the United States organize a militia and arm themselves. It is not by chance, either, that in the so-called free world there exist committees for the defence of Jewish minorities in U.S.S.R., nor an accident if General de Gaulle in one of his orations sheds tears over the millions of Moslems oppressed by Communist dictatorship. Both capitalism and imperialism are convinced that the struggle against racialism and the movements towards national freedom are purely and simply directed by remote control, fomented from outside. So they decide to use that very efficacious tactic, the Radio Free Europe Station, voice of the Committee for the aid of over-ruled minorities. . . . They practise anti-colonialism, as did the French colonels in Algeria when they carried on subversive warfare with the S.A.S.* or the psychological services. They 'use the people against the people'. We have seen with what results.

This atmosphere of violence and menaces, these rockets brandished by both sides, do not frighten nor deflect the colonized peoples. We have seen that all their recent history has prepared them to understand and grasp the situation. Between the

---

* Section Administrative Spéciale. An officers' corps whose task was to strengthen contact with the Algerians in non-military matters.

violence of the colonies and that peaceful violence that the world is steeped in, there is a kind of complicit agreement, a sort of homogeneity. The colonized peoples are well adapted to this atmosphere; for once, they are up to date. Sometimes people wonder that the native, rather than give his wife a dress, buys instead a transistor radio. There is no reason to be astonished. The natives are convinced that their fate is in the balance, here and now. They live in the atmosphere of doomsday, and they consider that nothing ought to be let pass unnoticed. That is why they understand very well Phouma and Phoumi, Lumumba and Tshombe, Ahidjo and Moumie, Kenyatta, and the men that are pushed forward regularly to replace him. They understand all these figures very well, for they can unmask the forces working behind them. The native and the under-developed man are today political animals in the most universal sense of the word.

It is true to say that independence has brought moral compensation to colonized peoples, and has established their dignity. But they have not yet had time to elaborate a society, or to build up and affirm values. The warming, light-giving centre where man and citizen develop and enrich their experience in wider and still wider fields does not yet exist. Set in a kind of irresolution, such men persuade themselves fairly easily that everything is going to be decided elsewhere, for everybody, at the same time. As for the political leaders, when faced with this situation, they first hesitate and then choose neutralism.

There is plenty to be said on the subject of neutralism. Some equate it with a sort of tainted mercantilism which consists of taking what it can get from both sides. In fact, neutralism, a state of affairs created by the cold war, if it allows under-developed countries to receive economic help from both sides, does not allow either party to aid under-developed areas to the extent that is necessary. Those literally astronomical sums of money which are invested in military research, those engineers who are transformed into technicians of nuclear war, could in the space of fifteen years raise the standard of living of under-developed countries by sixty per cent. So we see that the true interests of under-developed countries do not lie in the protraction nor in the accentuation of this cold war. But it so happens that no one asks their advice. Therefore, when they can, they cut loose from it. But can they really remain outside it? At this very moment, France is trying out her atomic bombs in Africa. Apart from the passing of motions, the holding of meetings and the shattering of diplomatic relations, we cannot say that the peoples of Africa have had much influence, in this particular sector, on France's attitude.

Neutralism produces in the citizen of the Third World a state of mind which is expressed in everyday life by a fearlessness and an ancestral pride strangely resembling defiance. The flagrant refusal to compromise and the tough will that sets itself against getting tied up is reminiscent of the behaviour of proud, poverty-stricken adolescents, who are always ready to risk their necks in order to have the last word. All this leaves Western observers dumbfounded, for to tell the truth there is a glaring divergence between what these men claim to be and what they have behind them. These countries without tramways, without troops and without money have no justification for the bravado that they display in broad daylight. Undoubtedly, they are impostors. The Third World often gives the impression that it rejoices in sensation and that it must have its weekly dose of crises. These men at the head of empty countries, who talk too loud, are most irritating. You'd like to shut them up. But, on the contrary, they are in great demand. They are given bouquets; they are invited to dinner. In fact, we quarrel over who shall have them. And this is neutralism. They are ninety-eight per cent illiterate, but they are the subject of a huge body of literature. They travel a great deal: the governing classes and students of under-developed countries are gold mines for airline companies. African and Asian officials may in the same month follow a course on socialist planning in Moscow and one on the advantages of the liberal economy in London or at Columbia University. African trade-union leaders leap ahead at a great rate in their own field. Hardly have they been appointed to posts in managerial organizations when they decide to form themselves into autonomous bodies. They haven't the requisite fifty years experience of practical trade-unionism in the framework of an industrial country, but they already know that non-political trade-unionism doesn't make sense. They haven't come to grips with the bourgeois machine, nor developed their consciousness in the class struggle; but perhaps this isn't necessary. Perhaps. We shall see that this will to sum everything up, which caricatures itself often in facile internationalism, is one of the most fundamental characteristics of under-developed countries.

Let us return to considering the single combat between native and settler. We have seen that it takes the form of an armed and open struggle. There is no lack of historical examples: Indo-China, Indonesia, and of course North Africa. But what we must not lose sight of is that this struggle could have broken out anywhere, in Guinea as well as Somaliland, and moreover today it could break out in every place where colonialism means to stay on, in Angola, for example. The existence of an armed struggle shows that the people are decided to trust to violent methods only. He of whom *they* have never stopped saying that the only language he understands is that of force, decides to give utterance by force. In fact, as always, the settler has shown him the way he should take if he is to become free. The argument the native chooses has been furnished by the settler, and by an ironic turning of the tables it is the native who now affirms that the colonialist understands nothing but force. The colonial regime owes its legitimacy to force and at no time tries to hide this aspect of things. Every statue, whether of Faidherbe or of Lyautey, of Bugeaud or of Sergeant Blandan – all these *conquistadors* perched on colonial soil do not cease from proclaiming one and the same thing: 'We are here by the force of bayonets. . . .'* The sentence is easily completed. During the phase of insurrection, each settler reasons on a basis of simple arithmetic. This logic does not surprise the other settlers, but it is important to point out that it does not surprise the natives either. To begin with, the affirmation of the principle: 'It's them or us' does not constitute a paradox, since colonialism, as we have seen, is in fact the organization of a Manichaean world, a world divided up into compartments. And when in laying down precise methods the settler asks each member of the oppressing minority to shoot down thirty or 100 or 200 natives, he sees that nobody shows

* Refers to Mirabeau's famous saying: 'I am here by the will of the People; I shall leave only by the force of bayonets' (*translator*).

any indignation and that the whole problem is to decide whether it can be done all at once or by stages.*

This chain of reasoning which presumes very arithmetically the disappearance of the colonized people does not leave the native overcome with moral indignation. He has always known that his duel with the settler would take place in the arena. The native loses no time in lamentations, and he hardly ever seeks for justice in the colonial framework. The fact is that if the settler's logic leaves the native unshaken, it is because the latter has practically stated the problem of his liberation in identical terms: 'We must form ourselves into groups of two hundred or five hundred, and each group must deal with a settler.' It is in this manner of thinking that each of the protagonists begins the struggle.

For the native, this violence represents the absolute line of action. The militant is also a man who works. The questions that the organization asks the militant bear the mark of this way of looking at things: 'Where have you worked? With whom? What have you accomplished?' The group requires that each individual perform an irrevocable action. In Algeria, for example, where almost all the men who called on the people to join in the national struggle were condemned to death or searched for by the French police, confidence was proportional to the hopelessness of each case. You could be sure of a new recruit when he could no longer go back into the colonial system. This mechanism, it seems, had existed in Kenya among the Mau-Mau, who required that each member of the group should strike a blow at the victim. Each one was thus personally responsible for the death of that victim. To work means to work for the death of the settler. This assumed responsibility for violence allows both strayed and outlawed members of the group to come back again and to find their place once more, to become integrated. Violence

* It is evident that this vacuum cleaning destroys the very thing that they want to preserve. Sartre points this out when he says: 'In short by the very fact of repeating them [concerning racist ideas] it is revealed that the simultaneous union of all against the natives is unrealizable. Such union only recurs from time to time and moreover it can only come into being as an active groupment in order to massacre the natives – an absurd though perpetual temptation to the settlers, which even if it was feasible would only suceed in abolishing colonization at one blow' (*Critique de la raison dialectique*, p. 346).

is thus seen as comparable to a royal pardon. The colonized man finds his freedom in and through violence. This rule of conduct enlightens the agent because it indicates to him the means and end. The poetry of Césaire takes on in this precise aspect of violence a prophetic significance. We may recall one of the most decisive pages of his tragedy where the Rebel (indeed!) explains his conduct:

THE REBEL (*harshly*): My name – an offence; my Christian name – humiliation; my status – a rebel; my age – the stone age.

THE MOTHER: My race – the human race. My religion – brotherhood.

THE REBEL: My race: that of the fallen. My religion . . . but it's not you that will show it to me with your disarmament . . .

'tis I myself, with my rebellion and my poor fists clenched and my woolly head . . . (*Very calm*) I remember one November day; it was hardly six months ago . . . The master came into the cabin in a cloud of smoke like an April moon. He was flexing his short muscular arms – he was a very good master – and he was rubbing his little dimpled face with his fat fingers. His blue eyes were smiling and he couldn't get the honeyed words out of his mouth quick enough. 'The kid will be a decent fellow,' he said looking at me, and he said other pleasant things too, the master – that you had to start very early, that twenty years was not too much to make a good Christian and a good slave, a steady, devoted boy, a good commander's chain-gang captain, sharp-eyed and strong-armed. And all that man saw of my son's cradle was that it was the cradle of a chain-gang captain.

We crept in knife in hand . . .

THE MOTHER: Alas, you'll die for it.

THE REBEL: Killed . . . I killed him with my own hands . . .

Yes, 'twas a fruitful death, a copious death . . .

It was night. We crept among the sugar canes.

The knives sang to the stars, but we did not heed the stars.

The sugar canes scarred our faces with streams of green blades.

THE MOTHER: And I had dreamed of a son to close his mother's eyes.

THE REBEL: But I chose to open my son's eyes upon another sun.

THE MOTHER: O my son, son of evil and unlucky death –

THE REBEL: Mother of living and splendid death,

THE MOTHER: Because he has hated too much,

THE REBEL: Because he has too much loved.

THE MOTHER: Spare me, I am choking in your bonds. I bleed from your wounds.

THE REBEL: And the world does not spare me ... There is not anywhere in the world a poor creature who's been lynched or tortured in whom I am not murdered and humiliated ...

THE MOTHER: God of Heaven, deliver him!

THE REBEL: My heart, thou wilt not deliver me from all that I remember ...

It was an evening in November ...

And suddenly shouts lit up the silence;

We had attacked, we the slaves; we, the dung underfoot, we the animals with patient hooves,

We were running like madmen; shots rang out ... We were striking. Blood and sweat cooled and refreshed us. We were striking where the shouts came from, and the shouts became more strident and a great clamour rose from the east: it was the outhouses burning and the flames flickered sweetly on our cheeks.

Then was the assault made on the master's house.

They were firing from the windows.

We broke in the doors.

The master's room was wide open. The master's room was brilliantly lighted, and the master was there, very calm ... and our people stopped dead ... it was the master ... I went in. 'It's you,' he said, very calm.

It was I, even I, and I told him so, the good slave, the faithful slave, the slave of slaves, and suddenly his eyes were like two cockroaches, frightened in the rainy season ... I struck, and the blood spurted; that is the only baptism that I remember today.*

It is understandable that in this atmosphere, daily life becomes quite simply impossible. You can no longer be a *fellah*, a pimp or an alcoholic as before. The violence of the colonial regime and the counter-violence of the native balance each other and respond to each other in an extraordinary reciprocal homogeneity. This reign of violence will be the more terrible in proportion to the size of the implantation from the mother country. The development of violence among the colonized people will be proportionate to the violence exercised by the threatened colonial regime. In the first phase of this insurrectional period, the home governments are the slaves of the settlers, and these settlers seek to intimidate the natives and their home governments at one and

---

* Aimé Cesaire: *Les Armes miraculeuses* (*Et les chiens se taisaient*), Gallimard, pp. 133–7.

the same time. They use the same methods against both of them. The assassination of the Mayor of Evian, in its method and motivation, is identifiable with the assassination of Ali Boumendjel. For the settlers, the alternative is not between *Algérie algérienne* and *Algérie française* but between an independent Algeria and a colonial Algeria, and anything else is mere talk or attempts at treason. The settler's logic is implacable and one is only staggered by the counter-logic visible in the behaviour of the native in so far as one has not clearly understood beforehand the mechanisms of the settler's ideas. From the moment that the native has chosen the methods of counter-violence, police reprisals automatically call forth reprisals on the side of the nationalists. However, the results are not equivalent, for machine-gunning from aeroplanes and bombardments from the fleet go far beyond in horror and magnitude any answer the natives can make. This recurring terror demystifies once and for all the most estranged members of the colonized race. They find out on the spot that all the piles of speeches on the equality of human beings do not hide the commonplace fact that the seven Frenchmen killed or wounded at the Col de Sakamody kindles the indignation of all civilized consciences, whereas the sack of the *douars** of Guergour and of the *dechras* of Djerah and the massacre of whole populations – which had merely called forth the Sakamody ambush as a reprisal – all this is of not the slightest importance. Terror, counter-terror, violence, counter-violence: that is what observers bitterly record when they describe the circle of hate, which is so tenacious and so evident in Algeria.

In all armed struggles, there exists what we might call the point of no return. Almost always it is marked off by a huge and all-inclusive repression which engulfs all sectors of the colonized people. This point was reached in Algeria in 1955 with the 12,000 victims of Phillippeville, and in 1956 with Lacoste's instituting of urban and rural militias.†

---

* Temporary village for the use of shepherds (*translator*).

† We must go back to this period in order to judge the importance of this decision on the part of the French government in Algeria. Thus we may read in *Résistance algérienne*, No. 4, dated 28 March 1957, the following: 'In reply to the wish expressed by the General Assembly of the United Nations, the

French Government has now decided to create urban militias in Algeria. "Enough blood has been spilled," was what the United Nations said; Lacoste replies, "Let us form militias." "Cease fire," advised U.N.A.; Lacoste vociferates, "We must arm the civilians." Whereas the two parties face-to-face with each other were on the recommendation of the United Nations invited to contact each other with a view to coming to an agreement and finding a peaceful and democratic solution, Lacoste decrees that henceforward every European will be armed and should open fire on any person who seems to him suspect. It was then agreed (in the Assembly) that savage and iniquitous repression verging on genocide ought at all costs to be opposed by the authorities: but Lacoste replies, "Let us systematize the repression and organize the Algerian man-hunt." And, symbolically, he entrusts the military with civil powers, and gives military powers to civilians. The ring is closed. In the middle, the Algerian, disarmed, famished, tracked down, jostled, struck, lynched, will soon be slaughtered as a suspect. Today, in Algeria, there is not a single Frenchman who is not authorized and even invited to use his weapons. There is not a single Frenchman, in Algeria, one month after the appeal for calm made by UNO, who is not permitted, and obliged to search out, investigate and pursue suspects.

'One month after the vote on the final motion of the General Assembly of the United Nations, there is not one European in Algeria who is not party to the most frightful work of extermination of modern times. A democratic solution? Right, Lacoste concedes; let's begin by exterminating the Algerians, and to do that, let's arm the civilians and give them *carte blanche*. The Paris Press, on the whole, has welcomed the creation of these armed groups with reserve. Fascist militias, they've been called. Yes; but on the individual level, on the plane of human rights, what is fascism if not colonialism when rooted in a traditionally colonialist country? The opinion has been advanced that they are systematically legalized and commended; but does not the body of Algeria bear for the last one hundred and thirty years wounds which gape still wider, more numerous and more deep-seated than ever? "Take care," advises Monsieur Kenne-Vignes, member of parliament for the M.R.P., "do we not by the creation of these militias risk seeing the gap widen between the two communities in Algeria?" Yes; but is not colonial status simply the organized reduction to slavery of a whole people? The Algerian revolution is precisely the affirmed contestation of that slavery and that abyss. The Algerian revolution speaks to the occupying nation and says: "Take your fangs out of the bleeding flesh of Algeria! Let the people of Algeria speak!"

'The creation of militias, they say, will lighten the tasks of the Army. It will free certain units whose mission it will be to protect the Moroccan and Tunisian borders. In Algeria, the Army is six hundred thousand strong. Almost all the Navy and the Air Force are based there. There is an enormous, speedy police force with a horribly good record since it has absorbed the ex-torturers from Morocco and Tunisia. The territorial units are one hundred thousand strong. The task of the Army, all the same, must be lightened. So let us create urban militias. The fact remains that the hysterical and criminal frenzy of Lacoste imposes them even on clear-sighted French people. The truth is that

Then it became clear to everybody, including even the settlers, that 'things couldn't go on as before'. Yet the colonized people do not chalk up the reckoning. They record the huge gaps made in their ranks as a sort of necessary evil. Since they have decided to reply by violence, they therefore are ready to take all its consequences. They only insist in return that no reckoning should be kept, either, for the others. To the saying 'All natives are the same' the colonized person replies 'All settlers are the same.' *

---

the creation of militias carries its contradiction even in its justification. The task of the French Army is never-ending. Consequently, when it is given as an objective the gagging of the Algerian people, the door is closed on the future for ever. Above all, it is forbidden to analyse, to understand or to measure the depth and the density of the Algerian Revolution: departmental leaders, housing-estate leaders, street leaders, house leaders, leaders who control each landing . . . Today, to the surface chequer-board is added an underground network.

'In forty-eight hours two thousand volunteers were enrolled. The Europeans of Algeria responded immediately to Lacoste's call to kill. From now on, each European must check up on all surviving Algerians in his sector; and in addition he will be responsible for information, for a "quick response" to acts of terrorism, for the detection of suspects, for the liquidation of runaways and for the reinforcement of police services. Certainly, the tasks of the Army must be lightened. Today, to the surface mopping-up is added a deeper harrowing. Today, to the killing which is all in the day's work is added planified murder. "Stop the bloodshed," was the advice given by UNO. "The best way of doing this," replied Lacoste, "is to make sure there remains no blood to shed." The Algerian people, after having been delivered up to Massu's hordes, is put under the protection of the urban militias. By his decision to create these militias, Lacoste shows quite plainly that he will brook no interference with *his* war. It is a proof that there are no limits once the rot has set in. True, he is at the moment a prisoner of the situation; but what a consolation to drag everyone down in one's fall!

'After each of these decisions, the Algerian people tense their muscles still more and fight still harder. After each of these organized, deliberately sought after assassinations, the Algerian people builds up its awareness of self, and consolidates its resistance. Yes; the tasks of the French Army are infinite: for oh, how infinite is the unity of the people of Algeria!'

* This is why there are no prisoners when the fighting first starts. It is only through educating the local leaders politically that those at the head of the movement can make the masses accept (1) that people coming from the mother country do not always act of their own free will and are sometimes even disgusted by the war; (2) that it is of immediate advantage to the movement that its supporters should show by their actions that they respect certain international conventions; (3) that an army which takes prisoners is an army, and ceases to be considered as a group of wayside bandits; (4) that whatever

When the native is tortured, when his wife is killed or raped, he complains to no one. The oppressor's government can set up commissions of inquiry and of information daily if it wants to; in the eyes of the native, these commissions do not exist. The fact is that soon we shall have had seven years of crimes in Algeria and there has not yet been a single Frenchman indicted before a French court of justice for the murder of an Algerian. In Indo-China, in Madagascar or in the colonies the native has always known that he need expect nothing from the other side. The settler's work is to make even dreams of liberty impossible for the native. The native's work is to imagine all possible methods for destroying the settler. On the logical plane, the Manichaeism of the settler produces a Manichaeism of the native. To the theory of the 'absolute evil of the native' the theory of the 'absolute evil of the settler' replies.

The appearance of the settler has meant in the terms of syncretism the death of the aboriginal society, cultural lethargy, and the petrification of individuals. For the native, life can only spring up again out of the rotting corpse of the settler. This, then is the correspondence, term by term, between the two trains of reasoning.

But it so happens that for the colonized people this violence, because it constitutes their only work, invests their characters with positive and creative qualities. The practice of violence binds them together as a whole, since each individual forms a violent link in the great chain, a part of the great organism of violence which has surged upwards in reaction to the settler's violence in the beginning. The groups recognize each other and the future nation is already indivisible. The armed struggle mobilizes the people; that is to say, it throws them in one way and in one direction.

The mobilization of the masses, when it arises out of the war of liberation, introduces into each man's consciousness the ideas of a common cause, of a national destiny and of a collective history. In the same way the second phase, that of the building-up of the nation, is helped on by the existence of this cement which

the circumstances, the possession of prisoners constitutes a means of exerting pressure which must not be overlooked in order to protect our men who are in enemy hands.

has been mixed with blood and anger. Thus we come to a fuller appreciation of the originality of the words used in these under-developed countries. During the colonial period the people are called upon to fight against oppression; after national liberation, they are called upon to fight against poverty, illiteracy and under-development. The struggle, they say, goes on. The people realize that life is an unending contest.

We have said that the native's violence unifies the people. By its very structure, colonialism is separatist and regionalist. Colonialism does not simply state the existence of tribes; it also reinforces it and separates them. The colonial system encourages chieftaincies and keeps alive the old Marabout confraternities. Violence is in action all-inclusive and national. It follows that it is closely involved in the liquidation of regionalism and of tribal-ism. Thus the national parties show no pity at all towards the *caids* and the customary chiefs. Their destruction is the pre-liminary to the unification of the people.

At the level of individuals, violence is a cleansing force. It frees the native from his inferiority complex and from his despair and inaction; it makes him fearless and restores his self-respect. Even if the armed struggle has been symbolic and the nation is demobilized through a rapid movement of decolonization, the people have the time to see that the liberation has been the business of each and all and that the leader has no special merit. From thence comes that type of aggressive reticence with regard to the machinery of protocol which young governments quickly show. When the people have taken violent part in the national liberation they will allow no one to set themselves up as 'libera-tors'. They show themselves to be jealous of the results of their action and take good care not to place their future, their destiny or the fate of their country in the hands of a living god. Yester-day they were completely irresponsible; today they mean to understand everything and make all decisions. Illuminated by violence, the consciousness of the people rebels against any pacification. From now on the demagogues, the opportunists and the magicians have a difficult task. The action which has thrown them into a hand-to-hand struggle confers upon the masses a voracious taste for the concrete. The attempt at mystifi-cation becomes, in the long run, practically impossible.

VIOLENCE IN THE INTERNATIONAL CONTEXT

We have pointed out many times in the preceding pages that in under-developed regions the political leader is for ever calling on his people to fight: to fight against colonialism, to fight against poverty and under-development, and to fight against sterile traditions. The vocabulary which he uses in his appeals is that of a chief of staff: 'mass mobilization'; 'agricultural front'; 'fight against illiteracy'; 'defeats we have undergone'; 'victories won'. The young independent nation evolves during the first years in an atmosphere of the battlefield, for the political leader of an under-developed country looks fearfully at the huge distance his country will have to cover. He calls to the people and says to them: 'Let us gird up our loins and set to work', and the country, possessed by a kind of creative madness, throws itself into a gigantic and disproportionate effort. The programme consists not only of climbing out of the morass but also of catching up with the other nations using the only means at hand. They reason that if the European nations have reached that stage of development, it is on account of their efforts: 'Let us therefore', they seem to say, 'prove to ourselves and to the whole world that we are capable of the same achievements.' This manner of setting out the problem of the evolution of under-developed countries seems to us to be neither correct nor reasonable.

The European states achieved national unity at a moment when the national middle classes had concentrated most of the wealth in their hands. Shopkeepers and artisans, clerks and bankers monopolized finance, trade and science in the national framework. The middle class was the most dynamic and prosperous of all classes. Its coming to power enabled it to undertake certain very important speculations: industrialization, the development of communications and soon the search for outlets overseas.

In Europe, apart from certain slight differences (England, for example, was some way ahead) the various states were at a more or less uniform stage economically when they achieved national unity. There was no nation which by reason of the character of its development and evolution caused affront to the others.

Today, national independence and the growth of national feeling in under-developed regions take on totally new aspects. In these regions, with the exception of certain spectacular advances, the different countries show the same absence of infrastructure. The mass of the people struggle against the same poverty, flounder about making the same gestures and with their shrunken bellies outline what has been called the geography of hunger. It is an under-developed world, a world inhuman in its poverty; but also it is a world without doctors, without engineers and without administrators. Confronting this world the European nations sprawl, ostentatiously opulent. This European opulence is literally scandalous, for it has been founded on slavery, it has been nourished with the blood of slaves and it comes directly from the soil and from the subsoil of that under-developed world. The well-being and the progress of Europe have been built up with the sweat and the dead bodies of Negroes, Arabs, Indians and the yellow races. We have decided not to overlook this any longer. When a colonialist country, embarrassed by the claims for independence made by a colony, proclaims to the nationalist leaders: 'If you wish for independence, take it, and go back to the middle ages', the newly independent people tend to acquiesce and to accept the challenge; in fact you may see colonialism withdrawing its capital and its technicians and setting up around the young state the apparatus of economic pressure.* The apotheosis of independence is transformed

* In the present international context, capitalism does not merely operate an economic blockade against African or Asiatic colonies. The United States with its anti-Castro operations is opening a new chapter in the long story of man's toiling advance towards freedom. Latin America, made up of new independent countries which sit at the United Nations and raise the wind there ought to be an object lesson for Africa. These former colonies since their liberation have suffered the brazen-faced rule of Western capitalism in terror and destitution.

The liberation of Africa and the growth of consciousness among mankind have made it possible for the Latin American peoples to break with the old merry-go-round of dictatorships where each succeeding regime exactly resembled the preceding one. Castro took over power in Cuba, and gave it to the people. This heresy is felt to be a national scourge by the Yankees, and the United States is now organizing counter-revolutionary brigades, puts into the curse of independence, and the colonial power through its immense resources of coercion condemns the young nation to regression. In plain words, the colonial power says: 'Since you want independence, take it and starve.' The nationalist leaders have no other choice but to turn to their people and ask from them a gigantic effort. A regime of austerity is imposed on these starving men; a disproportionate amount of work is required from their atrophied muscles. An autarkic regime is set up and each state, with the miserable resources it has in hand, tries to find an answer to the nation's great hunger and poverty. We see the mobilization of a people which toils to exhaustion in front of a suspicious and bloated Europe.

Other countries of the Third World refuse to undergo this ordeal and agree to get over it by accepting the conditions of the former guardian power. These countries use their strategic position – a position which accords them privileged treatment in the struggle between the two *blocs* – to conclude treaties and give undertakings. The former dominated country becomes an economically dependent country. The ex-colonial power, which has kept intact and sometimes even reinforced its colonialist trade channels agrees to provision the budget of the independent nation by small injections. Thus we see that the accession to independence of the colonial countries places an important question before the world, for the national liberation of colonized countries unveils their true economic state and makes it seem even more unendurable. The fundamental duel which seemed to be that between colonialism and anti-colonialism,

---

together a provisional government, burns the sugar-cane crops, and generally has decided to strangle the Cuban people mercilessly. But this will be difficult. The people of Cuba will suffer, but they will conquer. The Brazilian president Janio Quadros has just announced in a declaration of historic importance that his country will defend the Cuban Revolution by all means. Perhaps even the United States may draw back when faced with the declared will of the peoples. When that day comes, we'll hang out the flags, for it will be a decisive moment for the men and women of the whole world. The all-mighty dollar, which when all is said or done is only guaranteed by slaves scattered all over the globe, in the oil-wells of the Middle East, the mines of Peru or of the Congo, and the United Fruit or Firestone plantations, will then cease to dominate with all its force these slaves which it has created and who continue, empty-headed and empty-bellied, to feed it from their substance.

and indeed between capitalism and socialism, is already losing some of its importance. What counts today, the question which is looming on the horizon, is the need for a redistribution of wealth. Humanity must reply to this question, or be shaken to pieces by it.

It might have been generally thought that the time had come for the world, and particularly for the Third World, to choose between the capitalist and socialist systems. The under-developed countries, which have used the fierce competition which exists between the two systems in order to assure the triumph of their struggle for national liberation, should however refuse to become a factor in that competition. The Third World ought not to be content to define itself in the terms of values which have preceded it. On the contrary, the under-developed countries ought to do their utmost to find their own particular values and methods and a style which shall be peculiar to them. The concrete problem we find ourselves up against is not that of a choice, cost what it may, between socialism and capitalism as they have been defined by men of other continents and of other ages. Of course we know that the capitalist regime, in so far as it is a way of life, cannot leave us free to perform our work at home, nor our duty in the world. Capitalist exploitation and cartels and monopolies are the enemies of under-developed countries. On the other hand the choice of a socialist regime, a regime which is completely orientated towards the people as a whole and based on the principle that man is the most precious of all possessions will allow us to go forward more quickly and more harmoniously, and thus make impossible that caricature of society where all economic and political power is held in the hands of a few who regard the nation as a whole with scorn and contempt.

But in order that this regime may work to good effect so that we can in every instance respect those principles which were our inspiration, we need something more than human output. Certain under-developed countries expend a huge amount of energy in this way. Men and women, young and old undertake enthusiastically what is in fact forced labour, and proclaim themselves the slaves of the nation. The gift of oneself, and the contempt for every preoccupation which is not in the common interest, bring into being a national *morale* which comforts the heart of man, gives him fresh confidence in the destiny of mankind and disarms the most reserved observers. But we cannot believe that such an effort can be kept up at the same frenzied pace for very long. These young countries have agreed to take up the challenge after the unconditional withdrawal of the ex-colonial countries. The country finds itself in the hands of new managers; but the fact is that everything needs to be reformed and everything thought out anew. In reality the colonial system was concerned with certain forms of wealth and certain resources only – precisely those which provisioned her own industries. Up to the present no serious effort had been made to estimate the riches of the soil or of mineral resources. Thus the young independent nation sees itself obliged to use the economic channels created by the colonial regime. It can, obviously, export to other countries and other currency areas, but the basis of its exports is not fundamentally modified. The colonial regime has carved out certain channels and they must be maintained or catastrophe will threaten. Perhaps it is necessary to begin everything all over again: to change the nature of the country's exports, and not only simply their destination, to re-examine the soil and mineral resources, the rivers, and – why not? – the sun's productivity. Now, in order to do all this other things are needed over and above human output – capital of all kinds, technicians, engineers, skilled mechanics and so on. Let's be frank: we do not believe that the colossal effort which the under-developed peoples are called upon to make by their leaders will give the desired results. If conditions of work are not modified, centuries will be needed to humanize this world which has been forced down to animal level by imperial powers.*

The truth is that we ought not to accept these conditions. We should flatly refuse the situation to which the Western countries wish to condemn us. Colonialism and imperialism have not paid their score when they withdraw their flags and

* Certain countries who have benefited by a large European settlement come to independence with houses and wide streets, and these tend to forget the poverty-stricken, starving hinterland. By the irony of fate, they give the impression by a kind of complicit silence that their towns are contemporaneous with independence.

their police forces from our territories. For centuries the capitalists have behaved in the under-developed world like nothing more than war criminals. Deportations, massacres, forced labour and slavery have been the main methods used by capitalism to increase its wealth, its gold or diamond reserves, and to establish its power. Not long ago Nazism transformed the whole of Europe into a veritable colony. The governments of the various European nations called for reparations and demanded the restitution in kind and money of the wealth which had been stolen from them: cultural treasures, pictures, sculptures and stained glass have been given back to their owners. There was only one slogan in the mouths of Europeans on the morrow of the 1945 V-day: 'Germany must pay.' Herr Adenauer, it must be said, at the opening of the Eichmann trial, and in the name of the German people, asked once more for forgiveness from the Jewish people. Herr Adenauer has renewed the promise of his people to go on paying to the state of Israel the enormous sums which are supposed to be compensation for the crimes of the Nazis.*

In the same way we may say that the imperialist states would make a great mistake and commit an unspeakable injustice if they contented themselves with withdrawing from our soil the military cohorts, and the administrative and managerial services whose function it was to discover the wealth of the country, to extract it and to send it off to the mother countries. We are

* It is true that Germany has not paid all her reparations. The indemnities imposed on the vanquished nation have not been claimed in full, for the injured nations have included Germany in their anti-communist system of defence. This same preoccupation is the permanent motivation of the colonialist countries when they try to obtain from their former colonies, if not their inclusion in the Western system, at least military bases and enclaves. On the other hand, they have decided unanimously to forget their demands for the sake of NATO strategy and to preserve the free world; and we have seen Germany receiving floods of dollars and machines. A Germany once more standing on its feet, strong and powerful, was a necessity for the Western camp. It was in the understood interests of so-called free Europe to have a prosperous and reconstructed Germany which would be capable of serving as a first rampart against the eventual Red hordes. Germany has made admirable use of the European crisis. At the same time the United States and other European states feel a legitimate bitterness when confronted with this Germany, yesterday at their feet, which today metes out to them cut-throat competition in the economic field.

not blinded by the moral reparation of national independence; nor are we fed by it. The wealth of the imperial countries is our wealth too. On the universal plane this affirmation, you may be sure, should on no account be taken to signify that we feel ourselves affected by the creations of Western arts or techniques. For in a very concrete way Europe has stuffed herself inordinately with the gold and raw materials of the colonial countries: Latin America, China and Africa. From all these continents, under whose eyes Europe today raises up her tower of opulence, there has flowed out for centuries towards that same Europe diamonds and oil, silk and cotton, wood and exotic products. Europe is literally the creation of the Third World. The wealth which smothers her is that which was stolen from the underdeveloped peoples. The ports of Holland, the docks of Bordeaux and Liverpool were specialized in the Negro slave-trade, and owe their renown to millions of deported slaves. So when we hear the head of a European state declare with his hand on his heart that he must come to the help of the poor underdeveloped peoples, we do not tremble with gratitude. Quite the contrary; we say to ourselves: 'It's a just reparation which will be paid to us.' Nor will we acquiesce in the help for underdeveloped countries being a programme of 'sisters of charity'. This help should be the ratification of a double realization: the realization by the colonized peoples that *it is their due*, and the realization by the capitalist powers that in fact *they must pay*.* For if, through lack of intelligence (we won't speak of lack of gratitude) the capitalist countries refuse to pay, then the relentless dialectic of their own system will smother them. It is a fact that young nations do not attract much private capital. There are many reasons which explain and render legitimate

* 'To make a radical difference between the building up of socialism in Europe and our relations with the Third World (as if our only relations with it were external ones) is, whether we know it or not, to set the pace for the distribution of the colonial inheritance over and above the liberation of the under-developed countries. It is to wish to build up a luxury socialism upon the fruits of imperialist robbery – as if, inside the gang, the swag is more or less shared out equally, and even a little of it is given to the poor in the form of charity, since it's been forgotten that they were the people it was stolen from.' Marcel Péju: 'To die for De Gaulle?' Article appearing in *Temps modernes*, No. 175–6, October–November 1960.

this reserve on the part of the monopolies. As soon as the capitalists know – and of course they are the first to know – that their government is getting ready to decolonize, they hasten to withdraw all their capital from the colony in question. The spectacular flight of capital is one of the most constant phenomena of decolonization.

Private companies, when asked to invest in independent countries, lay down conditions which are shown in practice to be unacceptable or unrealizable. Faithful to the principle of immediate returns which is theirs as soon as they go 'overseas', the capitalists are very chary concerning all long-term investments. They are unamenable and often openly hostile to the prospective programmes of planning laid down by the young teams who form the new government. At a pinch they willingly agree to lend money to the young states, but only on condition that this money is used to buy manufactured products and machines: in other words, that it serves to keep the factories in the mother country going.

In fact the cautiousness of the Western financial groups may be explained by their fear of taking any risk. They also demand political stability and a calm social climate which are impossible to obtain when account is taken of the appalling state of the population as a whole immediately after independence. Therefore, vainly looking for some guarantee which the former colony cannot give, they insist on garrisons being maintained or the inclusion of the young state in military or economic pacts. The private companies put pressure on their own governments at least to set up military bases in these countries for the purpose of assuring the protection of their interests. In the last resort these companies ask their government to guarantee the investments which they decide to make in such-and-such an underdeveloped region.

It happens that few countries fulfil the conditions demanded by the trusts and monopolies. Thus capital, failing to find a safe outlet, remains blocked in Europe, and is frozen. It is all the more frozen because the capitalists refuse to invest in their own countries. The returns in this case are in fact negligible and treasury control is the despair of even the boldest spirits.

In the long run the situation is catastrophic. Capital no

longer circulates, or else its circulation is considerably diminished. In spite of the huge sums swallowed up by military
budgets, international capitalism is in desperate straits.

But another danger threatens it as well. In so far as the Third
World is in fact abandoned and condemned to regression or at
least to stagnation by the selfishness and wickedness of Western
nations, the under-developed peoples will decide to continue
their evolution inside a collective autarky. Thus the Western
industries will quickly be deprived of their overseas markets.
The machines will pile up their products in the warehouses and
a merciless struggle will ensue on the European market between
the trusts and the financial groups. The closing of factories, the
paying off of workers and unemployment will force the European working class to engage in an open struggle against the
capitalist regime. Then the monopolies will realize that their
true interests lie in giving aid to the under-developed countries –
unstinted aid with not too many conditions. So we see that the
young nations of the Third World are wrong in trying to make
up to the capitalist countries. We are strong in our own right,
and in the justice of our point of view. We ought on the contrary
to emphasize and explain to the capitalist countries that the
fundamental problem of our time is not the struggle between
the socialist regime and them. The Cold War must be ended, for
it leads nowhere. The plans for nuclearizing the world must
stop, and large-scale investments and technical aid must be
given to under-developed regions. The fate of the world depends
on the answer that is given to this question.

Moreover, the capitalist regime must not try to enlist the aid
of the socialist regime over 'the fate of Europe' in face of the
starving multitudes of coloured peoples. The exploit of Colonel
Gagarin doesn't seem to displease General de Gaulle, for is it
not a triumph which brings honour to Europe? For some time
past the statesmen of the capitalist countries have adopted an
equivocal attitude towards the Soviet Union. After having
united all their forces to abolish the socialist regime, they now
realize that they'll have to reckon with it. So they look as pleasant
as they can, they make all kinds of advances, and they remind the
Soviet people the whole time that they 'belong to Europe'.

They will not manage to divide the progressive forces which

mean to lead mankind towards happiness by brandishing the threat of a Third World which is rising like the tide to swallow up all Europe. The Third World does not mean to organize a great crusade of hunger against the whole of Europe. What it expects from those who for centuries have kept it in slavery is that they will help it to rehabilitate mankind, and make man victorious everywhere, once and for all. But it is clear that we are not so naïve as to think that this will come about with the co-operation and the good will of the European governments. This huge task which consists of reintroducing mankind into the world, the whole of mankind, will be carried out with the indispensable help of the European peoples, who themselves must realize that in the past they have often joined the ranks of our common masters where colonial questions were concerned. To achieve this, the European peoples must first decide to wake up and shake themselves, use their brains, and stop playing the stupid game of the Sleeping Beauty.

2. Spontaneity: Its Strength and Weakness

THIS consideration of violence has led us to take account of the frequent existence of a time-lag, or a difference of rhythm, between the leaders of a nationalist party and the mass of the people. In every political or trade-union organization there is a traditional gap between the rank-and-file, who demand the total and immediate bettering of their lot, and the leaders, who, since they are aware of the difficulties which may be made by the employers, seek to limit and restrain the workers' demands. This is why you often are aware of a dogged discontentment among the rank-and-file as regards their leaders. After a day spent in demonstrating for their demands, the leaders celebrate the victory, whereas the rank-and-file have a strong suspicion that they have been cheated. It is through a multiplicity of demonstrations in support of their claims and through an increase in trade-union demands that the rank-and-file achieve their political education. A politically informed trade-union member is a man who knows that a local conflict is not a decisive settlement between himself and the employers. The native intellectuals, who have studied in their respective 'mother countries' the working of political parties, carefully organize similar institutions in order to mobilize the masses and bring pressure to bear on the colonial administration. The birth of nationalist parties in the colonized countries is contemporary with the formation of an intellectual *élite* engaged in trade. The *élite* will attach a fundamental importance to organization, so much so that the fetish of organization will often take precedence over a reasoned study of colonial society. The notion of the party is a notion imported from the mother country. This instrument of modern political warfare is thrown down just as it is, without the slightest modification, upon real life with all its infinite variations and lack of balance, where slavery, serfdom, barter, a skilled working class and high finance exist side by side.

The weakness of political parties does not only lie in the

mechanical application of an organization which was created to carry on the struggle of the working class inside a highly industrialized, capitalist society. If we limit ourselves to the *type* of organization, it is clear that innovations and adaptations ought to have been made. The great mistake, the inherent defect in the majority of political parties in under-developed regions has been, following traditional lines, to approach in the first place those elements which are the most politically conscious: the working classes in the towns, the skilled workers and the civil servants – that is to say, a tiny portion of the population, which hardly represents more than one per cent.

But although this proletariat has read the party publications and understood its propaganda, it is much less ready to obey in the event of orders being given which set in motion the fierce struggle for national liberation. It cannot be too strongly stressed that in the colonial territories the proletariat is the nucleus of the colonized population which has been most pampered by the colonial regime. The embryonic proletariat of the towns is in a comparatively privileged position. In capitalist countries, the working class has nothing to lose; it is they who in the long run have everything to gain. In the colonial countries the working class has everything to lose; in reality it represents that fraction of the colonized nation which is necessary and irreplaceable if the colonial machine is to run smoothly: it includes tram conductors, taxi-drivers, miners, dockers, interpreters, nurses and so on. It is these elements which constitute the most faithful followers of the nationalist parties, and who because of the privileged place which they hold in the colonial system constitute also the 'bourgeois' fraction of the colonized people.

So we understand that the followers of the nationalist political parties are above all town-dwellers – shop-stewards, industrial workers, intellectuals and shopkeepers all living for the most part in the towns. Their way of thinking is already marked in many points by the comparatively well-to-do class, distinguished by technical advances, that they spring from. Here 'modern ideas' reign. It is these classes that will struggle against obscurantist traditions, that will change old customs, and that will thus enter into open conflict with the old granite block upon which the nation rests.

The overwhelming majority of nationalist parties show a deep distrust towards the people of the rural areas. The fact is that as a body these people appear to them to be bogged down in fruitless inertia. The members of the nationalist parties (town workers and intellectuals) pass the same unfavourable judgement on country districts as the settlers. But if we try to understand the reasons for this mistrust on the part of the political parties with regard to the rural areas, we must remember that colonialism has often strengthened or established its domination by organizing the petrification of the country districts. Ringed round by marabouts, witch-doctors and customary chieftains, the majority of country-dwellers are still living in the feudal manner, and the full power of this medieval structure of society is maintained by the settlers' military and administrative officials.

So now the young nationalist middle class, which is above all a class interested in trade, is going to compete with these feudal lords in many and various fields. There are marabouts and medicine-men who bar the way to sick people who otherwise could consult the doctor, oracles which pass judgement and thus render lawyers useless, *caids* who make use of their political and administrative powers to set up in trade or to start a transport service, customary chiefs who oppose, in the names of religion and tradition, the setting up of businesses and the introduction of new goods. The rising class of native traders and wholesalers needs the disappearance of these prohibitions and barriers in order to develop. The native customers, the preserve of feudal lords, who now become aware that they are more or less forbidden to buy the new products, therefore become a market to be contended for.

The feudal leaders form a screen between the young Westernized nationalists and the bulk of the people. Each time the *élite* tries to get through to the country people, the tribal chieftains, leaders of confraternities and traditional authorities intensify their warnings, their threats and their excommunications. These traditional authorities who have been upheld by the occupying power view with disfavour the attempts made by the *élite* to penetrate the country districts. They know very well that the ideas which are likely to be introduced by these influences coming from the towns call in question the very nature of unchanging, everlasting feudalism. Thus their enemy is not at all the occupying power with which they get along on the whole very well, but these people with modern ideas who mean to dislocate the aboriginal society, and who in doing so will take the bread out of their mouths.

The Westernized elements experience feelings with regard to the bulk of the peasantry which are reminiscent of those found among the town workers of industrialized countries. The history of middle-class and working-class revolutions has shown that the bulk of the peasants often constitute a brake on the revolution. Generally in industrialized countries the peasantry as a whole are the least aware, the worst organized and at the same time the most anarchical element. They show a whole range of characteristics – individualism, lack of discipline, liking for money and propensities towards waves of uncontrollable rage and deep discouragement which define a line of behaviour that is objectively reactionary.

We have seen that the nationalist parties copy their methods from those of the Western political parties; and also, for the most part, that they do not direct their propaganda towards the rural masses. In fact, if a reasoned analysis of colonized society had been made, it would have shown them that the native peasantry lives against a background of tradition, where the traditional structure of society has remained intact, whereas in the industrialized countries it is just this traditional setting which has been broken up by the progress of industrialization. In the colonies, it is at the very core of the embryonic working class that you find individual behaviour. The landless peasants, who make up the *lumpen-proletariat*, leave the country districts, where vital statistics are just so many insoluble problems, rush towards the towns, crowd into tin-shack settlements, and try to make their way into the ports and cities founded by colonial domination. The bulk of the country people for their part continue to live within a rigid framework, and the extra mouths to feed have no other alternative than to emigrate towards the centres of population. The peasant who stays put defends his traditions stubbornly, and in a colonized society stands for the disciplined element whose interests lie in maintaining the social structure. It is true that this unchanging way of life, which hangs on like grim death to rigid social structures, may occasionally give birth to movements which are based on religious fanaticism or tribal wars. But in their spontaneous movements the country people as a whole remain disciplined and altruistic. The individual stands aside in favour of the community.

The country people are suspicious of the townsman. The latter dresses like a European; he speak the European's language, works with him, sometimes even lives in the same district; so he is considered by the peasants as a turncoat who has betrayed everything that goes to make up the national heritage. The townspeople are 'traitors and knaves' who seem to get on well with the occupying powers, and do their best to get on within the framework of the colonial system. This is why you often hear the country people say of town-dwellers that they have no morals. Here, we are not dealing with the old antagonism between town and country; it is the antagonism which exists between the native who is excluded from the advantages of colonialism and his counterpart who manages to turn colonial exploitation to his account.

What is more, the colonialists make use of this antagonism in their struggle against the nationalist parties. They mobilize the people of the mountains and the up-country-dwellers against the townsfolk. They pitch the hinterland against the seaboard, they rouse up the tribespeople, and we need not be surprised to see Kalondji crowned king of Kasai, just as it was not surprising to see, some years ago, the assembly of the chiefs of Ghana making N'kruma dance to their tune.

The political parties do not manage to organize the country districts. Instead of using existing structures and giving them a nationalist or progressive character, they mean to try and destroy living tradition in the colonial framework. They believe it lies in their power to give the initial impulse to the nation, whereas in reality the chains forged by the colonial system still weigh it down heavily. They do not go out to find the mass of the people. They do not put their theoretical knowledge to the service of the people; they only try to erect a framework around the people which follows an *a priori* schedule. Thus from the capital city they will 'parachute' organizers into the villages who are either unknown or too young, and who, armed with instructions from the central authority, mean to treat the *douar* or village like a factory cell.

The traditional chiefs are ignored, sometimes even persecuted. The makers of the future nation's history trample unconcernedly over small local disputes, that is to say the only existing national events, whereas they ought to make of village history – the history of traditional conflicts between clans and tribes – a harmonious whole, at one with the decisive action to which they call on the people to contribute. The old men, surrounded by respect in all traditional societies and usually invested with unquestionable moral authority, are publicly held up to ridicule. The occupying power's local authorities do not fail to use the resentment thus engendered, and keep in touch with the slightest decisions adopted by this caricature of authority. Police repression, well-informed because it is based on precise information, strikes. The parachuted leaders and the consequential members of the new assembly are arrested.

Such setbacks confirm the 'theoretical analysis' of the nationalist parties. The disastrous experience of trying to enrol the country people as a whole reinforces their distrust and crystallizes their aggressiveness towards that section of the people. Even after the struggle for national freedom has succeeded, the same mistakes are made and such mistakes make for the maintenance of decentralizing and autonomist tendencies. Tribalism in the colonial phase gives way to regionalism in the national phase, and finds its expression as far as institutions are concerned in federalism.

But it may happen that the country people, in spite of the slight hold that the nationalist parties have over them, play a decisive part either in the process of the maturing of the national consciousness, or through working in with the action of nationalist parties, or, less frequently, by substituting themselves purely and simply for the sterility of these parties. For the propaganda of nationalist parties always finds an echo in the heart of the peasantry. The memory of the anti-colonial period is very much alive in the villages, where women still croon in their children's ears songs to which the warriors marched when they went out to fight the conquerors. At twelve or thirteen years of age the village children know the names of the old men who were in the last rising, and the dreams they dream in the *douars* or in the villages are not those of money or of getting through their exams like the children of the towns, but dreams of indentification with some rebel or another, the story of whose heroic death still today moves them to tears.

Just when the nationalist parties are trying to organize the embryonic working class in the towns, we notice certain seemingly completely inexplicable explosions in the country districts. Take for example the famous rebellion of 1947 in Madagascar. The colonial authorities were categorical: it was a peasant rising. In fact we now know that as usual things were much more complicated than that. During the Second World War the big colonial companies greatly increased their power and became the possessors of all the land that up to then was still free. At the same time there was talk of planting the island eventually with Jewish, Kabylian and West Indian refugees. Another rumour was equally rife – that the whites of South Africa were soon going to invade the island with the collusion of the settlers. Thus, after the war the candidates on the nationalist list were triumphantly elected. Immediately after, organized repression began of the cells of the *Mouvement Democratique de la Rénovation Malgache* (Democratic Movement for Madagascan Restoration). Colonialism, in order to reach its ends, used the usual traditional methods: frequent arrests, racist propaganda between tribes, and the creation of a party out of the unorganized elements of the *lumpen-proletariat*. This party, with the name of the Disinherited Madagascans, gave the colonial authorities by its distinctly provocative actions the legal excuse to maintain order. It happened that this very frequent operation of liquidating a party which had been set up in advance took on in this context gigantic proportions. The rural masses, on the defensive for the last three or four years, suddenly felt themselves in deadly peril and decided to oppose colonialist forces savagely. Armed with spears, or more often simply with sticks and stones, the people flung themselves into the general revolt for national liberty. We know the end of the story.

Such armed rebellions only represent one of the means used by the country-dwellers to join in the national struggle.

Sometimes when the nationalist party in the towns is tracked down by police repression the peasants carry on the tradition of urban agitation. News of the repression comes to the country districts in a grossly exaggerated form; the tale runs that the leaders are arrested, that machine-gunning is rife, that the town is running red with the blood of Negroes, or that the small settlers are bathing in Arab blood. Thereupon the accumulated, exacerbated hate explodes. The neighbouring police barracks is captured, the policemen are hacked to pieces, the local schoolmaster is murdered, the doctor only gets away with his life because he was not at home, etc. Pacifying forces are hurried to the spot and the air-force bombards it. Then the banner of revolt is unfurled, the old warrior-like traditions spring up again, the women cheer, the men organize and take up positions in the mountains, and guerrilla war begins. The peasantry spontaneously gives concrete form to the general insecurity; and colonialism takes fright and either continues the war or negotiates.

What is the reaction of the nationalist parties to this eruption of the peasant masses into the national struggle? We have seen that the majority of nationalist parties have not written into their propaganda the necessity for armed intervention. They do not oppose the continuing of the rebellion, but they content themselves with leaving it to the spontaneous action of the country people. As a whole they treat this new element as a sort of manna fallen from heaven, and pray to goodness that it'll go on falling. They make the most of the manna, but do not attempt to organize the rebellion. They don't send leaders into the countryside to educate the people politically, or to increase their awareness or put the struggle on to a higher level. All they do is to hope that, carried onwards by its own momentum, the action of the people will not come to a standstill. There is no contamination of the rural movement by the urban movement; each develops according to its own dialectic.

The nationalist parties do not attempt to give definite orders to the country people, although the latter are perfectly ready to listen to them. They offer them no objective; they simply hope that this new movement will go on indefinitely and that the bombardments will not put an end to it. Thus we see that even when such an occasion offers, the nationalist parties make no use at all of the opportunity which is offered to them to integrate the people of the countryside, to educate them politically and to raise the level of their struggle. The old attitude of mistrust towards the countryside is criminally evident.

The political leaders go underground in the towns, give the impression to the colonialists that they have no connexion with the rebels, or seek refuge abroad. It very seldom happens that they join the people in the hills. In Kenya, for example, during the Mau-Mau rebellion, not a single well-known nationalist declared his affiliation with the movement, or even tried to defend the men involved in it.

The different strata of the nation never have it out with each other to any advantage; there is no settling of accounts between them. Thus, when independence is achieved, after the repression practised on the country people, after the *entente* between colonialism and the national parties, it is no wonder that you find this incomprehension to an even greater degree. The country-dwellers are slow to take up the structural reforms proposed by the government; and equally slow in following their social reforms, even though they may be very progressive if viewed objectively, precisely because the people now at the head of affairs did not explain to the people as a whole during the colonial period what were the aims of the party, the national trends, or the problems of international politics.

The mistrust which country-dwellers and those still living within the feudal system feel towards nationalist parties during the colonial period is followed by a similarly strong hostility during the national period. The colonial secret services which were not disbanded after independence keep up the discontentment and still manage to make serious difficulties for the young governments. All in all, the government is only being made to pay for its laziness during the period of liberation, and its unfailing mistrust of the country people. The nation may well have a reasonable, even progressive, head to it; its body will remain weak, stubborn and non-cooperative.

The temptation therefore will be to break up this body by centralizing the administration and surrounding the people by a firm administrative framework. This is one of the reasons why you often hear it said that in under-developed countries a small dose of dictatorship is needed. The men at the head of things distrust the people of the countryside; moreover this distrust takes on serious proportions. This is the case for example of certain governments which, long after national independence is declared, continue to consider the interior of the country as a non-pacified area where the chief of state or his ministers only go when the national army is carrying out manoeuvres there. For all practical purposes, the interior ranks with the unknown. Paradoxically, the national government in its dealings with the country people as a whole is reminiscent of certain features of the former colonial power. 'We don't quite know how the mass of these people will react' is the cry; and the young ruling class does not hesitate to assert that 'they need the thick end of the stick if this country is to get out of the Middle Ages'. But as we have seen, the off-hand way in which the political parties treated the rural population during the colonial phase could only prejudice national unity at the very moment when the young nation needs to get off to a good start.

Sometimes colonialism attempts to dislocate or create diversions around the upward thrust of nationalism. Instead of organizing the sheiks and the chiefs against the 'revolutionaries' in the towns, native committees organize the tribes and confraternities into parties. Confronted with the urban party which was beginning to 'embody the national will' and to constitute a danger for the colonial regime, splinter groups are born, and tendencies and parties which have their origin in ethnical or regional differences spring up. It is the entire tribe which is turning itself into a political party, closely advised by the colonialists. The conference table can now be pulled out. The party which advocates unity will be drowned in the computations of the various splinter groups, while the tribal parties will oppose centralization and unity, and will denounce the party of unity as a dictatorship.

Later on, the same tactics will be used by the national opposition. The occupying power has made its choice from among the two or three nationalist parties which led the struggle for liberation. The ways of choosing are well known: when a party has achieved national unanimity and has imposed itself on the occupying power as the sole spokesman of the nation, the colonial power starts complicated manoeuvrings and delays the opening of negotiations as much as ever it can. Such a delay will be used to fritter away the demands of this party or get its leaders to put certain 'extremist' elements into the background.

If on the other hand no party really succeeds in imposing itself the occupying power is content to extend privileges to the party which it considers to be the most 'reasonable'. The nationalist parties which have not taken part in the negotiations engage in denunciations of the agreement reached between the other party and the occupying power. The party which takes over the reins from the colonialists, conscious of the danger with which the extremely demagogical and confused attitude of the rival party threatens it, tries to disband its competitor and to condemn it to illegality. The persecuted party has no alternative but to seek refuge in the outskirts of the towns and in the country districts. It tries to rouse the people of the country against the 'traitors of the seaboard and the corrupt politicians of the capital'. Any excuse is good enough: religious feeling, innovations made by the new government which break from tradition, and so on. The obscurantist tendencies of the country dwellers are exploited to the full. The so-called revolutionary doctrine in fact rests on the retrograde, emotional and spontaneous nature of the country districts. Here and there it is whispered that the mountain is moving, that the countryside is discontented. It's said that in a certain place the police have opened fire on the peasantry, that reinforcements have been sent out, and that the government is on the point of falling. The parties in opposition, since they have no clear programme, have no other end in view but to take the place of the governing party; and with this as their goal they place their destiny in the hands of the obscure, spontaneous mass of the peasantry.

Inversely, it sometimes happens that the opposition no longer relies for support on the country people, but rather on the progressive elements found in the trade unions of the young nation. In this case the government calls upon the country-folk to oppose the demands of the workers, which they denounce as the manoeuvres of anti-traditionalist adventurers. The facts we have established regarding the political parties are once more observed, *mutatis mutandis*, on the level of the trade unions. In the beginning the trade-union organizations in colonial territories are regularly local branches of the trade unions of the mother country, and their orders are the echo of those given in the mother country.

Once the decisive phase of the struggle for liberation emerges, some native trade unionists will decide upon the creation of national unions. The old structure, imported from the mother country, will suffer heavy losses as the native members desert it. This creating of new unions is a fresh element of pressure in the hands of the population of the towns upon colonialism. We have seen that the working class in the colonies is in an embryonic state and represents that fraction of the people which is the most favoured. The national unions are born out of the struggle for independence organized in the towns, and their programme is above all a political programme and a nationalist programme. Such a national union which comes into being during the decisive phase of the fight for independence is in fact the legal enlistment of conscious, dynamic nationalist elements.

The mass of the country-dwellers, looked down upon by the political parties, continue to be kept at a distance. Of course there will be an agricultural workers' union there, but its creation is simply to supply an answer to the categorical necessity to 'present a united front to colonialism'. The trade-union officials who have won their colours in the field of the union organizations of the mother country have no idea how to organize the mass of country people. They have lost all contact with the peasantry and their primary preoccupation is to enlist dockers, metallurgists and state-employed gas and electricity workers in their ranks.

During the colonial phase, the nationalist trade-union organizations constitute an impressive striking power. In the towns, the trade unionist can bring to a standstill, or at any rate slow down at any given moment, the colonialist economy. Since the European settlement is often confined to the towns, the psychological effects of demonstrations on that settlement are considerable: there is no electricity, no gas, the dust-bins are left unemptied, and goods rot on the quays.

These little islands of the mother country which the towns constitute in the colonial structure are deeply conscious of trade-union action; the fortress of colonialism which the capital represents staggers under their blows. But the 'interior' – the mass of country-dwellers – knows nothing of this conflict.

Thus we see that there is a lack of proportion from the national point of view between the importance of the trade unions and the rest of the nation. After independence, the workers who have joined the unions get the impression that they are living in a vacuum. The limited objective that they set themselves turns out to be, at the very moment that it is attained, extremely precarious, having regard to the immensity of the task of national reconstruction. When faced with the national middle class whose connexions with the government are often closely linked, the trade-union leaders discover that they can no longer limit themselves to working-class agitation. Isolated by their very nature from the country people, and incapable of giving directions once outside the suburbs, the unions become more and more political in their attitude. In fact, the unions become candidates for governmental power. They try by every means to corner the middle classes: they protest against the maintenance of foreign bases on the national territory, they denounce trade agreements, and they oppose the national government's foreign policy. The workers, now that they have their 'independence', do not know where to go from there. For the day after independence is declared the trade unions realize that if their social demands were to be expressed, they would scandalize the rest of the nation: for the workers are in fact the most favoured section of the population, and represent the most comfortably off fraction of the people. Any movement starting off to fight for the bettering of living conditions for the dockers and workmen would not only be very unpopular, but would also run the risk of provoking the hostility of the disinherited rural population. The trade unions, to whom all trade-union activity is forbidden, merely mark time.

This unhealthy state of affairs simply shows the objective necessity of a social programme which will appeal to the nation as a whole. Suddenly the unions discover that the back-country too ought to be enlightened and organized. But since at no time have they taken care to establish working links between themselves and the mass of the peasants, and since this peasantry precisely constitutes the only spontaneously revolutionary force of the country, the trade unions will give proof of their inefficiency and find out for themselves the anachronistic nature of their programmes.

The trade-union leaders, steeped in working-class political action, automatically go from there to the preparation of a *coup d'état*. But here again the back-country is left out; this is a limited settling of accounts only, between the national middle class and the union workers. The national middle class, taking up the old traditions of colonialism, makes a show of its military and police forces, while the unions organize mass meetings and mobilize tens of thousands of members. The peasants confronted with this national middle class and these workers, who, after all, can eat their fill, look on, shrugging their shoulders; and they shrug their shoulders because they know very well that both sides look on them as a make-weight. The unions, the parties or the government in a kind of immoral Machiavellian fashion all make use of the peasant masses as a blind, inert tactical force: brute force, as it were.

On the other hand, in certain circumstances the country people are going to intervene in decisive fashion both in the struggle for national freedom and in the way that the future nation marks out for itself. This phenomenon takes on a fundamental importance for under-developed countries; this is why we propose to study it in detail.

We have seen that inside the nationalist parties, the will to break colonialism is linked with another quite different will: that of coming to a friendly agreement with it. Within these parties, the two processes will sometimes continue side by side. In the first place, when the intellectual elements have carried out a prolonged analysis of the true nature of colonialism and of the international situation, they will begin to criticize their party's lack of ideology and the poverty of its tactics and strategy. They begin to question their leaders ceaselessly on crucial points: 'What is nationalism? What sense do you give to this word? What is its meaning? Independence for what? And in the first place, how do you propose to achieve it?' They ask these questions, and at the same time require that the problems of methodology should be vigorously tackled. They are ready to suggest that electoral resources should be supplemented by 'all other means'. After the first skirmishes, the official leaders speedily dispose of this effervescence which they are quick to label as childishness. But since these demands are not simply effervescence, nor the sign of immaturity, the revolutionary elements which subscribe to them will rapidly be isolated. The official leaders, draped in their years of experience, will pitilessly disown these 'adventurers and anarchists'.

The party machine shows itself opposed to any innovation. The revolutionary minority finds itself alone, confronted with leaders who are terrified and worried by the idea that they could be swept away by a maelstrom whose nature, force or direction they cannot even imagine. The second process concerns the main leaders, or their seconds in command, who were marked out for police repression under the colonialists. It must be emphasized that these men have come to the head of the party by their untiring work, their spirit of sacrifice and a most exemplary patriotism. Such men, who have worked their way up from the bottom, are often unskilled workers, seasonal labourers or even sometimes chronically unemployed. For them the fact of militating in a national party is not simply taking part in politics; it is choosing the only means whereby they can pass from the status of an animal to that of a human being. Such men, hampered by the excessive legalism of the party, will show within the limits of the activities for which they are responsible a spirit of initiative, courage and a sense of the importance of the struggle which mark them out almost automatically as targets for colonialist repression. Arrested, condemned, tortured, finally amnestied, they use their time in prison to clarify their ideas and strengthen their determination. Through hunger-strikes and the violent brotherhood of the prisons' quicklime they live on, hoping for their freedom, looking on it as an opportunity to start an armed struggle. But at one and the same time outside the prison walls colonialism, attacked from all sides, is making advances to the nationalist moderates.

So we can observe the process whereby the rupture occurs between the illegal and legal tendencies in the party. The illegal minority is made to feel that they are undesirables and are shunned by the people that matter. The legal members of their party come to their aid with great precaution, but already there is a rift between the two tendencies. The illegalists, therefore, will get into touch with the intellectual elements whose attitude they were able to understand a few years back; and an underground party, an off-shoot of the legal party, will be the result of this meeting. But the repression of these wayward elements intensifies as the legal party draws nearer to colonialism and attempts to modify it 'from the inside'. The illegal minority thus finds itself in a historical blind alley.

Boycotted by the towns, these men first settle in the outskirts of the suburbs. But the police network traps them and forces them to leave the towns for good, and to quit the scenes of political action. They fall back towards the countryside and the mountains, towards the peasant people. From the beginning, the peasantry closes in around them, and protects them from being pursued by the police. The militant nationalist who decides to throw in his lot with the country people instead of playing at hide-and-seek with the police in urban centres will lose nothing. The peasant's cloak will wrap him around with a gentleness and firmness that he never suspected. These men, who are in fact exiled to the backwoods, who are cut off from the urban background against which they had defined their ideas of the nation and of the political fight, these men have in fact become 'Maquisards'. Since they are obliged to move about the whole time in order to escape from the police, often at night so as not to attract attention, they will have good reason to wander through their country and to get to know it. The cafés are forgotten; so are the arguments about the next elections or the spitefulness of some policeman or other. Their ears hear the true voice of the country, and their eyes take in the great and infinite poverty of their people. They realize the precious time that has been wasted in useless commentaries upon the colonial regime. They finally come to understand that the change-over will not be a reform, nor a bettering of things. They come to understand, with a sort of bewilderment that will from henceforth never quite leave them, that political action in the towns will always be powerless to modify or overthrow the colonial regime.

These men get used to talking to the peasants. They discover that the mass of the country people have never ceased to think of the problem of their liberation except in terms of violence, in terms of taking back the land from the foreigners, in terms of national struggle, and of armed insurrection. It is all very simple. These men discover a coherent people who go on living, as it were, statically, but who keep their moral values and their devotion to the nation intact. They discover a people that is generous, ready to sacrifice themselves completely, an impatient people, with a stony pride. It is understandable that the meeting between these militants with the police on their track and these mettlesome masses of people, who are rebels by instinct, can produce an explosive mixture of unusual potentiality. The men coming from the towns learn their lessons in the hard school of the people; and at the same time these men open classes for the people in military and political education. The people furbish up their weapons; but in fact the classes do not last long, for the masses come to know once again the strength of their own muscles, and push the leaders on to prompt action. The armed struggle has begun.

The rising disconcerts the political parties. Their doctrine, in fact, has always affirmed the uselessness of a trial of force, and their very existence is a constant condemnation of all rebellion. Secretly, certain political parties share the optimism of the settlers, and congratulate themselves on being well away from this act of madness which, it's said, will be put down with bloodshed. But once the match is lit, the blaze spreads like wild-fire through the whole country. The armoured cars and the aeroplanes do not win through with unqualified success. Faced with the full extent of the trouble, colonialism begins to reflect on the matter. At the very core of the oppressing nation voices are raised, and listened to, which draw attention to the gravity of the situation.

As for the people, they join in the new rhythm of the nation, in their mud huts and in their dreams. Under their breath and from their hearts' core they sing endless songs of praise to the glorious fighters. The tide of rebellion has already flooded the whole nation. Now it is the parties' turn to be isolated.

The leaders of the rising, however, realize that some day or another the rebellion must come to include the towns. This awareness is not fortuitous; it is the crowning point of the dialectic which reigns over the development of an armed struggle for national liberation. Although the country districts represent inexhausible reserves of popular energy, and groups of armed men ensure that insecurity is rife there, colonialism does not doubt the strength of its system. It does not feel that it is endangered fundamentally. The rebel leaders therefore decide to bring the war into the enemy's camp, that is to say into his grandiose, peaceful cities.

The organizing of the rising in the centres of population sets the leaders some difficult problems. We have seen that the greater part of the leaders, born or brought up in the towns, have fled from their normal background because they were wanted by the colonialist police, and were in general unappreciated by the cautious, reasonable administrators of the political parties. Their retreat into the country was both a flight from persecution and a sign of their distrust for the old political structure. The natural receiving stations in the towns for these leaders are well-known nationalists who are in the thick of the political parties. But we have seen that their recent history was precisely an off-shoot from these timid, nervous officials who spend their time in ceaseless lamentation over the misdeeds of colonialism.

Moreover, the first overtures which the men of the Maquis make towards their former friends – precisely those whom they consider to be the most towards the Left – will confirm their fears and will take away even the wish to see their old companions again. In fact the rebellion, which began in the country districts, will filter into the towns through that fraction of the peasant population which is blocked on the outer fringe of the urban centres, that fraction which has not yet succeeded in finding a bone to gnaw in the colonial system. The men whom the growing population of the country districts and colonial expropriation have brought to desert their family holdings circle tirelessly around the different towns, hoping that one day or another they will be allowed inside. It is within this mass of humanity, this people of the shanty towns, at the core of the *lumpen-proletariat* that the rebellion will find its urban spear-head. For the *lumpen-proletariat*, that horde of starving men, uprooted from their tribe and from their clan, constitutes one of the most spontaneous and the most radically revolutionary forces of a colonized people.

In Kenya, in the years preceding the Mau-Mau revolt, it was noticeable how the British colonial authorities multiplied intimidatory measures against the *lumpen-proletariat*. The police forces and the missionaries coordinated their efforts, in the years 1950–51, in order to make a suitable response to the enormous influx of young Kenyans coming from the country districts and the forests who, when they did not manage to find a market for their labour, took to stealing, debauchery and alcoholism. Juvenile delinquency in the colonized countries is the direct result of the existence of a *lumpen-proletariat*. In parallel fashion, in the Congo, Draconian measures were taken from 1957 onwards to send back to the countryside the 'young hooligans' who were disturbing the social order. Resettlement camps were opened and put under the charge of evangelical missions, protected, of course, by the Belgian army.

The constitution of a *lumpen-proletariat* is a phenomenon which obeys its own logic, and neither the brimming activity of the missionaries nor the decrees of the central government can check its growth. This *lumpen-proletariat* is like a horde of rats; you may kick them and throw stones at them, but despite your efforts they'll go on gnawing at the roots of the tree.

The shanty-town sanctions the native's biological decision to invade, at whatever cost and if necessary by the most cryptic methods, the enemy fortress. The *lumpen-proletariat*, once it is constituted, brings all its forces to endanger the 'security' of the town, and is the sign of the irrevocable decay, the gangrene ever present at the heart of colonial domination. So the pimps, the hooligans, the unemployed and the petty criminals, urged on from behind, throw themselves into the struggle for liberation like stout working men. These classless idlers will by militant and decisive action discover the path that leads to nation-hood. They won't become reformed characters to please colonial society, fitting in with the morality of its rulers; quite on the contrary, they take for granted the impossibility of their entering the city save by hand-grenades and revolvers. These workless less-than-men are rehabilitated in their own eyes and in the eyes of history. The prostitutes too, and the maids who are paid two pounds a month, all the hopeless dregs of humanity, all who turn in circles between suicide and madness will recover their balance, once more go forward, and march proudly in the great procession of the awakened nation.

The nationalist parties do not understand this new phenomenon which precipitates their disintegration. The outbreak of the rebellion in the towns changes the nature of the struggle. Whereas before the colonialist troops were entirely concerned with the country districts, we now see them falling back in haste on the towns in order to ensure the safety of the town population and their property. The forces of repression spread out; danger is present everywhere; now it's the very soil of the nation, the whole of the colony, which goes into a trance. The armed groups of peasants look on while the mailed fist loses its grip. The rising in the towns is like an unhoped-for gas balloon.

The leaders of the rising who see an ardent and enthusiastic people striking decisive blows at the colonialist machine are strengthened in their mistrust of traditional policy. Every success confirms their hostility towards what in future they will describe as mouth-wash, word-spinning, blather and fruitless agitation. They feel a positive hatred for the 'politics' of demagogy, and that is why in the beginning we observe a veritable triumph for the cult of spontaneity.

The many peasant risings which have their roots in the country districts bear witness wherever they occur to the ubiquitous and usually solidly massed presence of the new nation. Every native who takes up arms is a part of the nation which from henceforward will spring to life. Such peasant revolts endanger the colonial regime; they mobilize its troops, making them spread out, and threaten at every turn to crush them. They hold one doctrine only: to act in such a way that the nation may exist. There is no programme; there are no speeches or resolutions, and no political trends. The problem is clear:

the foreigners must go: so let us form a common front against the oppressor and let us strengthen our hands by armed combat.

So long as the uncertainty of colonialism continues, the national cause goes on progressing, and becomes the cause of each and all. The plans for liberation are sketched out; already they include the whole country. During this period spontaneity is king, and initiative is localized. On every hill a government in miniature is formed and takes over power. Everywhere – in the valleys and in the forests, in the jungle and in the villages – we find a national authority. Each man or woman brings the nation to life by his or her action, and is pledged to ensure its triumph in their locality. We are dealing with a strategy of immediacy which is both radical and totalitarian: the aim and the programme of each locally constituted group is local liberation. If the nation is everywhere, then she is here. One step further, and only here is she to be found. Tactics are mistaken for strategy. The art of politics is simply transformed into the art of war; the political militant is the rebel. To fight the war and to take part in politics: the two things become one and the same.

This people that has lost its birthright, that is used to living in the narrow circle of feuds and rivalries, will now proceed in an atmosphere of solemnity to cleanse and purify the face of the nation as it appears in the various localities. In a veritable collective ecstasy, families which have always been traditional enemies decide to rub out old scores and to forgive and forget. There are numerous reconciliations. Long-buried but unforgettable hatreds are brought to light once more, so that they may more surely be rooted out. The taking on of nationhood involves a growth of awareness. The national unity is first the unity of a group, the disappearance of old quarrels and the final liquidation of unspoken grievances. At the same time, forgiveness and purification include those natives who by their activities and by their complicity with the occupier have dishonoured their country. On the other hand, traitors and those who have sold out to the enemy will be judged and punished. In undertaking this onward march, the people legislates, finds itself and wills itself to sovereignty. In every corner that is thus awakened from colonial slumber, life is lived at an impossibly high temperature. There is a permanent outpouring in all the villages of spectacular generosity, of disarming kindness, and willingness, which cannot ever be doubted, to die for the 'cause'. All this is evocative of a confraternity, a church and a mystical body of belief at one and the same time. No native can remain unmoved by this new rhythm which leads the nation on. Messengers are dispatched to neighbouring tribes. They constitute the first system of intercommunication in the rebellion, and bring movement and cadence to districts which are still motionless. Even tribes whose stubborn rivalry is well known now disarm with joyful tears and pledge help and succour to each other. Marching shoulder to shoulder in the armed struggle these men join with those who yesterday were their enemies. The circle of the nation widens and fresh ambushes to entrap the enemy hail the entry of new tribes upon the scene. Each village finds that it is itself both an absolute agent of revolution, and also a link in the chain of action. Solidarity between tribes and between villages, national solidarity, is in the first place expressed by the increasing blows struck at the enemy. Every new group which is formed, each fresh salvo that bursts out is an indication that each is on the enemy's track, and that each is prepared to meet him.

This solidarity will be much more clearly shown during the second period, which is characterized by the putting into operation of the enemy offensive. The colonial forces, once the explosion has taken place, regroup and reorganize, inaugurating methods of warfare which correspond to the nature of the rising. This offensive will call in question the ideal, Utopian atmosphere of the first period. The enemy attacks, and concentrates large forces on certain definite points. The local group is quickly overrun, all the more so because it tends to seek the forefront of the battle. The optimism which reigned in the first period makes the local group fearless, or rather careless. It is persuaded that its own mountain peak is the nation, and because of this it refuses to abandon it, or to beat a retreat. But the losses are serious, and doubts spring up and begin to weigh heavily upon the rebels. The group faces a local attack as if it were a decisive test. It behaves as if the fate of the whole country was literally at stake, here and now.

But we should make it quite clear that this spontaneous

impetuosity which is determined to settle the fate of the colonial system immediately is condemned, in so far as it is a doctrine of instantaneity, to self-repudiation. For the most everyday, practical realism takes the place of yesterday's effusion, and substitutes itself for the illusion of eternity. The hard lesson of facts, the bodies mown down by machine-guns: these call forth a complete re-interpretation of events. The simple instinct to survive engenders a less rigid, more mobile attitude. This modification in fighting technique characterized the first months of the war of liberation of the people of Angola. We may remember that on 15 March 1961 a group of two or three thousand Angolan peasants threw themselves against the Portuguese positions. Men, women and children, armed and unarmed, afire with courage and enthusiasm, then flung themselves in successive waves of compact masses upon the districts where the settler, the soldier and the Portuguese flag held sway. Villages and aerodromes were encircled and subjected to frequent attacks, but it must be added that thousands of Angolans were mown down by colonialist machine-guns. It did not take long for the leaders of the Angolan rising to realize that they must find some other methods if they really wanted to free their country. So during the last few months* the Angolan leader Holden Roberto has reorganized the National Angolan Army, using the experience gained in various other wars of liberation, and employing guerrilla techniques.

The fact is that in guerrilla warfare the struggle no longer concerns the place where you are, but the place where you are going. Each fighter carries his warring country between his bare toes. The national army of liberation is not an army which engages once and for all with the enemy; it is rather an army which goes from village to village, falling back on the forests, and dancing for joy when in the valley below there comes into view the white column of dust that the enemy columns kick up. The tribes go into action, and the various groups move about, changing their grounds. The people of the North move towards the West; the people of the plains go up into the mountains. There is absolutely no strategically privileged position. The enemy thinks he is pursuing us; but we always manage to

* Written in 1961 (*translator*).

harry his rear-guard, striking back at him at the very moment when he thinks he has annihilated us. From now on, it is *we* who pursue *him*; in spite of all his technical advantages and his superior artillery power the enemy gives the impression that he is floundering and getting bogged down. And as for us, we sing, we go on singing.

Meantime, however, the leaders of the rising realize that the various groups must be enlightened; that they must be educated and indoctrinated, and that an army and a central authority must be created. The scattering of the nation, which is the manifestation of a nation in arms, needs to be corrected and to become a thing of the past. Those leaders who have fled from the useless political activity of the towns rediscover politics, no longer as a way of lulling people to sleep nor as a means of mystification, but as the only method of intensifying the struggle and of preparing the people to undertake the governing of their country clearly and lucidly. The leaders of the rebellion come to see that even very large-scale peasant risings need to be controlled and directed into certain channels. These leaders are led to renounce the movement in so far as it can be termed a peasant revolt, and to transform it into a revolutionary war. They discover that the success of the struggle presupposes clear objectives, a definite methodology and above all the need for the mass of the people to realize that their unorganized efforts can only be a temporary dynamic. You can hold out for three days – maybe even for three months – on the strength of the admixture of sheer resentment contained in the mass of the people; but you won't win a national war, you'll never overthrow the terrible enemy machine, and you won't change human beings if you forget to raise the standard of consciousness of the rank-and-file. Neither stubborn courage nor fine slogans are enough.

Moreover, as it develops, the war of liberation can be counted upon to strike a decisive blow at the faith of the leaders. The enemy, in fact, changes his tactics. At opportune moments he combines his policy of brutal repression with spectacular gestures of friendship, manoeuvres calculated to sow division, and 'psychological action'. Here and there he tries with success to revive tribal feuds, using *agents provocateurs* and practising what might be called counter-subversion. Colonialism will use two types of native to gain its ends; and the first of these are the traditional collaborators – chiefs, *caids* and witch-doctors. The mass of the peasantry is steeped, as we have seen, in a changeless ever-recurring life without incident; and they continue to revere their religious leaders who are descended from ancient families. The tribe follows, as one man, the way marked out for it by its traditional chief. Colonialism secures for itself the services of these confidential agents by pensioning them off at a ransom price.

Colonialism will also find in the *lumpen-proletariat* a considerable space for manoeuvring. For this reason any movement for freedom ought to give its fullest attention to this *lumpen-proletariat*. The peasant masses will always answer the call to rebellion, but if the rebellion's leaders think it will be able to develop without taking the masses into consideration, the *lumpen-proletariat* will throw itself into the battle and will take part in the conflict – but this time on the side of the oppressor. And the oppressor, who never loses a chance of setting the niggers against each other, will be extremely skilful in using that ignorance and incomprehension which are the weaknesses of the *lumpen-proletariat*. If this available reserve of human effort is not immediately organized by the forces of rebellion, it will find itself fighting as hired soldiers side by side with the colonial troops. In Algeria, it is the *lumpen-proletariat* which furnished the *harkish* and the *messalists*;* in Angola, it supplied the road-openers who nowadays precede the Portuguese armed columns; in the Congo, we find once more the *lumpen-proletariat* in regional manifestations in Kasai and Katanga, while at Leopold-ville the Congo's enemies made use of it to organize 'spontaneous' mass meetings against Lumumba.

The enemy is aware of ideological weaknesses, for he analyses the forces of rebellion and studies more and more carefully the aggregate enemy which makes up a colonial people; he is also aware of the spiritual instability of certain layers of the population. The enemy discovers the existence, side by side with the disciplined and well-organized advance guard of rebellion, of a mass of men whose participation is constantly at the mercy of

* Algerians enlisted in the French army (*translator*).

their being for too long accustomed to physiological wretchedness, humiliation and irresponsibility. The enemy is ready to pay a high price for the services of this mass. He will create spontaneity with bayonets and exemplary floggings. Dollars and Belgian francs pour into the Congo, while in Madagascar levies against Hova increase and in Algeria native recruits, who are in fact hostages, are enlisted in the French forces. The leaders of the rebellion literally see the nation capsizing. Whole tribes join up as *harkis*, and, using the modern weapons that they have been given, go on the war-path and invade the territory of the neighbouring tribe, which for this occasion has been labelled as nationalist. That unanimity in battle, so fruitful and grandiose in the first days of the rebellion, undergoes a change. National unity crumbles away; the rising is at a decisive turning of the way. Now the political education of the masses is seen to be a historic necessity.

That spectacular volunteer movement which meant to lead the colonized people to supreme sovereignty at one fell swoop, that certainty which you had that all portions of the nation would be carried along with you at the same speed and led onwards by the same light, that strength which gave you hope: all now are seen in the light of experience to be symptoms of a very great weakness. While the native thought that he could pass without transition from the status of a colonized person to that of a self-governing citizen of an independent nation, he made no real progress along the road to knowledge. His consciousness remained rudimentary. We have seen that the native enters passionately into the fight, above all if that fight is an armed one. The peasants threw themselves into the rebellion with all the more enthusiasm in that they had never stopped clutching at a way of life which was in practice anti-colonial. From all eternity, by means of manifold tricks and through a system of checks and balances reminiscent of a conjurer's most successful sleight-of-hand, the country people had more or less kept their individuality free from colonial impositions. They even believed that colonialism was not the victor. The peasant's pride, his hesitation to go down into the towns and to mingle with the world that the foreigner had built, his perpetual shrinking back at the approach of the agents of colonial administration: all these reactions signified that to the dual world of the settler he opposed his own duality.

Racial feeling, as opposed to racial prejudice, and that determination to fight for one's life which characterizes the native's reply to oppression are obviously good enough reasons for joining in the fight. But you do not carry on a war, nor suffer brutal and widespread repression, nor look on while all other members of your family are wiped out in order to make racialism or hatred triumph. Racialism and hatred and resentment – 'a legitimate desire for revenge' – cannot sustain a war of liberation. Those lightning flashes of consciousness which fling the body into stormy paths or which throw it into an almost pathological trance where the face of the other beckons me on to giddiness, where my blood calls for the blood of the other, where by sheer inertia my death calls for the death of the other – that intense emotion of the first few hours falls to pieces if it is left to feed on its own substance. It is true that the never-ending exactions of the colonial forces re-introduce emotional elements into the struggle, and give the militant fresh motives for hating and new reasons to go off hunting for a settler to shoot. But the leader realizes, day in and day out, that hatred alone cannot draw up a programme. You will only risk the defeat of your own ends if you depend on the enemy (who of course will always manage to commit as many crimes as possible) to widen the gap, and to throw the whole people on the side of the rebellion. At all events, as we have noticed, the enemy tries to win the support of certain sectors of the population, of certain districts and of certain chiefs. As the struggle is carried on, instructions are issued to the settlers and to the police forces; their behaviour takes on a different complexion: it becomes more 'human'. They even go as far as to call a native 'Mister' when they have dealings with him. Attentions and acts of courtesy come to be the rule. The native is in fact made to feel that things are changing.

The native, who did not take up arms simply because he was dying of hunger and because he saw his own social forms disintegrating before his eyes, but also because the settler considered him to be an animal, and treated him as such, reacts very favourably to such measures. Hatred is disarmed by these psychological windfalls. Technologists and sociologists shed their light on colonialist manoeuvres, and studies on the various 'complexes' pour forth: the frustration complex, the belligerency complex, and the colonizability complex. The native is promoted; they try to disarm him with their psychology, and of course they throw in a few shillings too. And these miserable methods, this eye-wash administered drop by drop, even meet with some success. The native is so starved for anything, anything at all that will turn him into a human being, any bone of humanity flung to him, that his hunger is incoercible, and these poor scraps of charity may, here and there, overwhelm him. His consciousness is so precarious and dim that it is affected by the slightest spark of kindliness. Now it is that the first great undifferentiated thirst for light is continually threatened by mystification. The violent, total demands which lit up the sky now become modest, and withdraw into themselves. The springing wolf which wanted to devour everything at sight, and the rising gust of wind which was to have brought about a real revolution run the risk of becoming quite unrecognizable if the struggle continues: and continue it does. The native may at any moment let himself be disarmed by some concession or another.

The discovery of this instability inherent in the native is a frightening experience for the leaders of the rebellion. At first they are completely bewildered; then they are made to realize by this new drift of things that explanation is very necessary, and that they must stop the native consciousness from getting bogged down. For the war goes on; and the enemy organizes, reinforces his position and comes to guess the native's strategy. The struggle for national liberation does not consist in spanning the gap at one stride; the drama has to be played out in all its difficulty every day, and the sufferings engendered far outmeasure any endured during the colonial period. Down in the towns the settlers seem to have changed. Our people are happier; they are respected. Day after day goes by; the native who is taking part in the struggle and the people who ought to go on giving him their help must not waver. They must not imagine that the end is already won. When the real objectives of the fight are shown to them, they must not think that they are impossible to attain. Once again, things must be explained to them; the people must see where they are going, and how they are to get there. The war is not a single battle, but rather a series of local engagements; and to tell the truth, none of these are decisive.

So we must be sparing of our strength, and not throw everything into the scales once and for all. Colonialism has greater and wealthier resources than the native. The war goes on; the enemy holds his own; the final settling of accounts will not be to-day nor yet tomorrow, for the truth is that the settlement was begun on the very first day of the war, and it will be ended not because there are no more enemies left to kill, but quite simply because the enemy, for various reasons, will come to realize that his interest lies in ending the struggle and in recognizing the sovereignty of the colonized people. The objectives of the struggle ought not to be chosen without discrimination, as they were in the first days of the struggle. If care is not taken, the people may begin to question the prolongation of the war at any moment that the enemy grants some concession. They are so used to the settler's scorn and to his declared intention to maintain his oppression at whatever cost that the slightest suggestion of any generous gesture or of any goodwill is hailed with astonishment and delight, and the native bursts into a hymn of praise. It must be clearly explained to the rebel that he must on no account be blindfolded by the enemy's concessions. These concessions are no more than sops; they have no bearing on the essential question; and from the native's point of view, we may lay down that a concession has nothing to do with the essentials if it does not affect the real nature of the colonial regime.

For, as a matter of fact, the more brutal manifestations of the presence of the occupying power may perfectly well disappear. Indeed, such a spectacular disappearance turns out to be both a saving of expense to the colonial power and a positive way of preventing its forces being spread out over a wide area. But such a disappearance will be paid for at a high price: the price of a much stricter control of the country's future destiny. Historic examples can be quoted to help the people to see that the masquerade of giving concessions, and even the mere acceptance of the principle of concessions at any price, have been bartered by not a few countries for a servitude that is less blatant but much more complete. The people and all their leaders ought to know

that historical law which lays down that certain concessions are
the cloak for a tighter rein. But when there has been no work of
clarification, it is astonishing with what complacency the leaders
of certain political parties enter into undefined compromises
with the former colonialist. The native must realize that colonialism never gives anything away for nothing. Whatever the
native may gain through political or armed struggle is not the
result of the kindliness or good will of the settler; it simply
shows that he cannot put off granting concessions any longer.
Moreover, the native ought to realize that it is not colonialism
that grants such concessions, but he himself that extorts them.
When the British government decides to bestow a few more
seats in the National Assembly of Kenya upon the African
population, it needs plenty of effrontery or else a complete
ignorance of facts to maintain that the British government has
made a concession. Is it not obvious that it is the Kenyan people
who have made the concession? The colonized peoples, the
peoples who have been robbed, must lose the habits of mind
which have characterized them up to now. If need be the native
can accept a compromise with colonialism, but never a surrender
of principle.

All this taking stock of the situation, this enlightening of
consciousness and this advance in the knowledge of the history
of societies are only possible within the framework of an organization, and inside the structure of a people. Such an organization
is set afoot by the use of revolutionary elements coming from
the towns at the beginning of the rising, together with those
rebels who go down into the country as the fight goes on. It is
this core which constitutes the embryonic political organization
of the rebellion. But on the other hand the peasants, who are all
the time adding to their knowledge in the light of experience,
will come to show themselves capable of directing the people's
struggle. Between the nation on a wartime footing and its
leaders there is established a mutual current of enlightenment
and enrichment. Traditional institutions are reinforced, deepened and sometimes literally transformed. The tribunals which
settle disputes, the *djemaas* and the village assemblies turn into
revolutionary tribunals and political and military committees.
In each fighting group and in every village hosts of political

commissioners spring up, and the people, who are beginning
to splinter upon the reefs of misunderstanding, will be shown
their bearings by these political pilots. Thus the latter will not
be afraid to tackle problems which if left unclarified would contribute to the bewilderment of the people. The rebel in arms is
in fact vexed to see that many natives go on living their lives in
the towns as if they were strangers to everything taking place in
the mountains and as if they failed to realize that the essential
movement for freedom has begun. The towns keep silent, and
their continuing their daily humdrum life gives the peasant the
bitter impression that a whole sector of the nation is content to
sit on the side-line. Such proofs of indifference disgust the
peasants and strengthen their tendency to condemn the townsfolk as a whole. The political educator ought to lead them to
modify this attitude by getting them to understand that certain
fractions of the population have particular interests and that
these do not always coincide with the national interest. The
people will thus come to understand that national independence
sheds light upon many facts which are sometimes divergent
and antagonistic. Such a taking stock of the situation at this
precise moment of the struggle is decisive, for it allows the
people to pass from total, undiscriminating nationalism to social
and economic awareness. The people who at the beginning of
the struggle had adopted the primitive Manichaeism of the settler
– Blacks and Whites, Arabs and Christians – realize as they go
along that it sometimes happens that you get Blacks who are
whiter than the Whites and that the fact of having a national
flag and the hope of an independent nation does not always
tempt certain strata of the population to give up their interests
or privileges. The people come to realize that natives like themselves do not lose sight of the main chance, but quite on the
contrary seem to make use of the war in order to strengthen
their material situation and their growing power. Certain
natives continue to profiteer and exploit the war, making their
gains at the expense of the people, who as usual are prepared to
sacrifice everything, and water their native soil with their blood.
The militant who faces the colonialist war machine with the bare
minimum of arms realizes that while he is breaking down colonial
oppression he is building up automatically yet another system

of exploitation. This discovery is unpleasant, bitter and sickening: and yet everything seemed to be so simple before: the bad people were on one side, and the good on the other. The clear, unreal, idyllic light of the beginning is followed by a semi-darkness that bewilders the senses. The people find out that the iniquitous fact of exploitation can wear a black face, or an Arab one; and they raise the cry of 'Treason!' But the cry is mistaken; and the mistake must be corrected. The treason is not national, it is social. The people must be taught to cry 'Stop thief!' In their weary road towards rational knowledge the people must also give up their too-simple conception of their overlords. The species is breaking up under their very eyes. As they look around them, they notice that certain settlers do not join in the general guilty hysteria; there are differences in the same species. Such men, who before were included without distinction and indiscriminately in the monolithic mass of the foreigner's presence, actually go so far as to condemn the colonial war. The scandal explodes when the prototypes of this division of the species go over to the enemy, become Negroes or Arabs, and accept suffering, torture and death.

Such examples disarm the general hatred that the native feels towards the foreign settlement. The native surrounds these few men with warm affection, and tends by a kind of emotional over-valuation to place absolute confidence in them. In the mother country, once looked upon as a bloodthirsty and implacable step-mother, many voices are raised, some those of prominent citizens, in condemnation of the policy of war that their government is following, advising that the national will of the colonized people should be taken into consideration. Certain soldiers desert from the colonialist ranks; others explicitly refuse to fight against the people's liberty and go to prison for the sake of the right of that people to independence and self-government.

The settler is not simply the man that must be killed. Many members of the mass of colonialists reveal themselves to be much, much nearer to the national struggle than certain sons of the nation. The barriers of blood and race-prejudice are broken down on both sides. In the same way, not every Negro or Moslem is issued automatically with a hall-mark of genuineness; and the gun or the knife is not inevitably reached for when a settler makes his appearance. Consciousness slowly dawns upon truths that are only partial, limited and unstable. As we may surmise, all this is very difficult. The task of bringing the people to maturity will be made easier by the thoroughness of the organization and by the high intellectual level of its leaders. The force of intellect increases and becomes more elaborate as the struggle goes on, as the enemy increases his manoeuvres and as victories are gained and defeats suffered. The leaders show their power and authority by criticizing mistakes, using every appraisal of past conduct to bring the lesson home, and thus insure fresh conditions for progress. Each local ebb of the tide will be used to review the question from the standpoint of *all* villages and of *all* political networks. The rebellion gives proof of its rational basis and expresses its maturity each time that it uses a particular case to advance the people's awareness. In defiance of those inside the movement who tend to think that shades of meaning constitute dangers and drive wedges into the solid block of popular opinion, the leaders stand firm upon those principles that have been sifted out in the national struggle, and in the world-wide struggle of mankind for his freedom. There exists a brutality of thought and a mistrust of subtlety which is typical of revolutions; but there also exists another kind of brutality which is astonishingly like the first and which is typically anti-revolutionary, hazardous and anarchist. This unmixed and total brutality, if not immediately combated, invariably leads to the defeat of the movement within a few weeks.

The nationalist militant who had fled from the town in disgust at the demagogic and reformist manoeuvres of the leaders there, disappointed by political life, discovers in real action a new form of political activity which is no way resembles the old. These politics are the politics of leaders and organizers living inside history who take the lead with their brains and their muscles in the fight for freedom. These politics are national, revolutionary and social and these new facts which the native will now come to know exist only in action. They are the essence of the fight which explodes the old colonial truths and reveals unexpected facets, which brings out new meanings and pinpoints the contradictions camouflaged by these facts. The people engaged in the struggle who because of it command and know these facts, go forward, freed from colonialism and forewarned of all attempts at mystification, inoculated against all national anthems. Violence alone, violence committed by the people, violence organized and educated by its leaders, makes it possible for the masses to understand social truths and gives the key to them. Without that struggle, without that knowledge of the practice of action, there's nothing but a fancy-dress parade and the blare of the trumpets. There's nothing save a minimum of readaptation, a few reforms at the top, a flag waving: and down there at the bottom an undivided mass, still living in the Middle Ages, endlessly marking time.

3. The Pitfalls of National Consciousness

HISTORY teaches us clearly that the battle against colonialism does not run straight away along the lines of nationalism. For a very long time the native devotes his energies to ending certain definite abuses: forced labour, corporal punishment, inequality of salaries, limitation of political rights, etc. This fight for democracy against the oppression of mankind will slowly leave the confusion of neo-liberal universalism to emerge, sometimes laboriously, as a claim to nationhood. It so happens that the unpreparedness of the educated classes, the lack of practical links between them and the mass of the people, their laziness, and, let it be said, their cowardice at the decisive moment of the struggle will give rise to tragic mishaps.

National consciousness, instead of being the all-embracing crystallization of the innermost hopes of the whole people, instead of being the immediate and most obvious result of the mobilization of the people, will be in any case only an empty shell, a crude and fragile travesty of what it might have been. The faults that we find in it are quite sufficient explanation of the facility with which, when dealing with young and independent nations, the nation is passed over for the race, and the tribe is preferred to the state. These are the cracks in the edifice which show the process of retrogression that is so harmful and prejudicial to national effort and national unity. We shall see that such retrograde steps with all the weaknesses and serious dangers that they entail are the historical result of the incapacity of the national middle class to rationalize popular action, that is to say their incapacity to see into the reasons for that action.

This traditional weakness, which is almost congenital to the national consciousness of under-developed countries, is not solely the result of the mutilation of the colonized people by the colonial regime. It is also the result of the intellectual laziness of the national middle class, of its spiritual penury, and of the profoundly cosmopolitan mould that its mind is set in.

The national middle class which takes over power at the end

of the colonial regime is an under-developed middle class. It has practically no economic power, and in any case it is in no way commensurate with the bourgeoisie of the mother country which it hopes to replace. In its wilful narcissism, the national middle class is easily convinced that it can advantageously replace the middle class of the mother country. But that same independence which literally drives it into a corner will give rise within its ranks to catastrophic reactions, and will oblige it to send out frenzied appeals for help to the former mother country. The university and merchant classes which make up the most enlightened section of the new state are in fact characterized by the smallness of their number and their being concentrated in the capital, and the type of activities in which they are engaged: business, agriculture and the liberal professions. Neither financiers nor industrial magnates are to be found within this national middle class. The national bourgeoisie of under-developed countries is not engaged in production, nor in invention, nor building, nor labour; it is completely canalized into activities of the intermediary type. Its innermost vocation seems to be to keep in the running and to be part of the racket. The psychology of the national bourgeoisie is that of the businessman, not that of a captain of industry; and it is only too true that the greed of the settlers and the system of embargoes set up by colonialism has hardly left them any other choice.

Under the colonial system, a middle class which accumulates capital is an impossible phenomenon. Now, precisely, it would seem that the historical vocation of an authentic national middle class in an under-developed country is to repudiate its own nature in so far as it is bourgeois, that is to say in so far as it is the tool of capitalism, and to make itself the willing slave of that revolutionary capital which is the people.

In an under-developed country an authentic national middle class ought to consider as its bounden duty to betray the calling fate has marked out for it, and to put itself to school with the people: in other words to put at the people's disposal the intellectual and technical capital that it has snatched when going through the colonial universities. But unhappily we shall see that very often the national middle class does not follow this heroic, positive, fruitful and just path; rather, it disappears with its soul set at peace into the shocking ways – shocking because anti-national – of a traditional bourgeoisie, of a bourgeoisie which is stupidly, contemptibly, cynically bourgeois.

The objective of nationalist parties as from a certain given period is, we have seen, strictly national. They mobilize the people with slogans of independence, and for the rest leave it to future events. When such parties are questioned on the economic programme of the state that they are clamouring for, or on the nature of the regime which they propose to install, they are incapable of replying, because, precisely, they are completely ignorant of the economy of their own country.

This economy has always developed outside the limits of their knowledge. They have nothing more than an approximate, bookish acquaintance with the actual and potential resources of their country's soil and mineral deposits; and therefore they can only speak of these resources on a general and abstract plane. After independence this under-developed middle class, reduced in numbers and without capital, which refuses to follow the path of revolution, will fall into deplorable stagnation. It is unable to give free rein to its genius, which formerly it was wont to lament, though rather too glibly, was held in check by colonial domination. The precariousness of its resources and the paucity of its managerial class forces it back for years into an artisan economy. From its point of view, which is inevitably a very limited one, a national economy is an economy based on what may be called local products. Long speeches will be made about the artisan class. Since the middle classes find it impossible to set up factories that would be more profit-earning both for themselves and for the country as a whole, they will surround the artisan class with a chauvinistic tenderness in keeping with the new awareness of national dignity, and which moreover will bring them in quite a lot of money. This cult of local products and this incapability to seek out new systems of management will be equally manifested by the bogging down of the national middle class in the methods of agricultural production which were characteristic of the colonial period.

The national economy of the period of independence is not set on a new footing. It is still concerned with the ground-nut harvest, with the cocoa crop and the olive yield. In the same way there is no change in the marketing of basic products, and not a single industry is set up in the country. We go on sending out raw materials; we go on being Europe's small farmers who specialize in unfinished products.

Yet the national middle class constantly demands the nationalization of the economy and of the trading sectors. This is because, from their point of view, nationalization does not mean placing the whole economy at the service of the nation and deciding to satisfy the needs of the nation. For them, nationalization does not mean governing the state with regard to the new social relations whose growth it has been decided to encourage. To them, nationalization quite simply means the transfer into native hands of those unfair advantages which are a legacy of the colonial period.

Since the middle class has neither sufficient material nor intellectual resources (by intellectual resources we mean engineers and technicians) it limits its claims to the taking over of business offices and commercial houses formerly occupied by the settlers. The national bourgeoisie steps into the shoes of the former European settlement: doctors, barristers, traders, commercial travellers, general agents and transport agents. It considers that the dignity of the country and its own welfare require that it should occupy all these posts. From now on it will insist that all the big foreign companies should pass through its hands, whether these companies wish to keep on their connexions with the country, or to open it up. The national middle class discovers its historic mission: that of intermediary.

Seen through its eyes, its mission has nothing to do with transforming the nation; it consists, prosaically, of being the transmission line between the nation and a capitalism, rampant though camouflaged, which today puts on the masque of neo-colonialism. The national bourgeoisie will be quite content with the role of the Western bourgeoisie's business agent, and it will play its part without any complexes in a most dignified manner. But this same lucrative role, this cheap-jack's function, this meanness of outlook and this absence of all ambition symbolize the incapability of the national middle class to fulfil its historic role of bourgeoisie. Here, the dynamic, pioneer aspect, the characteristics of the inventor and of the discoverer of new worlds which are found in all national bourgeoisies are lamentably absent. In the colonial countries, the spirit of indulgence is dominant at the core of the bourgeoisie; and this is because the national bourgeoisie identifies itself with the Western bourgeoisie, from whom it has learnt its lessons. It follows the Western bourgeoisie along its path of negation and decadence without ever having emulated it in its first stages of exploration and invention, stages which are an acquisition of that Western bourgeoisie whatever the circumstances. In its beginnings, the national bourgeoisie of the colonial countries identifies itself with the decadence of the bourgeoisie of the West. We need not think that it is jumping ahead; it is in fact beginning at the end. It is already senile before it has come to know the petulance, the fearlessness or the will to succeed of youth.

The national bourgeoisie will be greatly helped on its way towards decadence by the Western bourgeoisies, who come to it as tourists avid for the exotic, for big-game hunting and for casinos. The national bourgeoisie organizes centres of rest and relaxation and pleasure resorts to meet the wishes of the Western bourgeoisie. Such activity is given the name of tourism, and for the occasion will be built up as a national industry. If proof is needed of the eventual transformation of certain elements of the ex-native bourgeoisie into the organizers of parties for their Western opposite numbers, it is worth while having a look at what has happened in Latin America. The casinos of Havana and of Mexico, the beaches of Rio, the little Brazilian and Mexican girls, the half-breed thirteen-year-olds, the ports of Acapulco and Copacabana – all these are the stigma of this depravation of the national middle class. Because it is bereft of ideas, because it lives to itself and cuts itself off from the people, undermined by its hereditary incapacity to think in terms of all the problems of the nation as seen from the point of view of the whole of that nation, the national middle class will have nothing better to do than to take on the role of manager for Western enterprise, and it will in practice set up its country as the brothel of Europe.

Once again we must keep before us the unfortunate example of certain Latin American republics. The banking magnates, the technocrats and the big businessmen of the United States have only to step on to a plane and they are wafted into sub-tropical climes, there for a space of a week or ten days to luxuriate in the delicious depravities which their 'reserves' hold for them.

The behaviour of the national landed proprietors is practically identical with that of the middle classes of the towns. The big farmers have, as soon as independence was proclaimed, demanded the nationalization of agricultural production. Through manifold scheming practices they manage to make a clean sweep of the farms formerly owned by settlers, thus reinforcing their hold on the district. But they do not try to introduce new agricultural methods, nor to farm more intensively, nor to integrate their farming systems into a genuinely national economy.

In fact, the landed proprietors will insist that the state should give them a hundred times more facilities and privileges than were enjoyed by the foreign settlers in former times. The exploitation of agricultural workers will be intensified and made legitimate. Using two or three slogans, these new colonists will demand an enormous amount of work from the agricultural labourers, in the name of the national effort of course. There will be no modernization of agriculture, no planning for development, and no initiative; for initiative throws these people into a panic since it implies a minimum of risk, and completely upsets the hesitant, prudent, landed bourgeoisie, which gradually slips more and more into the lines laid down by colonialism. In the districts where this is the case, the only efforts made to better things are due to the government; it orders them, encourages them and finances them. The landed bourgeoisie refuses to take the slightest risk, and remains opposed to any venture and to any hazard. It has no intention of building upon sand; it demands solid investments and quick returns. The enormous profits which it pockets, enormous if we take into account the national revenue, are never reinvested. The money-in-the-stocking mentality is dominant in the psychology of these landed proprietors. Sometimes, especially in the years immediately following independence, the bourgeoisie does not hesitate to invest in foreign banks the profits that it makes out of its native soil.

On the other hand large sums are spent on display: on cars, country houses, and on all those things which have been justly described by economists as characterizing an under-developed bourgeoisie.

We have said that the native bourgeoisie which comes to power uses its class aggressiveness to corner the positions formerly kept for foreigners. On the morrow of independence, in fact, it violently attacks colonial personalities: barristers, traders, landed proprietors, doctors and higher civil servants. It will fight to the bitter end against these people 'who insult our dignity as a nation'. It waves aloft the notion of the nationalization and Africanization of the ruling classes. The fact is that such action will become more and more tinged by racism, until the bourgeoisie bluntly puts the problem to the government by saying 'We must have these posts'. They will not stop their snarling until they have taken over every one.

The working class of the towns, the masses of unemployed, the small artisans and craftsmen for their part line up behind this nationalist attitude; but in all justice let it be said, they only follow in the steps of their bourgeoisie. If the national bourgeoisie goes into competition with the Europeans, the artisans and craftsmen start a fight against non-national Africans. In the Ivory Coast, the anti-Dahoman and anti-Voltaic troubles are in fact racial riots. The Dahoman and Voltaic peoples, who control the greater part of the petty trade, are, once independence is declared, the object of hostile manifestations on the part of the people of the Ivory Coast. From nationalism we have passed to ultra-nationalism, to chauvinism, and finally to racism. These foreigners are called on to leave; their shops are burned, their street stalls are wrecked, and in fact the government of the Ivory Coast commands them to go, thus giving their nationals satisfaction. In Senegal it is the anti-Sudanese demonstrations which called forth these words from Mr Mamadou Dia:

The truth is that the Senegalese people have only adopted the Mali mystique through attachment to its leaders. Their adhesion to the Mali has no other significance than that of a fresh act of faith in the political policy of the latter. The Senegalese territory was no less real, in fact it was all the more so in that the presence of the Sudanese in Dakar was too obviously manifested for it to be forgotten. It is this fact which explains that, far from being regretted, the break-up of the Federation has been greeted with relief by the mass of the people and nowhere was a hand raised to maintain it.*

While certain sections of the Senegalese people jump at the chance which is afforded them by their own leaders to get rid of the Sudanese, who hamper them in commercial matters or in administrative posts, the Congolese, who stood by hardly daring to believe in the mass exodus of the Belgians, decide to bring pressure to bear on the Senegalese who have settled in Leopoldville and Elizabethville and to get them to leave.

As we see it, the mechanism is identical in the two sets of circumstances. If the Europeans get in the way of the intellectuals and business bourgeoisie of the young nation, for the mass of the people in the towns competition is represented principally by Africans of another nation. On the Ivory Coast these competitors are the Dahomans; in Ghana they are the Nigerians; in Senegal, they are the Sudanese.

When the bougeoisie's demands for a ruling class made up exclusively of Negroes or Arabs do not spring from an authentic movement of nationalization but merely correspond to an anxiety to place in the bourgeoisie's hands the power held hitherto by the foreigner, the masses on their level present the same demands, confining, however, the notion of Negro or Arab within certain territorial limits. Between resounding assertions of the unity of the continent and this behaviour of the masses which has its inspiration in their leaders, many different attitudes may be traced. We observe a permanent see-saw between African unity, which fades quicker and quicker into the mists of oblivion, and a heart-breaking return to chauvinism in its most bitter and detestable form.

On the Senegalese side, the leaders who have been the main theoreticians of African unity, and who several times over have sacrificed their local political organizations and their personal positions to this idea, are, though in all good faith, undeniably responsible. Their mistake – our mistake – has been, under pretext of fighting 'Balkanization', not to have taken into consideration the pre-colonial fact of territorial-

* Mamadou Dia: *Nations africaines et solidarité mondial*, Presses Universitaires de France, p. 140.

ism. Our mistake has been not to have paid enough attention in our analyses to this phenomenon, which is the fruit of colonialism if you like, but also a sociological fact which no theory of unity, be it ever so laudable or attractive, can abolish. We have allowed ourselves to be seduced by a mirage; that of the structure which is the most pleasing to our minds; and, mistaking our ideal for reality, we have believed it enough to condemn territorialism, and its natural sequel, micro-nationalism, for us to get the better of them, and to assure the success of our chimerical undertaking.*

From the chauvinism of the Senegalese to the tribalism of the Yolofs is not a big step. For, in fact, everywhere that the national bourgeoisie has failed to break through to the people as a whole, to enlighten them, and to consider all problems in the first place with regard to them – a failure due to the bourgeoisie's attitude of mistrust and to the haziness of its political tenets – everywhere where that national bourgeoisie has shown itself incapable of extending its vision of the world sufficiently, we observe a falling back towards old tribal attitudes, and, furious and sick at heart, we perceive that race feeling in its most exacerbated form is triumphing. Since the sole motto of the bourgeoisie is 'Replace the foreigner', and because it hastens in every walk of life to secure justice for itself and to take over the posts that the foreigner has vacated, the 'small people' of the nation – taxi-drivers, cake-sellers and shoeblacks – will be equally quick to insist that the Dahomans go home to their own country, or will even go further and demand that the Foulbis and the Peuhls return to their jungle or their mountains.

It is from this view-point that we must interpret the fact that in young, independent countries, here and there federalism triumphs. We know that colonial domination has marked certain regions out for privilege. The colony's economy is not integrated into that of the nation as a whole. It is still organized in order to complete the economy of the different mother countries. Colonialism hardly ever exploits the whole of a country. It contents itself with bringing to light the natural resources, which it extracts, and exports to meet the needs of the mother country's industries, thereby allowing certain sectors of the colony to become relatively rich. But the rest of the colony

* Mamadou Dia, op. cit.

follows its path of under-development and poverty, or at all events sinks into it more deeply.

Immediately after independence, the nationals who live in the more prosperous regions realize their good luck, and show a primary and profound reaction in refusing to feed the other nationals. The districts which are rich in ground-nuts, in cocoa and in diamonds come to the forefront, and dominate the empty panorama which the rest of the nation presents. The nationals of these rich regions look upon the others with hatred, and find in them envy and covetousness, and homicidal impulses. Old rivalries which were there before colonialism, old inter-racial hatred come to the surface. The Balubas refuse to feed the Luluas; Katanga forms itself into a state, and Albert Kalondji gets himself crowned king of South Kasai.

African unity, that vague formula, yet one to which the men and women of Africa were passionately attached, and whose operative value served to bring immense pressure to bear on colonialism, African unity takes off the mask, and crumbles into regionalism inside the hollow shell of nationality itself. The national bourgeoisie, since it is strung up to defend its immediate interests, and sees no farther than the end of its nose, reveals itself incapable of simply bringing national unity into being, or of building up the nation on a stable and productive basis. The national front which has forced colonialism to withdraw cracks up, and wastes the victory it has gained.

This merciless fight engaged upon by races and tribes, and this aggressive anxiety to occupy the posts left vacant by the departure of the foreigner, will equally give rise to religious rivalries. In the country districts and the bush, minor confraternities, local religions and maraboutic cults will show a new vitality and will once more take up their round of excommunications. In the big towns, on the level of the administrative classes, we will observe the coming to grips of the two great revealed religions, Islam and Catholicism.

Colonialism, which had been shaken to its very foundations by the birth of African unity, recovers its balance and tries now to break that will to unity by using all the movement's weaknesses. Colonialism will set the African peoples moving by revealing to them the existence of 'spiritual' rivalries. In Senegal, it is the newspaper *New Africa* which week by week distils hatred of Islam and of the Arabs. The Lebanese, in whose hands is the greater part of the small trading enterprises on the western seaboard, are marked out for national obloquy. The missionaries find it opportune to remind the masses that long before the advent of European colonialism the great African empires were disrupted by the Arab invasion. There is no hesitation in saying that it was the Arab occupation which paved the way for European colonialism; Arab imperialism is commonly spoken of, and the cultural imperialism of Islam is condemned. Moslems are usually kept out of the more important posts. In other regions the reverse is the case, and it is the native Christians who are considered as conscious, objective enemies of national independence.

Colonialism pulls every string shamelessly, and is only too content to set at loggerheads those Africans who only yesterday were leagued against the settlers. The idea of a Saint Bartholomew takes shape in certain minds, and the advocates of colonialism laugh to themselves derisively when they hear magnificent declarations about African unity. Inside a single nation, religion splits up the people into different spiritual communities, all of them kept up and stiffened by colonialism and its instruments. Totally unexpected events break out here and there. In regions where Catholicism or Protestantism predominates, we see the Moslem minorities flinging themselves with unaccustomed ardour into their devotions. The Islamic feastdays are revived, and the Moslem religion defends itself inch by inch against the violent absolutism of the Catholic faith. Ministers of state are heard to say for the benefit of certain individuals that if they are not content they have only to go to Cairo. Sometimes American Protestantism transplants its anti-Catholic prejudices into African soil, and keeps up tribal rivalries through religion.

Taking the continent as a whole, this religious tension may be responsible for the revival of the commonest racial feeling. Africa is divided into Black and White, and the names that are substituted – Africa south of the Sahara, Africa north of the Sahara – do not manage to hide this latent racism. Here, it is affirmed that White Africa has a thousand-year-old tradition of culture; that she is Mediterranean, that she is a continuation of Europe and that she shares in Graeco-Latin civilization. Black Africa is looked on as a region that is inert, brutal, uncivilized – in a word, savage. There, all day long you may hear unpleasant remarks about veiled women, polygamy and the supposed disdain the Arabs have for the feminine sex. All such remarks are reminiscent in their aggressiveness of those that are so often heard coming from the settler's lips. The national bourgeoisie of each of these two great religions, which has totally assimilated colonialist thought in its most corrupt form, takes over from the Europeans and establishes in the continent a racial philosophy which is extremely harmful for the future of Africa. By its laziness and will to imitation, it promotes the ingrafting and stiffening of racism which was characteristic of the colonial era. Thus it is by no means astonishing to hear in a country that calls itself African remarks which are neither more nor less than racist, and to observe the existence of paternalist behaviour which gives you the bitter impression that you are in Paris, Brussels or London.

In certain regions of Africa, drivelling paternalism with regard to the blacks and the loathsome idea derived from Western culture that the black man is impervious to logic and the sciences reign in all their nakedness. Sometimes it may be ascertained that the black minorities are hemmed in by a kind of semi-slavery which renders legitimate that species of wariness, or in other words mistrust, which the countries of Black Africa feel with regard to the countries of White Africa. It is all too common that a citizen of Black Africa hears himself called a 'Negro' by the children when walking in the streets of a big town in White Africa, or finds that civil servants address him in pidgin English.

Yes, unfortunately it is not unknown that students from Black Africa who attend secondary schools north of the Sahara hear their schoolfellows asking if in their country there are houses, if they know what electricity is, or if they practise cannibalism in their families. Yes, unfortunately it is not unknown that in certain regions north of the Sahara Africans coming from countries south of the Sahara meet nationals who implore them to take them 'anywhere at all on condition we meet Negroes'. In parallel fashion, in certain young states of Black Africa members of parliament, or even ministers, maintain without a trace of humour that the danger is not at all of a reoccupation of their country by colonialism but of an eventual invasion by 'those vandals of Arabs coming from the North'.

As we see it, the bankruptcy of the bourgeoisie is not apparent in the economic field only. They have come to power in the name of a narrow nationalism and representing a race; they will prove themselves incapable of triumphantly putting into practice a programme with even a minimum humanist content, in spite of fine-sounding declarations which are devoid of meaning since the speakers bandy about in irresponsible fashion phrases that come straight out of European treatises on morals and political philosophy. When the bourgeoisie is strong, when it can arrange everything and everybody to serve its power, it does not hesitate to affirm positively certain democratic ideas which claim to be universally applicable. There must be very exceptional circumstances if such a bourgeoisie, solidly based economically, is forced into denying its own humanist ideology. The Western bourgeoisie, though fundamentally racist, most often manages to mask this racism by a multiplicity of nuances which allow it to preserve intact its proclamation of mankind's outstanding dignity.

The Western bourgeoisie has prepared enough fences and railings to have no real fear of the competition of those whom it exploits and holds in contempt. Western bourgeois racial prejudice as regards the nigger and the Arab is a racism of contempt; it is a racism which minimizes what it hates. Bourgeois ideology, however, which is the proclamation of an essential equality between men, manages to appear logical in its own eyes by inviting the sub-men to become human, and to take as their prototype Western humanity as incarnated in the Western bourgeoisie.

The racial prejudice of the young national bourgeoisie is a racism of defence, based on fear. Essentially it is no different from vulgar tribalism, or the rivalries between septs or confraternities. We may understand why keen-witted international observers have hardly taken seriously the great flights of oratory about African unity, for it is true that there are so many cracks in that unity visible to the naked eye that it is only reasonable to insist that all these contradictions ought to be resolved before the day of unity can come.

The people of Africa have only recently come to know themselves. They have decided, in the name of the whole continent, to weigh in strongly against the colonial regime. Now the nationalist bourgeoisies, who in region after region hasten to make their own fortunes and to set up a national system of exploitation, do their utmost to put obstacles in the path of this 'Utopia'. The national bourgeoisies, who are quite clear as to what their objectives are, have decided to bar the way to that unity, to that coordinated effort on the part of two hundred and fifty million men to triumph over stupidity, hunger and inhumanity at one and the same time. This is why we must understand that African unity can only be achieved through the upward thrust of the people, and under the leadership of the people, that is to say, in defiance of the interests of the bourgeoisie.

As regards internal affairs and in the sphere of institutions, the national bourgeoisie will give equal proof of its incapacity. In a certain number of under-developed countries the parliamentary game is faked from the beginning. Powerless economically, unable to bring about the existence of coherent social relations, and standing on the principle of its domination as a class, the bourgeoisie chooses the solution that seems to it the easiest, that of the single party. It does not yet have the quiet conscience and the calm that economic power and the control of the state machine alone can give. It does not create a state that reassures the ordinary citizen, but rather one that rouses his anxiety.

The state, which by its strength and discretion ought to inspire confidence and disarm and lull everybody to sleep, on the contrary seeks to impose itself in spectacular fashion. It makes a display, it jostles people and bullies them, thus intimating to the citizen that he is in continual danger. The single party is the modern form of the dictatorship of the bourgeoisie, unmasked, unpainted, unscrupulous and cynical.

It is true that such a dictatorship does not go very far. It cannot halt the processes of its own contradictions. Since the bourgeoisie has not the economic means to ensure its domination and to throw a few crumbs to the rest of the country; since, moreover, it is preoccupied with filling its pockets as rapidly as possible but also as prosaically as possible, the country sinks all the more deeply into stagnation. And in order to hide this stagnation and to mask this regression, to reassure itself and to give itself something to boast about, the bourgeoisie can find nothing better to do than to erect grandiose buildings in the capital and to lay out money on what are called prestige expenses.

The national bourgeoisie turns its back more and more on the interior and on the real facts of its undeveloped country, and tends to look towards the former mother country and the foreign capitalists who count on its obliging compliance. As it does not share its profits with the people, and in no way allows them to enjoy any of the dues that are paid to it by the big foreign companies, it will discover the need for a popular leader to whom will fall the dual role of stabilizing the regime and of perpetuating the domination of the bourgeoisie. The bourgeois dictatorship of under-developed countries draws its strength from the existence of a leader. We know that in the well-developed countries the bourgeois dictatorship is the result of the economic power of the bourgeoisie. In the under-developed countries on the contrary the leader stands for moral power, in whose shelter the thin and poverty-stricken bourgeoisie of the young nation decides to get rich.

The people who for years on end have seen this leader and heard him speak, who from a distance in a kind of dream have followed his contests with the colonial power, spontaneously put their trust in this patriot. Before independence, the leader generally embodies the aspirations of the people for independence, political liberty and national dignity. But as soon as independence is declared, far from embodying in concrete form the needs of the people in what touches bread, land and the restoration of the country to the sacred hands of the people, the leader will reveal his inner purpose: to become the general president of that company of profiteers impatient for their returns which constitutes the national bourgeoisie.

In spite of his frequently honest conduct and his sincere declarations, the leader as seen objectively is the fierce defender of these interests, today combined, of the national bourgeoisie and the ex-colonial companies. His honesty, which is his soul's true bent, crumbles away little by little. His contact with the masses is so unreal that he comes to believe that his authority is hated and that the services that he has rendered his country are being called in question. The leader judges the ingratitude of the masses harshly, and every day that passes ranges himself a little more resolutely on the side of the exploiters. He therefore knowingly becomes the aider and abettor of the young bourgeoisie which is plunging into the mire of corruption and pleasure.

The economic channels of the young state sink back inevitably into neo-colonialist lines. The national economy, formerly protected, is today literally controlled. The budget is balanced through loans and gifts, while every three or four months the chief ministers themselves or else their governmental delegations come to the erstwhile mother countries or elsewhere, fishing for capital.

The former colonial power increases its demands, accumulates concessions and guarantees and takes fewer and fewer pains to mask the hold it has over the national government. The people stagnate deplorably in unbearable poverty; slowly they awaken to the unutterable treason of their leaders. This awakening is all the more acute in that the bourgeoisie is incapable of learning its lesson. The distribution of wealth that it effects is not spread out between a great many sectors; it is not ranged among different levels, nor does it set up a hierarchy of half-tones. The new caste is an affront all the more disgusting in that the immense majority, nine-tenths of the population, continue to die of starvation. The scandalous enrichment, speedy and pitiless, of this caste is accompanied by a decisive awakening on the part of the people, and a growing awareness that promises stormy days to come. The bourgeois caste, that section of the nation which annexes for its own profit all the wealth of the country, by a kind of unexpected logic will pass disparaging judgements upon the other Negroes and the other Arabs that more often than not are reminiscent of the racist doctrines of the former representatives of the colonial power. At one and the same time the poverty of the people, the immoderate money-making of the bourgeois caste, and its widespread scorn for the rest of the nation will harden thought and action.

But such threats will lead to the re-affirmation of authority and the appearance of dictatorship. The leader, who has behind him a lifetime of political action and devoted patriotism, constitutes a screen between the people and the rapacious bourgeoisie since he stands surety for the ventures of that caste and closes his eyes to their insolence, their mediocrity and their fundamental immorality. He acts as a braking-power on the awakening consciousness of the people. He comes to the aid of the bourgeois caste and hides his manoeuvres from the people, thus becoming the most eager worker in the task of mystifying and bewildering the masses. Every time he speaks to the people he calls to mind his often heroic life, the struggles he has led in the name of the people and the victories in their name he has achieved, thereby intimating clearly to the masses that they ought to go on putting their confidence in him. There are plenty of examples of African patriots who have introduced into the cautious political advance of their elders a decisive style characterized by its nationalist outlook. These men came from the backwoods, and they proclaimed, to the scandal of the dominating power and the shame of the nationals of the capital, that they came from the backwoods and that they spoke in the name of the Negroes. These men, who have sung the praises of their race, who have taken upon themselves the whole burden of the past, complete with cannibalism and degeneracy, find themselves today, alas, at the head of a team of administrators who turn their back on the jungle and who proclaim that the vocation of their people is to obey, to go on obeying and to be obedient till the end of time.

The leader pacifies the people. For years on end after independence has been won, we see him, incapable of urging on the people to a concrete task, unable really to open the future to them or of flinging them into the path of national reconstruction, that is to say, of their own reconstruction; we see him reassessing the history of independence and recalling the sacred unity of the struggle for liberation. The leader, because he refuses to break up the national bourgeoisie, asks the people to fall back into the past and to become drunk on the remembrance of the epoch which led up to independence. The leader, seen objectively, brings the people to a halt and persists in either expelling them from history or preventing them from taking root in it. During the struggle for liberation the leader awakened the people and promised them a forward march, heroic and unmitigated. Today, he uses every means to put them to sleep, and three or four times a year asks them to remember the colonial period and to look back on the long way they have come since then.

Now it must be said that the masses show themselves totally incapable of appreciating the long way they have come. The peasant who goes on scratching out a living from the soil, and the unemployed man who never finds employment do not manage, in spite of public holidays and flags, new and brightly-coloured though they may be, to convince themselves that anything has really changed in their lives. The bourgeoisie who are in power vainly increase the number of processions; the masses have no illusions. They are hungry; and the police officers, though now they are Africans, do not serve to reassure them particularly. The masses begin to sulk; they turn away from this nation in which they have been given no place and begin to lose interest in it.

From time to time, however, the leader makes an effort; he speaks on the radio or makes a tour of the country to pacify the people, to calm them and bemuse them. The leader is all the more necessary in that there is no party. During the period of the struggle for independence there was one right enough, a party led by the present leader. But since then this party has sadly disintegrated; nothing is left but the shell of a party, the name, the emblem and the motto. The living party, which ought to make possible the free exchange of ideas which have been elaborated according to the real needs of the mass of the people, has been transformed into a trade union of individual interests. Since the proclamation of independence the party no longer helps the people to set out its demands, to become more aware of its needs and better able to establish its power. Today, the party's mission is to deliver to the people the instructions which issue from the summit. There no longer exists the fruitful give-and-take from the bottom to the top and from the top to the bottom which creates and guarantees democracy in a party. Quite on the contrary, the party has made itself into a screen between the masses and the leaders. There is no longer any party life, for the branches which were set up during the colonial period are today completely demobilized.

The militant champs on his bit. Now it is that the attitude taken up by certain militants during the struggle for liberation is seen to be justified, for the fact is that in the thick of the fight more than a few militants asked the leaders to formulate a dogma, to set out their objectives and to draw up a programme. But under the pretext of safeguarding national unity, the leaders categorically refused to attempt such a task. The only worthwhile dogma, it was repeatedly stated, is the union of the nation against colonialism. And on they went, armed with an impetuous slogan which stood for principles, while their only ideological activity took the form of a series of variants on the theme of the right of peoples to self-determination, borne on the wind of history which would inevitably sweep away colonialism. When the militants asked whether the wind of history couldn't be a little more clearly analysed, the leaders gave them instead hope and trust, the necessity of decolonialization and its inevitability, and more to that effect.

After independence, the party sinks into an extraordinary lethargy. The militants are only called upon when so-called popular manifestations are afoot, or international conferences, or independence celebrations. The local party leaders are given administrative posts, the party becomes an administration, and the militants disappear into the crowd and take the empty title of citizen. Now that they have fulfilled their historical mission of leading the bourgeoisie to power, they are firmly invited to retire so that the bourgeoisie may carry out *its* mission in peace and quiet. But we have seen that the national bourgeoisie of under-developed countries is incapable of carrying out any mission whatever. After a few years, the break-up of the party becomes obvious, and any observer, even the most superficial, can notice that the party, today the skeleton of its former self, only serves to immobilize the people. The party, which during the battle had drawn to itself the whole nation, is falling to pieces. The intellectuals who on the eve of independence rallied to the party, now make it clear by their attitude that they gave their support with no other end in view than to secure their slices of the cake of independence. The party is becoming a means of private advancement.

There exists inside the new regime, however, an inequality in the acquisition of wealth and in monopolization. Some have a double source of income and demonstrate that they are specialized in opportunism. Privileges multiply and corruption triumphs, while morality declines. Today the vultures are too numerous and too voracious in proportion to the lean spoils of the national wealth. The party, a true instrument of power in the hands of the bourgeoisie, reinforces the machine, and ensures that the people are hemmed in and immobilized. The party helps the government to hold the people down. It becomes more and more clearly anti-democratic, an implement of coercion. The party is objectively, sometimes subjectively, the accomplice of the merchant bourgeoisie. In the same way that the national bourgeoisie conjures away its phase of construction in order to throw itself into the enjoyment of its wealth, in parallel fashion in the institutional sphere it jumps the parliamentary phase and chooses a dictatorship of the national-socialist type. We know today that this fascism at high interest which has triumphed for half a century in Latin America is the dialectic result of states which were semi-colonial during the period of independence.

In these poor, under-developed countries, where the rule is that the greatest wealth is surrounded by the greatest poverty, the army and the police constitute the pillars of the regime; an army and a police force (another rule which must not be forgotten) which are advised by foreign experts. The strength of the police force and the power of the army are proportionate to the stagnation in which the rest of the nation is sunk. By dint of yearly loans, concessions are snatched up by foreigners; scandals are numerous, ministers grow rich, their wives doll themselves up, the members of parliament feather their nests and there is not a soul down to the simple policeman or the customs officer who does not join in the great procession of corruption.

The opposition becomes more aggressive and the people at

once catch on to its propaganda. From now on their hostility to the bourgeoisie is plainly visible. This young bourgeoisie which appears to be afflicted with precocious senility takes no heed of the advice showered upon it, and reveals itself incapable of understanding that it would be in its interest to draw a veil, even if only the flimsiest kind, over its exploitation. It is the most Christian newspaper *The African Weekly*, published in Brazzaville, which addresses the princes of the regime thus:

You who are in good positions, you and your wives, today you enjoy many comforts; perhaps a good education, a fine house, good contacts and many missions on which you are delegated which open new horizons to you. But all your wealth forms a hard shell which prevents your seeing the poverty that surrounds you. Take care.

This warning coming from *The African Weekly* and, addressed to the henchmen of Monsieur Youlou has, we may imagine, nothing revolutionary about it. What *The African Weekly* wants to point out to the starvers of the Congolese people is that God will punish their conduct. It continues: 'If there is no room in your heart for consideration towards those who are beneath you, there will be no room for you in God's house.'

It is clear that the national bourgeoisie hardly worries at all about such an indictment. With its wave-lengths tuned in to Europe, it continues firmly and resolutely to make the most of the situation. The enormous profits which it derives from the exploitation of the people are exported to foreign countries. The young national bourgeoisie is often more suspicious of the regime that it has set up than are the foreign companies. The national bourgeoisie refuses to invest in its own country and behaves towards the state that protects and nurtures it with, it must be remarked, astonishing ingratitude. It acquires foreign securities in the European markets, and goes off to spend the week-end in Paris or Hamburg. The behaviour of the national bourgeoisie of certain under-developed countries is reminiscent of the members of a gang, who after every hold-up hide their share in the swag from the other members who are their accomplices and prudently start thinking about their retirement. Such behaviour shows that more or less consciously the national bourgeoisie is playing to lose if the game goes on too long.

They guess that the present situation will not last indefinitely but they intend to make the most of it. Such exploitation and such contempt for the state, however, inevitably gives rise to discontent among the mass of the people. It is in these conditions that the regime becomes harsher. In the absence of a parliament it is the army that becomes the arbiter: but sooner or later it will realize its power and will hold over the government's head the threat of a manifesto.

As we see it, the national bourgeoisie of certain under-developed countries has learned nothing from books. If they had looked closer at the Latin American countries they doubtless would have recognized the dangers which threaten them. We may thus conclude that this bourgeoisie in miniature that thrusts itself into the forefront is condemned to mark time, accomplishing nothing. In under-developed countries the bourgeois phase is impossibly arid. Certainly, there is a police dictatorship and a profiteering caste, but the construction of an elaborate bourgeois society seems to be condemned to failure. The ranks of decked-out profiteers whose grasping hands scrape up the bank-notes from a poverty-stricken country will sooner or later be men of straw in the hands of the army, cleverly handled by foreign experts. In this way the former mother country practises indirect government, both by the bourgeoisie that it upholds and also by the national army led by its experts, an army that pins the people down, immobilizing and terrorizing them.

The observations that we have been able to make about the national bourgeoisie bring us to a conclusion which should cause no surprise. In under-developed countries, the bourgeoisie should not be allowed to find the conditions necessary for its existence and its growth. In other words, the combined effort of the masses led by a party and of intellectuals who are highly conscious and armed with revolutionary principles ought to bar the way to this useless and harmful middle class.

The theoretical question that for the last fifty years has been raised whenever the history of under-developed countries is under discussion – whether or not the bourgeois phase can be skipped – ought to be answered in the field of revolutionary action, and not by logic. The bourgeois phase in under-developed countries can only justify itself in so far as the national bourgeoisie has sufficient economic and technical strength to build up a bourgeois society, to create the conditions necessary for the development of a large-scale proletariat, to mechanize agriculture and finally to make possible the existence of an authentic national culture.

A bourgeoisie similar to that which developed in Europe is able to elaborate an ideology and at the same time strengthen its own power. Such a bourgeoisie, dynamic, educated and secular, has fully succeeded in its undertaking of the accumulation of capital and has given to the nation a minimum of prosperity. In under-developed countries, we have seen that no true bourgeoisie exists; there is only a sort of little greedy caste, avid and voracious, with the mind of a huckster, only too glad to accept the dividends that the former colonial power hands out to it. This get-rich-quick middle class shows itself incapable of great ideas or of inventiveness. It remembers what it has read in European textbooks and imperceptibly it becomes not even the replica of Europe, but its caricature.

The struggle against the bourgeoisie of under-developed countries is far from being a theoretical one. It is not concerned with making out its condemnation as laid down by the judgement of history. The national bourgeoisie of under-developed countries must not be opposed because it threatens to slow down the total, harmonious development of the nation. It must simply be stoutly opposed because, literally, it is good for nothing. This bourgeoisie, expressing its mediocrity in its profits, its achievements and in its thought, tries to hide this mediocrity by buildings which have prestige value at the individual level, by chromium plating on big American cars, by holidays on the Riviera and week-ends in neon-lit night-clubs.

This bourgeoisie which turns its back more and more on the people as a whole does not even succeed in extracting spectacular concessions from the West, such as investments which would be of value for the country's economy or the setting up of certain industries. On the contrary, assembly plants spring up and consecrate the type of neo-colonialist industrialization in which the country's economy flounders. Thus it must not be said that the national bourgeoisie retards the country's evolution, that it makes it lose time or that it threatens to lead the nation up blind alleys. In fact, the bourgeois phase in the history of under-developed countries is a completely useless phase. When this caste has vanished, devoured by its own contradictions, it will be seen that nothing new has happened since independence was proclaimed, and that everything must be started again from scratch. The change-over will not take place at the level of the structures set up by the bourgeoisie during its reign, since that caste has done nothing more than take over unchanged the legacy of the economy, the thought and the institutions left by the colonialists.

It is all the easier to neutralize this bourgeois class in that, as we have seen, it is numerically, intellectually and economically weak. In the colonized territories, the bourgeois caste draws its strength after independence chiefly from agreements reached with the former colonial power. The national bourgeoisie has all the more opportunity to take over from the oppressor since it has been given time for a leisurely *tête-à-tête* with the ex-colonial power. But deep-rooted contradictions undermine the ranks of that bourgeoisie; it is this that gives the observer an impression of instability. There is not as yet a homogeneity of caste. Many intellectuals, for example, condemn this regime based on the domination of the few. In under-developed countries, there are certain members of the *élite*, intellectuals and civil servants, who are sincere, who feel the necessity for a planned economy, the outlawing of profiteers and the strict prohibition of attempts at mystification. In addition, such men fight in a certain measure for the mass participation of the people in the ordering of public affairs.

In those under-developed countries which accede to independence, there almost always exists a small number of honest intellectuals, who have no very precise ideas about politics, but who instinctively distrust the race for positions and pensions which is symptomatic of the early days of independence in colonized countries. The personal situation of these men (breadwinners of large families) or their background (hard struggles and a strictly moral upbringing) explain their manifest contempt for profiteers and schemers. We must know how to use these men in the decisive battle that we mean to engage upon which will lead to a healthier outlook for the nation. Closing the road to the national bourgeoisie is, certainly, the means whereby the vicissitudes of new-found independence may be avoided, and with them the decline of morals, the installing of corruption within the country, economic regression, and the immediate disaster of an anti-democratic regime depending on force and intimidation. But it is also the only means towards progress.

What holds up the taking of a decision by the profoundly democratic elements of the young nation and adds to their timidity is the apparent strength of the bourgeoisie. In newly independent under-developed countries, the whole of the ruling class swarms into the towns built by colonialism. The absence of any analysis of the total population induces on-lookers to think that there exists a powerful and perfectly organized bourgeoisie. In fact, we know today that the bourgeoisie in under-developed countries is non-existent. What creates a bourgeoisie is not the bourgeois spirit, nor its taste or manners, nor even its aspirations. The bourgeoisie is above all the direct product of precise economic conditions.

Now, in the colonies, the economic conditions are conditions of a foreign bourgeoisie. Through its agents, it is the bourgeoisie of the mother country that we find present in the colonial towns. The bourgeoisie in the colonies is, before independence, a Western bourgeoisie, a true branch of the bourgeoisie of the mother country, that derives its legitimacy, its force and its stability from the bourgeoisie of the homeland. During the period of unrest that precedes independence, certain native elements, intellectuals and traders, who live in the midst of that imported bourgeoisie, try to identify themselves with it. A permanent wish for identification with the bourgeois representatives of the mother country is to be found among the native intellectuals and merchants.

This native bourgeoisie, which has adopted unreservedly and with enthusiasm the ways of thinking characteristic of the mother country, which has become wonderfully detached from its own thought and has based its consciousness upon foundations which are typically foreign, will realize, with its mouth watering, that it lacks something essential to a bourgeoisie: money. The bourgeoisie of an under-developed country is a bourgeoisie in spirit only. It is not its economic strength, nor the dynamism of its leaders, nor the breadth of its ideas that ensures its peculiar quality of bourgeoisie. Consequently it remains at the beginning and for a long time afterwards a bourgeoisie of the civil service. It is the positions that it holds in the new national administration which will give it strength and serenity. If the government gives it enough time and opportunity, this bourgeoisie will manage to put away enough money to stiffen its domination. But it will always reveal itself as incapable of giving birth to an authentic bourgeois society with all the economic and industrial consequences which this entails.

From the beginning the national bourgeoisie directs its efforts towards activities of the intermediary type. The basis of its strength is found in its aptitude for trade and small business enterprises, and in securing commissions. It is not its money that works, but its business acumen. It does not go in for investments and it cannot achieve that accumulation of capital necessary to the birth and blossoming of an authentic bourgeoisie. At that rate it would take centuries to set on foot an embryonic industrial revolution, and in any case it would find the way barred by the relentless opposition of the former mother country, which will have taken all precautions when setting up neo-colonialist trade conventions.

If the government wants to bring the country out of its stagnation and set it well on the road towards development and progress, it must first and foremost nationalize the middleman's trading sector. The bourgeoisie, who wish to see both the triumph of the spirit of money-making and the enjoyment of consumer goods, and at the same time the triumph of their contemptuous attitude towards the mass of the people and the scandalous aspect of profit-making (should we not rather call it robbery?), in fact invest largely in this sector. The intermediary market which formerly was dominated by the settlers will be invaded by the young national bourgeoisie. In a colonial economy the intermediary sector is by far the most important. If you want to progress, you must decide in the first few hours to nationalize this sector. But it is clear that such a nationalization ought not to take on a rigidly state-controlled aspect. It is not a question of placing at the head of these services citizens who have had no political education. Every time such a procedure has been adopted it has been seen that the government has in fact contributed to the triumph of a dictatorship of civil servants who had been set in the mould of the former mother country, and who quickly showed themselves incapable of thinking in terms of the nation as a whole. These civil servants very soon began to sabotage the national economy and to throw its structure out of joint; under them, corruption, prevarication, the diversion of stocks and the black market came to stay. Nationalizing the intermediary sector means organizing wholesale and retail cooperatives on a democratic basis; it also means decentralizing these cooperatives by getting the mass of the people interested in the ordering of public affairs. You will not be able to do all this unless you give the people some political education. Previously, it was realized that this key problem should be clarified once and for all. Today, it is true that the principle of the political education of the masses is generally subscribed to in under-developed countries. But it does not seem that this primordial task is really taken to heart. When people stress the need to educate the people politically, they decide to point out at the same time that they want to be supported by the people in the action that they are taking. A government which declares that it wishes to educate the people politically thus expresses its desire to govern with the people and for the people. It ought not to speak a language destined to camouflage a bourgeois administration. In the capitalist countries, the bourgeois governments have long since left this infantile stage of authority behind. To put it bluntly, they govern with the help of their laws, their economic strength and their police. Now that their power is firmly established they no longer need to lose time in striking demagogic attitudes. They govern in their own interests, and they have the courage of their own strength. They have created legitimacy, and they are strong in their own right.

The bourgeois caste in newly independent countries have not yet the cynicism nor the unruffled calm which are founded on the strength of long-established bourgeoisies. From this springs the fact that they show a certain anxiety to hide their real convictions, to side-track, and in short to set themselves up as a popular force. But the inclusion of the masses in politics does not consist in mobilizing three or four times a year ten thousand or a hundred thousand men and women. These mass meetings and spectacular gatherings are akin to the old tactics that date from before independence, whereby you exhibited your forces in order to prove to yourself and to others that you had the people behind you. The political education of the masses proposes not to treat the masses as children but to make adults of them.

This brings us to consider the role of the political party in an under-developed country. We have seen in the preceding pages that very often simple souls, who moreover belong to the newly born bourgeoisie, never stop repeating that in an under-developed country the direction of affairs by a strong authority, in other words a dictatorship, is a necessity. With this in view the party is given the task of supervising the masses. The party plays understudy to the administration and the police, and controls the masses, not in order to make sure that they really participate in the business of governing the nation, but in order to remind them constantly that the government expects from them obedience and discipline. That famous dictatorship, whose supporters believe that it is called for by the historical process and consider it an indispensable prelude to the dawn of independence, in fact symbolizes the decision of the bourgeois caste to govern the under-developed country first with the help of the people, but soon against them. The progressive transformation of the party into an information service is the indication that the government holds itself more and more on the defensive. The incoherent mass of the people is seen as a blind force that must be continually held in check either by mystification or by the fear inspired by the police force. The party acts as a barometer and as an information service. The militant is turned into an informer. He is entrusted with punitive expeditions against the villages. The embryo opposition parties are liquidated by beatings and stonings. The opposition candidates see their houses set on fire. The police increase their provocations. In these conditions, you may be sure, the party is unchallenged and 99·99 per cent of the votes are cast for the governmental candidate. We should add that in Africa a certain number of governments actually behave in this way. All the opposition parties, which moreover are usually progressive and would therefore tend to work for the greater influence of the masses in the conduct of public matters, and who desire that the proud, money-making bourgeoisie should be brought to heel, have been by dint of baton charges and prisons condemned first to silence and then to a clandestine existence.

The political party in many parts of Africa which are today independent is puffed up in a most dangerous way. In the presence of a member of the party, the people are silent, behave like a flock of sheep and publish panegyrics in praise of the government of the leader. But in the street when evening comes, away from the village, in the cafés or by the river, the bitter disappointment of the people, their despair but also their unceasing anger makes itself heard. The party, instead of welcoming the expression of popular discontentment, instead of taking for its fundamental purpose the free flow of ideas from the people up to the government, forms a screen, and forbids such ideas. The party leaders behave like common sergeant-majors, frequently reminding the people of the need for 'silence in the ranks'. This party which used to call itself the servant of the people, which used to claim that it worked for the full expression of the people's will, as soon as the colonial power puts the country into its control hastens to send the people back to their caves. As far as national unity is concerned the party will also make many mistakes, as for example when the so-called national party behaves as a party based on ethnical differences. It becomes, in fact, the tribe which makes itself into a party. This party which of its own will proclaims that it is a national party, and which claims to speak in the name of the totality of the people, secretly, sometimes even openly organizes an authentic ethnical dictatorship. We no longer see the rise of a bourgeois dictatorship, but a tribal dictatorship. The ministers, the members of the cabinet, the ambassadors and local commissioners are chosen from the same ethnological group as the leader, sometimes directly from his own family. Such regimes of the family sort seem to go back to the old laws of inbreeding, and not anger but shame is felt when we are faced with such stupidity, such an imposture, such intellectual and spiritual poverty. These heads of the government are the true traitors in Africa, for they sell their country to the most terrifying of all its enemies: stupidity. This tribalizing of the central authority, it is certain, encourages regionalist ideas and separatism. All the decentralizing tendencies spring up again and triumph, and the nation falls to pieces, broken in bits. The leader, who once used to call for 'African unity' and who thought of his own little family wakes up one day to find himself saddled with five tribes, who also want to have their own ambassadors and ministers; and irresponsible as ever, still unaware and still despicable, he denounces their 'treason'.

We have more than once drawn attention to the baleful influence frequently wielded by the leader. This is due to the fact that the party in certain districts is organized like a gang, with the toughest person in it as its head. The ascendancy of such a leader and his power over others is often mentioned, and people have no hesitation in declaring, in a tone of slightly admiring complicity that he strikes terror into his nearest collaborators. In order to avoid these many pitfalls an unceasing battle must be waged, a battle to prevent the party ever becoming a willing tool in the hands of a leader. 'Leader': the word comes from the English verb 'to lead', but a frequent French translation is 'to drive'. The driver, the shepherd of the people no longer exists today. The people are no longer a herd; they do not need to be driven. If the leader drives me on, I want him to realize that at the same time I show him the way; the nation ought not to be something bossed by a Grand Panjandrum. We may understand the panic caused in governmental circles each time one of these leaders falls ill; they are obsessed by the question of who is to succeed him. What will happen to the country if the leader disappears? The ruling classes who have abdicated in favour of the leader, irresponsible, oblivious of everything and essentially preoccupied with the pleasures of their everyday life, their cocktail parties, their journeys paid for by government money, the profits they can make out of various schemes – from time to time these people discover the spiritual waste land at the heart of the nation.

A country that really wishes to answer the questions that history puts to it, that wants to develop not only its towns but also the brains of its inhabitants, such a country must possess a trustworthy political party. The party is not a tool in the hands of the government. Quite on the contrary, the party is a tool in the hands of the people; it is they who decide on the policy that the government carries out. The party is not, and ought never to be, the only political bureau where all the members of the government and the chief dignitaries of the regime may meet freely together. Only too frequently the political bureau, unfortunately, consists of all the party and its members who reside permanently in the capital. In an underdeveloped country, the leading members of the party ought to avoid the capital as if it had the plague. They ought, with some few exceptions, to live in the country districts. The centralization of all activity in the city ought to be avoided. No excuse of administrative discipline should be taken as legitimizing that excrescence of a capital which is already overpopulated and over-developed with regard to nine-tenths of the country. The party should be decentralized in the extreme. It is the only way to bring life to regions which are dead, those regions which are not yet awakened to life.

In practice, there will be at least one member of the political bureau in each area and he will deliberately not be appointed as head of that area. He will have no administrative powers. The regional member of the political bureau is not expected to hold the highest rank in the regional administrative organization. He ought not automatically to belong to the regional administrative body. For the people, the party is not an authority, but an organism through which they as the people exercise their authority and express their will. The less there is of confusion and duality of powers, the more the party will play its part of guide and the more surely it will constitute for the people a decisive guarantee. If the party is mingled with the government, the fact of being a party militant means that you take the short cut to gain private ends, to hold a post in the government, step up the ladder, get promotion and make a career for yourself.

In an under-developed country, the setting up of dynamic district officials stops the progress whereby the towns become top-heavy, and the incoherent rush towards the cities of the mass of country people. The setting up early in the days of independence of regional organizations and officials who have full authority to do everything in their power to awaken such a region, to bring life to it and to hasten the growth of consciousness in it is a necessity from which there is no escape for a country that wishes to progress. Otherwise, the government bigwigs and the party officials group themselves around the leader. The government services swell to huge proportions, not because they are developing and specializing, but because new-found cousins and fresh militants are looking for jobs and hope to edge themselves into the government machine. And the dream of every citizen is to get up to the capital, and to have his share of the cake. The local districts are deserted; the mass of the country people with no one to lead them, uneducated and unsupported, turn their backs on their poorly-laboured fields and flock towards the outer ring of suburbs, thus swelling out of all proportion the ranks of the *lumpen-proletariat*.

The moment for a fresh national crisis is not far off. To avoid it, we think that a quite different policy should be followed: that the interior, the back-country ought to be the most privileged part of the country. Moreover, in the last resort, there is nothing inconvenient in the government choosing its seat elsewhere than in the capital. The capital must be deconsecrated; the outcast masses must be shown that we have decided to work for them. It is with this idea in mind that the government of Brazil tried to found Brazilia. The dead city of Rio de Janeiro was an insult to the Brazilian people. But, unfortunately, Brazilia is just another new capital, as monstrous as the first. The only advantage of this achievement is that, today, there exists a road through the bush to it.

No, there is no serious reason which can be opposed to the choice of another capital, or to the moving of the government as a whole towards one of the most under-populated regions. The capital of under-developed countries is a commercial notion inherited from the colonial period. But we who are citizens of the under-developed countries, we ought to seek every occasion for contacts with the rural masses. We must create a national policy, in other words a policy for the masses. We ought never to lose contact with the people which has battled for its independence and for the concrete betterment of its existence.

The native civil servants and technicians ought not to bury themselves in diagrams and statistics, but rather in the heart of the people. They ought not to bristle up every time there is question of a move to be made to the 'interior'. We should no longer see the young women of the country threaten their husbands with divorce if they do not manage to avoid being appointed to a rural post. For these reasons, the political bureau of the party ought to treat these forgotten districts in a very privileged manner; and the life of the capital, an altogether artificial life which is stuck on to the real, national life like a foreign body ought to take up the least space possible in the life of the nation, which is sacred and fundamental.

In an under-developed country the party ought to be organized in such fashion that it is not simply content with having contacts with the masses. The party should be the direct expression of the masses. The party is not an administration responsible for transmitting government orders; it is the energetic spokesman and the incorruptible defender of the masses. In order to arrive at this conception of the party, we must above all rid ourselves of the very Western, very bourgeois and therefore contemptuous attitude that the masses are incapable of governing themselves. In fact, experience proves that the masses understand perfectly the most complicated problems. One of the greatest services that the Algerian revolution will have rendered to the intellectuals of Algeria will be to have placed them in contact with the people, to have allowed them to see the extreme, ineffable poverty of the people, at the same time allowing them to watch the awakening of the people's intelligence and the onward progress of their consciousness. The Algerian people, that mass of starving illiterates, those men and women plunged for centuries in the most appalling obscurity have held out against tanks and aeroplanes, against napalm and 'psychological services', but above all against corruption and brain-washing, against traitors and against the 'national' armies of General Bellounis. This people has held out in spite of hesitant or feeble individuals, and in spite of would-be dictators. This people has held out because for seven years its struggle has opened up for it vistas that it never dreamed existed. Today, arms factories are working in the midst of the mountains several yards underground; today, the people's tribunals are functioning at every level, and local planning commissions are organizing the division of large-scale holdings, and working out the Algeria of tomorrow. An isolated individual may obstinately refuse to understand a problem, but the group or the village understands with disconcerting rapidity. It is true that if care is taken to use only a language that is understood by graduates in law and economics, you can easily prove that the masses have to be managed from above. But if you speak the language of every day; if you are not obsessed by the perverse desire to spread confusion and to rid yourself of the people, then you will realize that the masses are quick to seize every shade of meaning and to learn all the tricks of the trade. If recourse is had to technical language, this signifies that it has been decided to consider the masses as uninitiated. Such a language is hard put to it to hide the lecturers' wish to cheat the people and to leave them out of things. The business of obscuring language is a mask behind which stands out the much greater business of plunder. The people's property and the people's sovereignty are to be stripped from them at one and the same time. Everything can be explained to the people, on the single condition that you really want them to understand. And if you think that you don't need them, and that on the contrary they may hinder the smooth running of the many limited liability companies whose aim it is to make the people even poorer, then the problem is quite clear.

For if you think that you can manage a country without letting the people interfere, if you think that the people upset the game by their mere presence, whether they slow it down or whether by their natural ignorance they sabotage it, then you must have no hesitation: you must keep the people out. Now, it so happens that when the people are invited to partake in the management of the country, they do not slow the movement down but on the contrary they speed it up. We Algerians have had occasion and the good fortune during the course of this war to handle a fair number of questions. In certain country districts, the politico-military leaders of the revolution found themselves in fact confronted with situations which called for radical solutions. We shall look at some of these situations.

During the years 1956–7, French colonialism had marked off certain zones as forbidden, and within these zones people's movements were strictly controlled. Thus the peasants could no longer go freely to the towns and buy provisions. During this period, the grocers made huge profits. The prices of tea, coffee, sugar, tobacco and salt soared. The black market flourished blatantly. The peasants who could not pay in money mortgaged their crops, in other words their land, or else lopped off field after field of their fathers' farms and during the second phase worked them for the grocer. As soon as the political commissioners realized the danger of the situation they reacted immediately. Thus a rational system of provisioning was instituted: the grocer who went to the town was obliged to buy from nationalist wholesalers who handed him an invoice which clearly showed the prices of the goods. When the retailer got back to the village, before doing anything else he had to go to the political commissioner who checked the invoice, decided on the margin of profit and fixed the price at which the various goods should be sold. However, the retailer soon discovered a new trick, and after three or four days declared that his stocks had run out. In fact, he went on with his business of selling on the black market on the sly. The reaction of the politico-military authorities was thorough-going. Heavy penalizations were decided on, and the fines collected were put into the village funds and used for social purposes or to pay for public works in the general interest. Sometimes it was decided to shut down the shop for a while. Then if there was a repetition of black marketeering, the business was at once confiscated and a managing committee elected to carry it on, which paid a monthly allowance to the former owner.

Taking these experiences as a starting-point, the functioning of the main laws of economics were explained to the people, with concrete examples. The accumulation of capital ceased to be a theory and became a very real and immediate mode of behaviour. The people understood how that once a man was in trade, he could become rich and increase his turnover. Then and then only did the peasants tell the tale of how the grocer gave them loans at exorbitant interest, and others recalled how he evicted them from their land and how from owners they became labourers. The more the people understand, the more watchful they become, and the more they come to realize that finally everything depends on them and their salvation lies in their own cohesion, in the true understanding of their interests and in knowing who are their enemies. The people come to understand that wealth is not the fruit of labour but the result of organized, protected robbery. Rich people are no longer respectable people; they are nothing more than flesh-eating animals, jackals and vultures which wallow in the people's blood. With another end in view the political commissioners have had to decide that nobody will work for anyone else any longer. The land belongs to those that till it. This is a principle which has through explanation become a fundamental law of the Algerian revolution. The peasants who used to employ agricultural labourers have been obliged to give a share of the land to their former employees.

So it may be seen that production per acre trebled, in spite of the many raids by the French, in spite of bombardments from the air, and the difficulty of getting manures. The *fellahs* who at harvest-time were able to judge and weigh the crops thus obtained wanted to know whence came such a phenomenon; and they were quick to understand that the idea of work is not as simple as all that, that slavery is opposed to work, and that work presupposes liberty, responsibility and consciousness.

In those districts where we have been able to carry out successfully these interesting experiments, where we have watched man being created by revolutionary beginnings, the peasants have very clearly caught hold of the idea that the more intelligence you bring to your work, the more pleasure you will have in it. We have been able to make the masses understand that work is not simply the output of energy, nor the functioning of certain muscles, but that people work more by using their brains and their hearts than with only their muscles and their sweat. In the same way in these liberated districts which are at the same time excluded from the old trade routes we have had to modify production, which formerly looked only towards the towns and towards export. We have organized production to meet consumers' needs for the people and for the units of the national army of liberation. We have quadrupled the production of lentils and organized the manufacture of charcoal. Green vegetables and charcoal have been sent through the mountains from the north to the south, whereas the southern districts send meat to the north. This coordination was decided upon by the F.L.N. and they it was who set up the system of communications. We did not have any technicians or planners coming from big Western universities; but in these liberated regions the daily ration went up to the hitherto unheard-of figure of 3,200 calories. The people were not content with coming triumphant out of this test. They started asking themselves theoretical questions: for example, why did certain districts never see an orange before the war of liberation, while thousands of tons are exported every year abroad? Why were grapes unknown to a great many Algerians whereas the European peoples enjoyed them by the million? Today, the people have a very clear notion of what belongs to them. The Algerian people today know that they are the sole owners of the soil and mineral wealth of their country. And if some individuals do not understand the unrelenting refusal of the F.L.N. to tolerate any encroachment on this right of ownership, and its fierce refusal to allow any compromise on principles, they must one and all remember that the Algerian people is today an adult people, responsible and fully conscious of its responsibilities. In short, the Algerians are men of property.

If we have taken the example of Algeria to illustrate our subject, it is not at all with the intention of glorifying our own people, but simply to show the important part played by the war in leading them towards consciousness of themselves. It is clear that other peoples have come to the same conclusion in different ways. We know for sure today that in Algeria the test of force was inevitable; but other countries through political action and through the work of clarification undertaken by a party have led their people to the same results. In Algeria, we have realized that the masses are equal to the problems which confront them. In an under-developed country, experience proves that the important thing is not that three hundred people form a plan and decide upon carrying it out, but that the whole people plan and decide even if it takes them twice or three times as long. The fact is that the time taken up by explaining, the time 'lost' in treating the worker as a human being, will be caught up in the execution of the plan. People must know where they are going, and why. The politician should not ignore the fact that the future remains a closed book so long as the consciousness of the people remains imperfect, elementary and cloudy. We African politicians must have very clear ideas on the situation of our people. But this clarity of ideas must be profoundly dialectical. The awakening of the whole people will not come about at once; the people's work in the building of the nation will not immediately take on its full dimensions: first because the means of communication and transmission are only beginning to be developed; secondly because the yardstick of time must no longer be that of the moment or up till the next harvest, but must become that of the rest of the world, and lastly because the spirit of discouragement which has been deeply rooted in people's minds by colonial domination is still very near the surface. But we must not overlook the fact that victory over those weaknesses which are the heritage of the material and spiritual domination of the country by another is a necessity from which no government will be able to escape. Let us take the example of work under the colonial regime. The settler never stopped complaining that the native is slow. Today, in certain countries which have become independent, we hear the ruling classes taking up the same cry. The fact is that the settler wanted the native to be enthusiastic. By a sort of process of mystification which constitutes the most sublime type of separation from reality, he wanted to persuade the slave that the land that he worked belonged to him, that the mines where he lost his health were owned by him. The settler was singularly forgetful of the fact that he was growing rich through the death-throes of the slave. In fact what the settler was saying to the native was 'Kill yourself that I may become rich'. Today, we must behave in a different fashion. We ought not to say to the people: 'Kill yourselves that the country may become rich.' If we want to increase the national revenue, and decrease the importing of certain products which are useless, or even harmful, if we want to increase agricultural production and overcome illiteracy, we must explain what we are about. The people must understand what is at stake. Public business ought to be the business of the public. So the necessity of creating a large number of well-informed nuclei at the bottom crops up again. Too often, in fact, we are content to establish national organizations at the top and always in the capital: the Women's Union, the Young People's Federation, Trade Unions, etc. But if one takes the trouble to investigate what is behind the office in the capital, if you go into the inner room where the reports ought to be, you will be shocked by the emptiness, the blank spaces, and the bluff. There must be a basis; there must be cells that supply content and life. The masses should be able to meet together, discuss, propose and receive directions. The citizens should be able to speak, to express themselves and to put forward new ideas. The branch meeting and the committee meeting are liturgical acts. They are privileged occasions given to a human being to listen and to speak. At each meeting, the brain increases its means of participation and the eye discovers a landscape more and more in keeping with human dignity.

The large proportion of young people in the under-developed countries raises specific problems for the government, which must be tackled with lucidity. The young people of the towns, idle and often illiterate, are a prey to all sorts of disintegrating influences. It is to the youth of an under-developed country that the industrialized countries most often offer their pastimes. Normally, there is a certain homogeneity between the mental and material level of the members of any given society and the pleasures which that society creates for itself. But in under-developed countries, young people have at their disposal leisure occupations designed for the youth of capitalist countries: detective novels, penny-in-the slot machines, sexy photographs, pornographic literature, films banned to those under sixteen, and above all alcohol. In the West, the family circle, the effects of education and the relatively high standard of living of the working classes provide a more or less efficient protection against the harmful action of these pastimes. But in an African country, where mental development is uneven, where the violent collision of two worlds has considerably shaken old traditions and thrown the universe of the perceptions out of focus, the impressionability and sensibility of the young African are at the mercy of the various assaults made upon them by the very nature of Western culture. His family very often proves itself incapable of showing stability and homogeneity when faced with such attacks.

In this domain, the government's duty is to act as a filter and a stabilizer. But the Youth Commissioners in under-developed countries often make the mistake of imagining their role to be that of Youth Commissioners in fully developed countries. They speak of strengthening the soul, of developing the body, and of facilitating the growth of sportsmanlike qualities. It is our opinion that they should beware of these conceptions. The young people of an under-developed country are above all idle: occupations must be found for them. For this reason the Youth Commissioners ought for practical purposes to be attached to the Ministry for Labour. The Ministry for Labour, which is a prime necessity in an under-developed country, functions in collaboration with the Ministry for Planning, which is another necessary institution in under-developed countries. The youth of Africa ought not to be sent to sports stadiums but into the fields and into the schools. The stadium ought not to be a show place erected in the towns, but a bit of open ground in the midst of the fields that the young people must reclaim, cultivate and give to the nation. The capitalist conception of sport is fundamentally different from that which should exist in an under-developed country. The African politician should not be preoccupied with turning out sportsmen, but with turning out fully conscious men, who play games as well. If games are not integrated into the national life, that is to say in the building of the nation, and if you turn out national sportsmen and not fully conscious men, you will very quickly see sport rotted by professionalism and commercialism. Sport should not be a pastime or a distraction for the bourgeoisie of the towns. The greatest task before us is to understand at each moment what is happening in our country. We ought not to cultivate the exceptional or to seek for a hero, who is another form of leader. We ought to uplift the people; we must develop their brains, fill them with ideas, change them and make them into human beings.

We once more come up against that obsession of ours – which we would like to see shared by all African politicians – about the need for effort to be well-informed, for work which is enlightened and free from its historic intellectual darkness. To hold a responsible position in an under-developed country is to know that in the end everything depends on the education of the masses, on the raising of the level of thought, and on what we are too quick to call 'political teaching'.

In fact, we often believe with criminal superficiality that to educate the masses politically is to deliver a long political harangue from time to time. We think that it is enough that the leader or one of his lieutenants should speak in a pompous tone about the principle events of the day for them to have fulfilled this bounden duty to educate the masses politically. Now, political education means opening their minds, awakening them, and allowing the birth of their intelligence; as Césaire said, it is 'to invent souls'. To educate the masses politically does not mean, cannot mean making a political speech. What it means is to try, relentlessly and passionately, to teach the masses that everything depends on them; that if we stagnate it is their responsibility, and that if we go forward it is due to them too, that there is no such thing as a demiurge, that there is no famous man who will take the responsibility for everything, but that the demiurge is the people themselves and the magic hands are finally only the hands of the people. In order to put all this into practice, in order really to incarnate the people, we repeat that there must be decentralization in the extreme. The movement from the top to the bottom and from the bottom to the top should be a fixed principle, not through concern for formalism but because simply to respect this principle is the guarantee of salvation. It is from the base that forces mount up which supply the summit with its dynamic, and make it possible dialectically for it to leap ahead. Once again we Algerians have been quick to understand these facts, for no member of the government at the head of any recognized state has had the chance of availing himself of such a mission of salvation. For it is the rank-and-file who are fighting in Algeria, and the rank-and-file know well that without their daily struggle, hard and heroic as it is, the summit would collapse; and in the same way those at the bottom know that without a head and without leadership the base would split apart in incoherence and anarchy. The summit only draws its worth and its strength from the existence of the people at war. Literally, it is the people who freely create a summit for themselves, and not the summit that tolerates the people.

The masses should know that the government and the party are at their service. A deserving people, in other words a people conscious of its dignity, is a people that never forgets these facts. During the colonial occupation the people were told that they must give their lives so that dignity might triumph. But the African peoples quickly came to understand that it was not only the occupying power that threatened their dignity. The African peoples were quick to realize that dignity and sovereignty were exact equivalents, and, in fact, a free people living in dignity is a sovereign people. It is no use demonstrating that the African peoples are childish or weak. A government or a party gets the people it deserves and sooner or later a people gets the government it deserves.

Practical experience in certain regions confirms this point of view. It sometimes happens at meetings that militants use sweeping, dogmatic formulae. The preference for this shortcut, in which spontaneity and over-simple sinking of differences dangerously combine to defeat intellectual elaboration, frequently triumphs. When we meet this shirking of responsibility in a militant it is not enough to tell him he is wrong. We must make him ready for responsibility, encourage him to follow up his chain of reasoning and make him realize the true nature, often shocking, inhuman and in the long run sterile, of such over-simplification.

Nobody, neither leader nor rank-and-file, can hold back the truth. The search for truth in local attitudes is a collective affair. Some are richer in experience, and elaborate their thought more rapidly, and in the past have been able to establish a greater number of mental links. But they ought to avoid riding rough-shod over the people, for the success of the decision which is adopted depends upon the coordinated, conscious effort of the whole of the people. No one can get out of the situation scot free. Everyone will be butchered or tortured; and in the framework of the independent nation everyone will go hungry and everyone will suffer in the slump. The collective struggle presupposes collective responsibility at the base and collegiate responsibility at the top. Yes; everybody will have to be compromised in the fight for the common good. No one has clean hands; there are no innocents and no onlookers. We all have dirty hands; we are all soiling them in the swamps of our country and in the terrifying emptiness of our brains. Every onlooker is either a coward or a traitor.

The duty of those at the head of the movement is to have the masses behind them. Allegiance presupposes awareness and understanding of the mission which has to be fulfilled; in short, an intellectual position, however embryonic. We must not voodoo the people, nor dissolve them in emotion and confusion. Only those under-developed countries led by revolutionary *élites* who have come up from the people can today allow the entry of the masses upon the scene of history. But, we must repeat, it is absolutely necessary to oppose vigorously and definitively the birth of a national bourgeoisie and a privileged caste. To educate the masses politically is to make the totality of the nation a reality to each citizen. It is to make the history of the nation part of the personal experience of each of its citizens. As President Sékou Touré aptly remarked in his message to the second congress of African writers:

In the realm of thought, man may claim to be the brain of the world; but in real life where every action affects spiritual and physical existence, the world is always the brain of mankind; for it is at this level that you will find the sum total of the powers and units of thought, and the dynamic forces of development and improvement; and it is there that energies are merged and the sum of man's intellectual values is finally added together.

Individual experience, because it is national and because it is a link in the chain of national existence, ceases to be individual, limited and shrunken and is enabled to open out into the truth of the nation and of the world. In the same way that during the period of armed struggle each fighter held the fortune of

the nation in his hand, so during the period of national construction each citizen ought to continue in his real, everyday activity
to associate himself with the whole of the nation, to incarnate
the continuous dialectical truth of the nation and to will the
triumph of man in his completeness here and now. If the building of a bridge does not enrich the awareness of those who work
on it, then that bridge ought not to be built and the citizens
can go on swimming across the river or going by boat. The
bridge should not be 'parachuted down' from above; it should
not be imposed by a *deus ex machina* upon the social scene;
on the contrary it should come from the muscles and the brains
of the citizens. Certainly, there may well be need of engineers
and architects, sometimes completely foreign engineers and
architects; but the local party leaders should be always present,
so that the new techniques can make their way into the cerebral
desert of the citizen, so that the bridge in whole and in part can
be taken up and conceived, and the responsibility for it assumed
by the citizen. In this way, and in this way only, everything is
possible.

A government which calls itself a national government ought
to take responsibility for the totality of the nation; and in an
under-developed country the young people represent one of the
most important sectors. The level of consciousness of young
people must be raised; they need enlightenment. If the work
of explanation had been carried on among the youth of the
nation, and if the Young People's National Union had carried
out its task of integrating them into the nation, those mistakes
would have been avoided which have threatened or already
undermined the future of the Latin American Republics. The
army is not always a school of war; more often, it is a school of
civic and political education. The soldier of an adult nation is not
a simple mercenary but a citizen who by means of arms defends
the nation. That is why it is of fundamental importance that the
soldier should know that he is in the service of his country
and not in the service of his commanding officer, however great
that officer's prestige may be. We must take advantage of the
national military and civil service in order to raise the level
of the national consciousness, and to detribalize and unite the
nation. In an under-developed country every effort is made to

mobilize men and women as quickly as possible; it must guard against the danger of perpetuating the feudal tradition which holds sacred the superiority of the masculine element over the feminine. Women will have exactly the same place as men, not in the clauses of the constitution but in the life of every day: in the factory, at school and in the parliament. If in the Western countries men are shut up in barracks, that is not to say that this is always the best procedure. Recruits need not necessarily be militarized. The national service may be civil or military, and in any case it is advisable that every able-bodied citizen can at any moment take his place in a fighting unit for the defence of national and social liberties.

It should be possible to carry out large-scale undertakings in the public interest by using recruited labour. This is a marvellous way of stirring up inert districts and of making known to a greater number of citizens the needs of their country. Care must be taken to avoid turning the army into an autonomous body which sooner or later, finding itself idle and without any definite mission, will 'go into politics' and threaten the government. Drawing-room generals, by dint of haunting the corridors of government departments, come to dream of manifestoes. The only way to avoid this menace is to educate the army politically, in other words to nationalize it. In the same way another urgent task is to increase the militia. In case of war, it is the whole nation which fights and works. It should not include any professional soldiers, and the number of permanent officers should be reduced to a minimum. This is in the first place because officers are very often chosen from the university class, who could be much more useful elsewhere; an engineer is a thousand times more indispensable to his country than an officer; and secondly, because the crystallization of the caste spirit must be avoided. We have seen in the preceding pages that nationalism, that magnificent song that made the people rise against their oppressors, stops short, falters and dies away on the day that independence is proclaimed. Nationalism is not a political doctrine, nor a programme. If you really wish your country to avoid regression, or at best halts and uncertainties, a rapid step must be taken from national consciousness to political and social consciousness. The nation does not exist except in a programme which has been worked out by revolutionary leaders and taken up with full understanding and enthusiasm by the masses. The nation's effort must constantly be adjusted into the general background of under-developed countries. The battle-line against hunger, against ignorance, against poverty and against unawareness ought to be ever present in the muscles and the intelligences of men and women. The work of the masses and their will to overcome the evils which have for centuries excluded them from the mental achievements of the past ought to be grafted on to the work and will of all under-developed peoples. On the level of under-developed humanity there is a kind of collective effort, a sort of common destiny. The news which interests the Third World does not deal with King Baudouin's marriage nor the scandals of the Italian ruling class. What we want to hear about are the experiments carried out by the Argentinians or the Burmese in their efforts to overcome illiteracy or the dictatorial tendencies of their leaders. It is these things which strengthen us, teach us and increase our efficiency ten times over. As we see it, a programme is necessary for a government which really wants to free the people politically and socially. There must be an economic programme; there must also be a doctrine concerning the division of wealth and social relations. In fact, there must be an idea of man and of the future of humanity; that is to say that no demagogic formula and no collusion with the former occupying power can take the place of a programme. The new peoples, unawakened at first but soon becoming more and more clear-minded, will make strong demands for this programme. The African people and indeed all under-developed peoples, contrary to common belief, very quickly build up a social and political consciousness. What can be dangerous is when they reach the stage of social consciousness before the stage of nationalism. If this happens, we find in under-developed countries fierce demands for social justice which paradoxically are allied with often primitive tribalism. The under-developed peoples behave like starving creatures; this means that the end is very near for those who are having a good time in Africa. Their government will not be able to prolong its own existence indefinitely. A bourgeoisie that provides nationalism alone as food for the masses fails in its mission and gets caught up in a whole series of mishaps. But if nationalism is not made explicit, if it is not enriched and deepened by a very rapid transformation into a consciousness of social and political needs, in other words into humanism, it leads up a blind alley. The bourgeois leaders of under-developed countries imprison national consciousness in sterile formalism. It is only when men and women are included on a vast scale in enlightened and fruitful work that form and body are given to that consciousness. Then the flag and the palace where sits the government cease to be the symbols of the nation. The nation deserts these brightly lit, empty shells and takes shelter in the country, where it is given life and dynamic power. The living expression of the nation is the moving consciousness of the whole of the people; it is the coherent, enlightened action of men and women. The collective building up of a destiny is the assumption of responsibility on the historical scale. Otherwise there is anarchy, repression and the resurgence of tribal parties and federalism. The national government, if it wants to be national, ought to govern by the people and for the people, for the outcasts and by the outcasts. No leader, however valuable he may be, can substitute himself for the popular will; and the national government, before concerning itself about international prestige, ought first to give back their dignity to all citizens, fill their minds and feast their eyes with human things, and create a prospect that is human because conscious and sovereign men dwell therein.

4. On National Culture

To take part in the African revolution it is not enough to write a revolutionary song; you must fashion the revolution with the people. And if you fashion it with the people, the songs will come by themselves, and of themselves.

In order to achieve real action, you must yourself be a living part of Africa and of her thought; you must be an element of that popular energy which is entirely called forth for the freeing, the progress and the happiness of Africa. There is no place outside that fight for the artist or for the intellectual who is not himself concerned with and completely at one with the people in the great battle of Africa and of suffering humanity.*

*

Each generation must, out of relative obscurity, discover its mission, fulfil it, or betray it. In under-developed countries the preceding generations have both resisted the work of erosion carried on by colonialism and also helped on the maturing of the struggles of today. We must rid ourselves of the habit, now that we are in the thick of the fight, of minimizing the action of our fathers or of feigning incomprehension when considering their silence and passivity. They fought as well as they could, with the arms that they possessed then; and if the echoes of their struggle have not resounded in the international arena, we must realize that the reason for this silence lies less in their lack of heroism than in the fundamentally different international situation of our time. It needed more than one native to say 'We've had enough'; more than one peasant rising crushed, more than one demonstration put down before we could today hold our own, certain in our victory. As for us who have decided to break the back of colonialism, our historic mission is to sanction all revolts, all desperate actions, all those abortive attempts drowned in rivers of blood.

In this chapter we shall analyse the problem, which is felt to

* Sékou Touré, 'The political leader as the representative of a culture'. Address to the second Congress of Black Writers and Artists, Rome, 1959.

be fundamental, of the legitimacy of the claims of a nation. It must be recognized that the political party which mobilizes the people hardly touches on this problem of legitimacy. The political parties start from living reality and it is in the name of this reality, in the name of the stark facts which weigh down the present and the future of men and women, that they fix their line of action. The political party may well speak in moving terms of the nation, but what it is concerned with is that the people who are listening understand the need to take part in the fight if, quite simply, they wish to continue to exist.

Today we know that in the first phase of the national struggle colonialism tries to disarm national demands by putting forward economic doctrines. As soon as the first demands are set out, colonialism pretends to consider them, recognizing with ostentatious humility that the territory is suffering from serious under-development which necessitates a great economic and social effort. And, in fact, it so happens that certain spectacular measures (centres of work for the unemployed which are opened here and there, for example) delay the crystallization of national consciousness for a few years. But, sooner or later, colonialism sees that it is not within its powers to put into practice a project of economic and social reforms which will satisfy the aspirations of the colonized people. Even where food supplies are concerned, colonialism gives proof of its inherent incapability. The colonialist state quickly discovers that if it wishes to disarm the nationalist parties on strictly economic questions then it will have to do in the colonies exactly what it has refused to do in its own country. It is not mere chance that almost everywhere today there flourishes the doctrine of Cartierism.

The disillusioned bitterness we find in Cartier when up against the obstinate determination of France to link to herself peoples which she must feed while so many French people live in want shows up the impossible situation in which colonialism finds itself when the colonial system is called upon to transform itself into an unselfish programme of aid and assistance. It is why, once again, there is no use in wasting time repeating that hunger with dignity is preferable to bread eaten in slavery. On the contrary, we must become convinced that colonialism is incapable of procuring for the colonized peoples the material conditions which might make them forget their concern for dignity. Once colonialism has realized where its tactics of social reform are leading, we see it falling back on its old reflexes, reinforcing police effectives, bringing up troops and setting up a reign of terror which is better adapted to its interests and its psychology.

Inside the political parties, and most often in offshoots from these parties, cultured individuals of the colonized race make their appearance. For these individuals, the demand for a national culture and the affirmation of the existence of such a culture represent a special battle-field. While the politicians situate their action in actual present-day events, men of culture take their stand in the field of history. Confronted with the native intellectual who decides to make an aggressive response to the colonialist theory of pre-colonial barbarism, colonialism will react only slightly, and still less because the ideas developed by the young colonized intelligentsia are widely professed by specialists in the mother country. It is in fact a commonplace to state that for several decades large numbers of research workers have, in the main, rehabilitated the African, Mexican and Peruvian civilizations. The passion with which native intellectuals defend the existence of their national culture may be a source of amazement; but those who condemn this exaggerated passion are strangely apt to forget that their own psyche and their own selves are conveniently sheltered behind a French or German culture which has given full proof of its existence and which is uncontested.

I am ready to concede that on the plane of factual being the past existence of an Aztec civilization does not change anything very much in the diet of the Mexican peasant of today. I admit that all the proofs of a wonderful Songhai civilization will not change the fact that today the Songhais are under-fed and illiterate, thrown between sky and water with empty heads and empty eyes. But it has been remarked several times that this passionate search for a national culture which existed before the colonial era finds its legitimate reason in the anxiety shared by native intellectuals to shrink away from that Western culture in which they all risk being swamped. Because they realize they are in danger of losing their lives and thus becoming lost to their people, these men, hot-headed and with anger in their hearts, relentlessly determine to renew contact once more with the oldest and most pre-colonial springs of life of their people.

Let us go farther. Perhaps this passionate research and this anger are kept up or at least directed by the secret hope of discovering beyond the misery of today, beyond self-contempt, resignation and abjuration, some very beautiful and splendid era whose existence rehabilitates us both in regard to ourselves and in regard to others. I have said that I have decided to go farther. Perhaps unconsciously, the native intellectuals, since they could not stand wonder-struck before the history of today's barbarity, decided to go back farther and to delve deeper down; and, let us make no mistake, it was with the greatest delight that they discovered that there was nothing to be ashamed of in the past, but rather dignity, glory and solemnity. The claim to a national culture in the past does not only rehabilitate that nation and serve as a justification for the hope of a future national culture. In the sphere of psycho-affective equilibrium it is responsible for an important change in the native. Perhaps we have not sufficiently demonstrated that colonialism is not simply content to impose its rule upon the present and the future of a dominated country. Colonialism is not satisfied merely with holding a people in its grip and emptying the native's brain of all form and content. By a kind of perverted logic, it turns to the past of the oppressed people, and distorts, disfigures and destroys it. This work of devaluing pre-colonial history takes on a dialectical significance today.

When we consider the efforts made to carry out the cultural estrangement so characteristic of the colonial epoch, we realize that nothing has been left to chance and that the total result looked for by colonial domination was indeed to convince the natives that colonialism came to lighten their darkness. The effect consciously sought by colonialism was to drive into the natives' heads the idea that if the settlers were to leave, they would at once fall back into barbarism, degradation and bestiality.

On the unconscious plane, colonialism therefore did not seek to be considered by the native as a gentle, loving mother who protects her child from a hostile environment, but rather as a mother who unceasingly restrains her fundamentally perverse offspring from managing to commit suicide and from giving free rein to its evil instincts. The colonial mother protects her child from itself, from its ego, and from its physiology, its biology and its own unhappiness which is its very essence.

In such a situation the claims of the native intellectual are no luxury but a necessity in any coherent programme. The native intellectual who takes up arms to defend his nation's legitimacy and who wants to bring proofs to bear out that legitimacy, who is willing to strip himself naked to study the history of his body, is obliged to dissect the heart of his people.

Such an examination is not specifically national. The native intellectual who decides to give battle to colonial lies fights on the field of the whole continent. The past is given back its value. Culture, extracted from the past to be displayed in all its splendour, is not necessarily that of his own country. Colonialism, which has not bothered to put too fine a point on its efforts, has never ceased to maintain that the Negro is a savage; and for the colonist, the Negro was neither an Angolan nor a Nigerian, for he simply spoke of 'the Negro'. For colonialism, this vast continent was the haunt of savages, a country riddled with superstitions and fanaticism, destined for contempt, weighed down by the curse of God, a country of cannibals – in short, the Negro's country. Colonialism's condemnation is continental in its scope. The contention by colonialism that the darkest night of humanity lay over pre-colonial history concerns the whole of the African continent. The efforts of the native to rehabilitate himself and to escape from the claws of colonialism are logically inscribed from the same point of view as that of colonialism. The native intellectual who has gone far beyond the domains of Western culture and who has got it into his head to proclaim the existence of another culture never does so in the name of Angola or of Dahomey. The culture which is affirmed is African culture. The Negro, never so much a Negro as since he has been dominated by the whites, when he decides to prove that he has a culture and to behave like a cultured person, comes to realize that history points out a well-defined path to him: he must demonstrate that a Negro culture exists.

And it is only too true that those who are most responsible

for this racialization of thought, or at least for the first movement towards that thought, are and remain those Europeans who have never ceased to set up white culture to fill the gap left by the absence of other cultures. Colonialism did not dream of wasting its time in denying the existence of one national culture after another. Therefore the reply of the colonized peoples will be straight away continental in its breadth. In Africa, the native literature of the last twenty years is not a national literature but a Negro literature. The concept of Negro-ism, for example, was the emotional if not the logical antithesis of that insult which the white man flung at humanity. This rush of Negro-ism against the white man's contempt showed itself in certain spheres to be the one idea capable of lifting interdictions and anathemas. Because the New Guinean or Kenyan intellectuals found themselves above all up against a general ostracism and delivered to the combined contempt of their overlords, their reaction was to sing praises in admiration of each other. The unconditional affirmation of African culture has succeeded the unconditional affirmation of European culture. On the whole, the poets of Negro-ism oppose the idea of an old Europe to a young Africa, tiresome reasoning to lyricism, oppressive logic to high-stepping nature, and on one side stiffness, ceremony, etiquette and scepticism, while on the other frankness, liveliness, liberty and – why not? – luxuriance: but also irresponsibility.

The poets of Negro-ism will not stop at the limits of the continent. From America, black voices will take up the hymn with fuller unison. The 'black world' will see the light and Busia from Ghana, Birago Diop from Senegal, Hampaté Ba from the Sudan and Saint-Clair Drake from Chicago will not hesitate to assert the existence of common ties and a motive power that is identical.

The example of the Arab world might equally well be quoted here. We know that the majority of Arab territories have been under colonial domination. Colonialism has made the same effort in these regions to plant deep in the minds of the native population the idea that before the advent of colonialism their history was one which was dominated by barbarism. The struggle for national liberty has been accompanied by a cultural phenomenon known by the name of the awakening of Islam.

The passion with which contemporary Arab writers remind their people of the great pages of their history is a reply to the lies told by the occupying power. The great names of Arabic literature and the great past of Arab civilization have been brandished about with the same ardour as those of the African civilizations. The Arab leaders have tried to return to the famous Dar El Islam which shone so brightly from the twelfth to the fourteenth century.

Today, in the political sphere, the Arab League is giving palpable form to this will to take up again the heritage of the past and to bring it to culmination. Today, Arab doctors and Arab poets speak to each other across the frontiers, and strive to create a new Arab culture and a new Arab civilization. It is in the name of Arabism that these men join together, and that they try to think together. Everywhere, however, in the Arab world, national feeling has preserved, even under colonial domination, a liveliness that we fail to find in Africa. At the same time that spontaneous communion of each with all, present in the African movement, is not to be found in the Arab League. On the contrary, paradoxically, everyone tries to sing the praises of the achievements of his nation. The cultural process is freed from the lack of differentiation which characterized it in the African world, but the Arabs do not always manage to stand aside in order to achieve their aims. The living culture is not national but Arab. The problem is not as yet to secure a national culture, not as yet to lay hold of a movement differentiated by nations, but to assume an African or Arabic culture when confronted by the all-embracing condemnation pronounced by the dominating power. In the African world, as in the Arab, we see that the claims of the man of culture in a colonized country are all-embracing, continental and, in the case of the Arabs, world-wide.

This historical necessity in which the men of African culture find themselves to racialize their claims and to speak more of African culture than of national culture will tend to lead them up a blind alley. Let us take for example the case of the African Cultural Society. This society had been created by African intellectuals who wished to get to know each other and to compare their experiences and the results of their respective research work. The aim of this society was therefore to affirm the exis-

tence of an African culture, to evaluate this culture on the plane
of distinct nations and to reveal the internal motive forces of
each of their national cultures. But at the same time this society
fulfilled another need: the need to exist side by side with the
European Cultural Society, which threatened to transform itself
into a Universal Cultural Society. There was therefore at the
bottom of this decision the anxiety to be present at the universal
trysting place fully armed, with a culture springing from the
very heart of the African continent. Now, this Society will very
quickly show its inability to shoulder these different tasks, and
will limit itself to exhibitionist demonstrations, while the
habitual behaviour of the members of this Society will be confined to showing Europeans that such a thing as African culture
exists, and opposing their ideas to those of ostentatious and
narcissistic Europeans. We have shown that such an attitude is
normal and draws its legitimacy from the lies propagated by
men of Western culture. But the degradation of the aims of this
Society will become more marked with the elaboration of the
concept of Negro-ism. The African Society will become the
cultural society of the black world and will come to include the
Negro dispersion, that is to say the tens of thousands of black
people spread over the American continents.

The Negroes who live in the United States and in Central or
Latin America in fact experience the need to attach themselves
to a cultural matrix. Their problem is not fundamentally different from that of the Africans. The whites of America did not
mete out to them any different treatment from that of the whites
that ruled over the Africans. We have seen that the whites were
used to putting all Negroes in the same bag. During the first
congress of the African Cultural Society which was held in Paris
in 1956, the American Negroes of their own accord considered
their problems from the same standpoint as those of their African brothers. Cultured Africans, speaking of African civilizations, decreed that there should be a reasonable status within
the state for those who had formerly been slaves. But little by
little the American Negroes realized that the essential problems
confronting them were not the same as those that confronted
the African Negroes. The Negroes of Chicago only resemble the
Nigerians or the Tanganyikans in so far as they were all defined

in relation to the whites. But once the first comparisons had been made and subjective feelings were assuaged, the American Negroes realized that the objective problems were fundamentally heterogeneous. The test cases of civil liberty whereby both whites and blacks in America try to drive back racial discrimination have very little in common in their principles and objectives with the heroic fight of the Angolan people against the detestable Portuguese colonialism. Thus, during the second congress of the African Cultural Society the American Negroes decided to create an American society for people of black cultures.

Negro-ism therefore finds its first limitation in the phenomena which take account of the formation of the historical character of men. Negro and African-Negro culture broke up into different entities because the men who wished to incarnate these cultures realized that every culture is first and foremost national, and that the problems which kept Richard Wright or Langston Hughes on the alert were fundamentally different from those which might confront Leopold Senghor or Jomo Kenyatta. In the same way certain Arab states, though they had chanted the marvellous hymn of Arab renaissance, had nevertheless to realize that their geographical position and the economic ties of their region were stronger even than the past that they wished to revive. Thus we find today the Arab states organically linked once more with societies which are Mediterranean in their culture. The fact is that these states are submitted to modern pressure and to new channels of trade while the network of trade relations which was dominant during the great period of Arab history has disappeared. But above all there is the fact that the political regimes of certain Arab states are so different, and so far away from each other in their conceptions that even a cultural meeting between these states is meaningless.

Thus we see that the cultural problem as it sometimes exists in colonized countries runs the risk of giving rise to serious ambiguities. The lack of culture of the Negroes, as proclaimed by colonialism, and the inherent barbarity of the Arabs ought logically to lead to the exaltation of cultural manifestations which are not simply national but continental, and extremely

racial. In Africa, the movement of men of culture is a movement towards the Negro-African culture or the Arab-Moslem
culture. It is not specifically towards a national culture. Culture
is becoming more and more cut off from the events of today. It
finds its refuge beside a hearth that glows with passionate emotion, and from there makes its way by realistic paths which are
the only means by which it may be made fruitful, homogeneous
and consistent.

If the action of the native intellectual is limited historically,
there remains nevertheless the fact that it contributes greatly
to upholding and justifying the action of politicians. It is true
that the attitude of the native intellectual sometimes takes on
the aspect of a cult or of a religion. But if we really wish to
analyse this attitude correctly we will come to see that it is
symptomatic of the intellectual's realization of the danger that
he is running of cutting his last moorings and of breaking adrift
from his people. This stated belief in a national culture is in
fact an ardent, despairing turning towards anything that will
afford him secure anchorage. In order to ensure his salvation
and to escape from the supremacy of the white man's culture
the native feels the need to turn backwards towards his unknown
roots and to lose himself at whatever cost in his own barbarous
people. Because he feels he is becoming estranged, that is to
say because he feels that he is the living haunt of contradictions
which run the risk of becoming insurmountable, the native
tears himself away from the swamp that may suck him down
and accepts everything, decides to take all for granted and confirms everything even though he may lose body and soul. The
native finds that he is expected to answer for everything, and to
all comers. He not only turns himself into the defender of his
people's past; he is willing to be counted as one of them, and
henceforward he is even capable of laughing at his past cowardice.

This tearing away, painful and difficult though it may be, is,
however, necessary. If it is not accomplished there will be serious
psycho-affective injuries and the result will be individuals without an anchor, without a horizon, colourless, stateless, rootless –
a race of angels. It will be also quite normal to hear certain
natives declare 'I speak as a Senegalese and as a Frenchman . . .'

'I speak as an Algerian and as a Frenchman . . .'. The intellectual who is Arab and French, or Nigerian and English, when he comes up against the need to take on two nationalities, chooses, if he wants to remain true to himself, the negation of one of these determinations. But most often, since they cannot or will not make a choice, such intellectuals gather together all the historical determining factors which have conditioned them and take up a fundamentally 'universal standpoint'.

This is because the native intellectual has thrown himself greedily upon Western culture. Like adopted children who only stop investigating the new family framework at the moment when a minimum nucleus of security crystallizes in their psyche, the native intellectual will try to make European culture his own. He will not be content to get to know Rabelais and Diderot, Shakespeare and Egar Allen Poe; he will bind them to his intelligence as closely as possible:

> *La dame n'était pas seule*
> *Elle avait un mari*
> *Un mari très comme il faut*
> *Qui citait Racine et Corneille*
> *Et Voltaire et Rousseau*
> *Et le Père Hugo et le jeune Musset*
> *Et Gide et Valéry*
> *Et tant d'autres encore.**

But at the moment when the nationalist parties are mobilizing the people in the name of national independence, the native intellectual sometimes spurns these acquisitions which he suddenly feels make him a stranger in his own land. It is always easier to proclaim rejection than actually to reject. The intellectual who through the medium of culture has filtered into Western civilization, who has managed to become part of the body of European culture – in other words who has exchanged his own culture for another – will come to realize that the cultural matrix, which now he wishes to assume since he is anxious to appear original, can hardly supply any figureheads which will

* The lady was not alone; she had a most respectable husband, who knew how to quote Racine and Corneille, Voltaire and Rousseau, Victor Hugo and Musset, Gide, Valéry and as many more again. (René Depestre: '*Face à la nuit*'.)

bear comparison with those, so many in number and so great in prestige, of the occupying power's civilization. History, of course, though nevertheless written by the Westerners and to serve their purposes, will be able to evaluate from time to time certain periods of the African past. But, standing face to face with his country at the present time, and observing clearly and objectively the events of today throughout the continent which he wants to make his own, the intellectual is terrified by the void, the degradation and the savagery he sees there. Now he feels that he must get away from white culture. He must seek his culture elsewhere, anywhere at all; and if he fails to find the substance of culture of the same grandeur and scope as displayed by the ruling power, the native intellectual will very often fall back upon emotional attitudes and will develop a psychology which is dominated by exceptional sensitivity and susceptibility. This withdrawal which is due in the first instance to a begging of the question in his internal behaviour mechanism and his own character brings out, above all, a reflex and contradiction which is muscular.

This is sufficient explanation of the style of those native intellectuals who decide to give expression to this phase of consciousness which is in process of being liberated. It is a harsh style, full of images, for the image is the drawbridge which allows unconscious energies to be scattered on the surrounding meadows. It is a vigorous style, alive with rhythms, struck through and through with bursting life; it is full of colour, too, bronzed, sun-baked and violent. This style, which in its time astonished the peoples of the West, has nothing racial about it, in spite of frequent statements to the contrary; it expresses above all a hand-to-hand struggle and it reveals the need that man has to liberate himself from a part of his being which already contained the seeds of decay. Whether the fight is painful, quick or inevitable, muscular action must substitute itself for concepts.

If in the world of poetry this movement reaches unaccustomed heights, the fact remains that in the real world the intellectual often follows up a blind alley. When at the height of his intercourse with his people, whatever they were or whatever they are, the intellectual decides to come down into the common paths of real life, he only brings back from his adventuring formulas which are sterile in the extreme. He sets a high value on the customs, traditions and the appearances of his people; but his inevitable, painful experience only seems to be a banal search for exoticism. The sari becomes sacred, and shoes that come from Paris or Italy are left off in favour of pampooties, while suddenly the language of the ruling power is felt to burn your lips. Finding your fellow countrymen sometimes means in this phase to will to be a nigger, not a nigger like all other niggers but a real nigger, a Negro cur, just the sort of nigger that the white man wants you to be. Going back to your own people means to become a dirty wog, to go native as much as you can, to become unrecognizable, and to cut off those wings that before you had allowed to grow.

The native intellectual decides to make an inventory of the bad habits drawn from the colonial world, and hastens to remind everyone of the good old customs of the people, that people which he had decided contains all truth and goodness. The scandalized attitude with which the settlers who live in the colonial territory greet this new departure only serves to strengthen the native's decision. When the colonialists, who had tasted the sweets of their victory over these assimilated people, realize that these men whom they considered as saved souls are beginning to fall back into the ways of niggers, the whole system totters. Every native won over, every native who had taken the pledge not only marks a failure for the colonial structure when he decides to lose himself and to go back to his own side, but also stands as a symbol for the uselessness and the shallowness of all the work that has been accomplished. Each native who goes back over the line is a radical condemnation of the methods and of the regime; and the native intellectual finds in the scandal he gives rise to a justification and an encouragement to persevere in the path he has chosen.

If we wanted to trace in the works of native writers the different phases which characterize this evolution we would find spread out before us a panorama on three levels. In the first phase, the native intellectual gives proof that he has assimilated the culture of the occupying power. His writings correspond point by point with those of his opposite numbers in the mother country. His inspiration is European and we can easily link up these works with definite trends in the literature of the mother country. This is the period of unqualified assimilation. We find in this literature coming from the colonies the Parnassians, the Symbolists and the Surrealists.

In the second phase we find the native is disturbed; he decides to remember what he is. This period of creative work approximately corresponds to that immersion which we have just described. But since the native is not a part of his people, since he only has exterior relations with his people, he is content to recall their life only. Past happenings of the bygone days of his childhood will be brought up out of the depths of his memory; old legends will be reinterpreted in the light of a borrowed aestheticism and of a conception of the world which was discovered under other skies.

Sometimes this literature of just-before-the-battle is dominated by humour and by allegory; but often too it is symptomatic of a period of distress and difficulty, where death is experienced, and disgust too. We spew ourselves up; but already underneath laughter can be heard.

Finally, in the third phase, which is called the fighting phase, the native, after having tried to lose himself in the people and with the people, will on the contrary shake the people. Instead of according the people's lethargy an honoured place in his esteem, he turns himself into an awakener of the people; hence comes a fighting literature, a revolutionary literature, and a national literature. During this phase a great many men and women who up till then would never have thought of producing a literary work, now that they find themselves in exceptional circumstances – in prison, with the Maquis or on the eve of their execution – feel the need to speak to their nation, to compose the sentence which expresses the heart of the people and to become the mouthpiece of a new reality in action.

The native intellectual nevertheless sooner or later will realize that you do not show proof of your nation from its culture but that you substantiate its existence in the fight which the people wage against the forces of occupation. No colonial system draws its justification from the fact that the territories it dominates are culturally non-existent. You will never make colonialism blush for shame by spreading out little-known cultural treasures under its eyes. At the very moment when the native intellectual is anxiously trying to create a cultural work he fails to realize that he is utilizing techniques and language which are borrowed from the stranger in his country. He contents himself with stamping these instruments with a hall-mark which he wishes to be national, but which is strangely reminiscent of exoticism. The native intellectual who comes back to his people by way of cultural achievements behaves in fact like a foreigner. Sometimes he has no hesitation in using a dialect in order to show his will to be as near as possible to the people; but the ideas that he expresses and the preoccupations he is taken up with have no common yardstick to measure the real situation which the men and the women of his country know. The culture that the intellectual leans towards is often no more than a stock of particularisms. He wishes to attach himself to the people; but instead he only catches hold of their outer garments. And these outer garments are merely the reflection of a hidden life, teeming and perpetually in motion. That extremely obvious objectivity which seems to characterize a people is in fact only the inert, already forsaken result of frequent, and not always very coherent adaptations of a much more fundamental substance which itself is continually being renewed. The man of culture, instead of setting out to find this substance, will let himself be hypnotized by these mummified fragments which because they are static are in fact symbols of negation and outworn contrivances. Culture has never the translucidity of custom; it abhors all simplification. In its essence it is opposed to custom, for custom is always the deterioration of culture. The desire to attach oneself to tradition or bring abandoned traditions to life again does not only mean going against the current of history but also opposing one's own people. When a people undertakes an armed struggle or even a political struggle against a relentless colonialism, the significance of tradition changes. All that has made up the technique of passive resistance in the past may, during this phase, be radically condemned. In an underdeveloped country during the period of struggle traditions are fundamentally unstable and are shot through by centrifugal tendencies. This is why the intellectual often runs the risk of being out of date. The peoples who have carried on the struggle are more impervious to demagogy; and those who wish to follow them reveal themselves as nothing more than common opportunists, in other words late-comers.

In the sphere of plastic arts, for example, the native artist who wishes at whatever cost to create a national work of art shuts himself up in a stereotyped reproduction of details. These artists, who have nevertheless thoroughly studied modern techniques and who have taken part in the main trends of contemporary painting and architecture, turn their back on foreign culture, deny it and set out to look for a true national culture, setting great store on what they consider to be the constant principles of national art. But these people forget that the forms of thought and what it feeds on, together with modern techniques of information, language and dress have dialectically reorganized the people's intelligences and that the constant principles which acted as safeguards during the colonial period are now undergoing extremely radical changes.

The artist who has decided to illustrate the truths of the nation turns paradoxically towards the past and away from actual events. What he ultimately intends to embrace are in fact the cast-offs of thought, its shells and corpses, a knowledge which has been stabilized once and for all. But the native intellectual who wishes to create an authentic work of art must realize that the truths of a nation are in the first place its realities. He must go on until he has found the seething pot out of which the learning of the future will emerge.

Before independence, the native painter was insensible to the national scene. He set a high value on non-figurative art, or more often was specialized in still-lifes. After independence his anxiety to rejoin his people will confine him to the most detailed representation of reality. This is representative art which has no internal rhythms, an art which is serene and immobile, evocative not of life but of death. Enlightened circles are in ecstasies when confronted with this 'inner truth' which is so well expressed; but we have the right to ask if this truth is in fact a reality, and if it is not already outworn and denied, called in question by the epoch through which the people are treading out their path towards history.

In the realm of poetry we may establish the same facts. After the period of assimilation characterized by rhyming poetry, the poetic tom-tom's rhythms break through. This is a poetry of revolt; but it is also descriptive and analytical poetry. The poet ought, however, to understand that nothing can replace the reasoned, irrevocable taking up of arms on the people's side. Let us quote Depestre once more:

> The lady was not alone;
> She had a husband,
> A husband who knew everything,
> But to tell the truth knew nothing,
> For you can't have culture without making concessions.
> You concede your flesh and blood to it,
> You concede your own self to others;
> By conceding you gain
> Classicism and Romanticism,
> And all that our souls are steeped in.*

The native poet who is preoccupied with creating a national work of art and who is determined to describe his people fails in his aim, for he is not yet ready to make that fundamental concession that Depestre speaks of. The French poet René Char shows his understanding of the difficulty when he reminds us that 'the poem emerges out of a subjective imposition and an objective choice. A poem is the assembling and moving together of determining original values, in contemporary relation with someone that these circumstances bring to the front'.†

Yes, the first duty of the native poet is to see clearly the people he has chosen as the subject of his work of art. He cannot go forward resolutely unless he first realizes the extent of his estrangement from them. We have taken everything from the other side; and the other side gives us nothing unless by a thousand detours we swing finally round in their direction, unless by ten thousand wiles and a hundred thousand tricks they manage to draw us towards them, to seduce us and to imprison us. Taking means in nearly every case being taken: thus it is not enough to try to free oneself by repeating proclamations and denials. It is not enough to try to get back to the people in that past out of which they have already emerged; rather we must join them in

* René Depestre: '*Face à la Nuit*'.   † René Char: '*Partage Formel*'.

that fluctuating movement which they are just giving a shape to, and which, as soon as it has started, will be the signal for everything to be called in question. Let there be no mistake about it; it is to this zone of occult instability where the people dwell that we must come; and it is there that our souls are crystallized and that our perceptions and our lives are transfused with light.

Keita Fodeba, today minister of internal affairs in the Republic of Guinea, when he was the director of the 'African Ballets' did not play any tricks with the reality which the people of Guinea offered him. He reinterpreted all the rhythmic images of his country from a revolutionary stand-point. But he did more. In his poetic works, which are not well known, we find a constant desire to define accurately the historic moments of the struggle and to mark off the field in which were to be unfolded the actions and ideas around which the popular will would crystallize. Here is a poem by Keita Fodeba which is a true invitation to thought, to de-mystification and to battle.

AFRICAN DAWN
(Guitar music)
Dawn was breaking. The little village, which had danced half the night to the sound of its tom-toms was awaking slowly. Ragged shepherds playing their flutes were leading their flocks down into the valley. The girls of the village with their canaries followed one by one along the winding path that leads to the fountain. In the marabout's courtyard a group of children were softly chanting in chorus some verses from the Koran.

(Guitar music)
Dawn was breaking – dawn, the fight between night and day. But the night was exhausted and could fight no more, and slowly died. A few rays of the sun, the forerunners of this victory of the day, still hovered on the horizon, pale and timid, while the last stars gently glided under the mass of clouds, crimson like the blooming flamboyant flowers.

(Guitar music)
Dawn was breaking. And down at the end of the vast plain with its purple contours, the silhouette of a bent man tilling the ground could be seen, the silhouette of Naman the labourer. Each time he lifted his hoe the frightened birds rose, and flew swiftly away to find the quiet banks of the Djoliba, the great Niger river. The man's grey cotton

trousers, soaked by the dew, flapped against the grass on either side. Sweating, unresting, always bent over he worked with his hoe; for the seed had to be sown before the next rains came.

(Cora music)

Dawn was breaking, still breaking. The sparrows circled amongst the leaves announcing the day. On the damp track leading to the plain a child, carrying his little quiver of arrows round him like a bandolier, was running breathless towards Naman. He called out: 'Brother Naman, the head man of the village wants you to come to the council tree.'

(Cora music)

The labourer, surprised by such a message so early in the morning, laid down his hoe and walked towards the village which now was shining in the beams of the rising sun. Already the old men of the village were sitting under the tree, looking more solemn than ever. Beside them a man in uniform, a district guard, sat impassively, quietly smoking his pipe.

(Cora music)

Naman took his place on the sheep-skin. The head man's spokesman stook up to announce to the assembly the will of the old men: 'The white men have sent a district guard to ask for a man from the village who will go to the war in their country. The chief men, after taking counsel together, have decided to send the young man who is the best representative of our race, so that he may go and give proof to the white men of that courage which has always been a feature of our *Manding*.'

(Guitar music)

Naman was thus officially marked out, for every evening the village girls praised his great stature and muscular appearance in musical couplets. Gentle Kadia, his young wife, overwhelmed by the news, suddenly ceased grinding corn, put the mortar away under the barn, and without saying a word shut herself into her hut to weep over her misfortune with stifled sobs. For death had taken her first husband; and she could not believe that now the white people had taken Naman from her, Naman who was the centre of all her new-sprung hopes.

(Guitar music)

The next day, in spite of her tears and lamentations, the full-toned drumming of the war tom-toms accompanied Naman to the village's little harbour where he boarded a trawler which was going to the district capital. That night, instead of dancing in the market-place as they usually did, the village girls came to keep watch in Naman's outer room, and there told their tales until morning around a wood fire.

(Guitar music)

Several months went by without any news of Naman reaching the village. Kadia was so worried that she went to the cunning fetish-worker from the neighbouring village. The village elders themselves held a short secret council on the matter, but nothing came of it.

(Cora music)

At last one day a letter from Naman came to the village, to Kadia's address. She was worried as to what was happening to her husband, and so that same night she came, after hours of tiring walking, to the capital of the district, where a translator read the letter to her.

Naman was in North Africa; he was well, and he asked for news of the harvest, of the feastings, the river, the dances, the council tree . . . in fact, for news of all the village.

(Balafo music)

That night the old women of the village honoured Kadia by allowing her to come to the courtyard of the oldest woman and listen to the talk that went on nightly among them. The head man of the village, happy to have heard news of Naman, gave a great banquet to all the beggars of the neighbourhood.

(Bafalo music)

Again several months went by and everyone was once more anxious, for nothing more was heard of Naman. Kadia was thinking of going again to consult the fetish-worker when she received a second letter. Naman after passing through Corsica and Italy was now in Germany and was proud of having been decorated.

(Balafo music)

But the next time there was only a postcard to say that Naman had been made prisoner by the Germans. This news weighed heavily on the village. The old men held council and decided that henceforward Naman would be allowed to dance the Douga, that sacred dance of the vultures that no one who has not performed some outstanding feat is allowed to dance, that dance of the Mali emperors of which every step is a stage in the history of the Mali race. Kadia found consolation in the fact that her husband had been raised to the dignity of a hero of his country.

(Guitar music)

Time went by. A year followed another, and Naman was still in Germany. He did not write any more.

(Guitar music)

One fine day, the village head man received word from Dakar that Naman would soon be home. The mutter of the tom-toms was at once heard. There was dancing and singing till dawn. The village girls composed new songs for his homecoming, for the old men who were the devotees of the Douga spoke no more about that famous dance of the *Manding*.

(Tom-toms)

But a month later, Corporal Moussa, a great friend of Naman's, wrote a tragic letter to Kadia: 'Dawn was breaking. We were at Tiaroye-sur-Mer. In the course of a widespread dispute between us and our white officers from Dakar, a bullet struck Naman. He lies in the land of Senegal.'

(Guitar music)

Yes; dawn was breaking. The first rays of the sun hardly touched the surface of the sea, as they gilded its little foam-flecked waves. Stirred by the breeze, the palm-trees gently bent their trunks down towards the ocean, as if saddened by the morning's battle. The crows came in noisy flocks to warn the neighbourhood by their cawing of the tragedy that was staining the dawn at Tiaroye with blood. And in the flaming blue sky, just above Naman's body, a huge vulture was hovering heavily. It seemed to say to him 'Naman! You have not danced that dance that is named after me. Others will dance it.'

(Cora music)

If I have chosen to quote this long poem, it is on account of its unquestioned pedagogical value. Here, things are clear; it is a precise, forward-looking exposition. The understanding of the poem is not merely an intellectual advance, but a political advance. To understand this poem is to understand the part one has played, to recognize one's advance and to furbish up one's weapons. There is not a single colonized person who will not receive the message that this poem holds. Naman, the hero of the battle-fields of Europe, Naman who eternally ensures the power and perenniality of the mother country, Naman is machine-gunned by the police force at the very moment that he comes back to the country of his birth: and this is Sétif in 1945, this is Fort-le-France, this is Saigon, Dakar, and Lagos. All those niggers, all those wogs who fought to defend the liberty of France or for British civilization recognize themselves in this poem by Keita Fodeba.

But Keita Fodeba sees farther. In colonized countries, colonialism, after having made use of the natives on the battle-fields, uses them as trained soldiers to put down the movements of independence. The ex-service associations are in the colonies one of the most anti-nationalist elements which exist. The poet Keita Fodeba was training the Minister for Internal Affairs of the Republic of Guinea to frustrate the plots organized by French colonialism. The French secret service intend to use, among other means, the ex-service men to break up the young independent Guinean state.

The colonized man who writes for his people ought to use the past with the intention of opening the future, as an invitation to action and a basis for hope. But to ensure that hope and to give it form, he must take part in action and throw himself body and soul into the national struggle. You may speak about everything under the sun; but when you decide to speak of that unique thing in man's life that is represented by the fact of opening up new horizons, by bringing light to your own country and by raising yourself and your people to their feet, then you must collaborate on the physical plane.

The responsibility of the native man of culture is not a responsibility *vis-à-vis* his national culture, but a global responsibility with regard to the totality of the nation, whose culture merely, after all, represents one aspect of that nation. The cultured native should not concern himself with choosing the level on which he wishes to fight or the sector where he decides to give battle for his nation. To fight for national culture means in the first place to fight for the liberation of the nation, that material keystone which makes the building of a culture possible. There is no other fight for culture which can develop apart from the popular struggle. To take an example: all those men and women who are fighting with their bare hands against French colonialism in Algeria are not by any means strangers to the national culture of Algeria. The national Algerian culture is taking on form and content as the battles are being fought out, in prisons, under the guillotine and in every French outpost which is captured or destroyed.

We must not therefore be content with delving into the past of a people in order to find coherent elements which will counteract colonialism's attempts to falsify and harm. We must work and fight with the same rhythm as the people to construct the future and to prepare the ground where vigorous shoots are already springing up. A national culture is not a folklore, nor an abstract populism that believes it can discover the people's true nature. It is not made up of the inert dregs of gratuitous actions, that is to say actions which are less and less attached to the ever-present reality of the people. A national culture is the whole body of efforts made by a people in the sphere of thought to describe, justify and praise the action through which that people has created itself and keeps itself in existence. A national culture in under-developed countries should therefore take its place at the very heart of the struggle for freedom which these countries are carrying on. Men of African cultures who are still fighting in the name of African-Negro culture and who have called many congresses in the name of the unity of that culture should today realize that all their efforts amount to is to make comparisons between coins and sarcophagi.

There is no common destiny to be shared between the national cultures of Senegal and Guinea; but there *is* a common destiny between the Senegalese and Guinean nations which are both dominated by the same French colonialism. If it is wished that the national culture of Senegal should come to resemble the national culture of Guinea, it is not enough for the rulers of the two peoples to decide to consider their problems – whether the problem of liberation is concerned, or the trade-union questions, or economic difficulties – from similar view-points. And even here there does not seem to be complete identity, for the rhythm of the people and that of their rulers are not the same. There can be no two cultures which are completely identical. To believe that it is possible to create a black culture is to forget that niggers are disappearing, just as those people who brought them into being are seeing the break-up of their economic and cultural supremacy.* There will never be such a thing as black

* At the last school prize-giving in Dakar, the president of the Senegalese Republic, Leopold Senghor, decided to include the study of the idea of Negro-ism in the curriculum. If this decision was due to an anxiety to study

culture because there is not a single politician who feels he has a vocation to bring black republics into being. The problem is to get to know the place that these men mean to give their people, the kind of social relations that they decide to set up and the conception that they have of the future of humanity. It is this that counts; everything else is mystification, signifying nothing.

In 1959 the cultured Africans who met at Rome never stopped talking about unity. But one of the people who was loudest in the praise of this cultural unity, Jacques Rabemananjara, is today a minister in the Madagascan government, and as such has decided, with his government, to oppose the Algerian people in the General Assembly of the United Nations. Rabemananjara, if he had been true to himself, ought to have resigned from the government and denounced those men who claim to incarnate the will of the Madagascan people. The ninety thousand dead of Madagascar have not given Rabemananjara authority to oppose the aspirations of the Algerian people in the General Assembly of the United Nations.

It is around the peoples' struggles that African-Negro culture takes on substance, and not around songs, poems or folklore. Senghor, who is also a member of the Society of African Culture and who has worked with us on the question of African culture, is not afraid for his part either to give the order to his delegation to support French proposals on Algeria. Adherence to African-Negro culture and to the cultural unity of Africa is arrived at in the first place by upholding unconditionally the peoples' struggle for freedom. No one can truly wish for the spread of African culture if he does not give practical support to the creation of the conditions necessary to the existence of that culture; in other words, to the liberation of the whole continent.

I say again that no speech-making and no proclamation concerning culture will turn us from our fundamental tasks: the liberation of the national territory; a continual struggle against colonialism in its new forms; and an obstinate refusal to enter the charmed circle of mutual admiration at the summit.

---

historical causes, no one can criticize it. But if on the other hand it was taken in order to create black self-consciousness, it is simply a turning of his back upon history which has already taken cognizance of the disappearance of the majority of Negroes.

RECIPROCAL BASES OF NATIONAL CULTURE AND THE FIGHT FOR FREEDOM

Colonial domination, because it is total and tends to over-simplify, very soon manages to disrupt in spectacular fashion the cultural life of a conquered people. This cultural obliteration is made possible by the negation of national reality, by new legal relations introduced by the occupying power, by the banishment of the natives and their customs to outlying districts by colonial society, by expropriation, and by the systematic enslaving of men and women.

Three years ago at our first congress I showed that, in the colonial situation, dynamism is replaced fairly quickly by a substantification of the attitudes of the colonizing power. The area of culture is then marked off by fences and signposts. These are in fact so many defence mechanisms of the most elementary type, comparable for more than one good reason to the simple instinct for preservation. The interest of this period for us is that the oppressor does not manage to convince himself of the objective non-existence of the oppressed nation and its culture. Every effort is made to bring the colonized person to admit the inferiority of his culture which has been transformed into instinctive patterns of behaviour, to recognize the unreality of his 'nation', and, in the last extreme, the confused and imperfect character of his own biological structure.

Vis-à-vis this state of affairs, the native's reactions are not unanimous. While the mass of the people maintain intact traditions which are completely different from those of the colonial situation, and the artisan style solidifies into a formalism which is more and more stereotyped, the intellectual throws himself in frenzied fashion into the frantic acquisition of the culture of the occupying power and takes every opportunity of unfavourably criticizing his own national culture, or else takes refuge in setting out and substantiating the claims of that culture in a way that is passionate but rapidly becomes unproductive.

The common nature of these two reactions lies in the fact that they both lead to impossible contradictions. Whether a turncoat or a substantialist the native is ineffectual precisely because the analysis of the colonial situation is not carried out on strict lines. The colonial situation calls a halt to national culture in almost every field. Within the framework of colonial domination there is not and there will never be such phenomena as new cultural departures or changes in the national culture. Here and there valiant attempts are sometimes made to reanimate the cultural dynamic and to give fresh impulses to its themes, its forms and its tonalities. The immediate, palpable and obvious interest of such leaps ahead is nil. But if we follow up the consequences to the very end we see that preparations are being thus made to brush the cobwebs off national consciousness, to question oppression and to open up the struggle for freedom.

A national culture under colonial domination is a contested culture whose destruction is sought in systematic fashion. It very quickly becomes a culture condemned to secrecy. This idea of a clandestine culture is immediately seen in the reactions of the occupying power which interprets attachment to traditions as faithfulness to the spirit of the nation and as a refusal to submit. This persistence in following forms of cultures which are already condemned to extinction is already a demonstration of nationality; but it is a demonstration which is a throw-back to the laws of inertia. There is no taking of the offensive and no redefining of relationships. There is simply a concentration on a hard core of culture which is becoming more and more shrivelled up, inert and empty.

By the time a century or two of exploitation has passed there comes about a veritable emaciation of the stock of national culture. It becomes a set of automatic habits, some traditions of dress and a few broken-down institutions. Little movement can be discerned in such remnants of culture; there is no real creativity and no overflowing life. The poverty of the people, national oppression and the inhibition of culture are one and the same thing. After a century of colonial domination we find a culture which is rigid in the extreme, or rather what we find are the dregs of culture, its mineral strata. The withering away of the reality of the nation and the death-pangs of the national culture are linked to each other in mutual dependence. This is why it is of capital importance to follow the evolution of these relations during the struggle for national freedom. The negation of the native's culture, the contempt for any manifestation of culture whether active or emotional and the placing outside the pale of all specialized branches of organization contribute to breed aggressive patterns of conduct in the native. But these patterns of conduct are of the reflexive type; they are poorly differentiated, anarchic and ineffective. Colonial exploitation, poverty and endemic famine drive the native more and more to open, organized revolt. The necessity for an open and decisive breach is formed progressively and imperceptibly, and comes to be felt by the great majority of the people. Those tensions which hitherto were non-existent come into being. International events, the collapse of whole sections of colonial empires and the contradictions inherent in the colonial system strengthen and uphold the native's combativity while promoting and giving support to national consciousness.

These new-found tensions which are present at all stages in the real nature of colonialism have their repercussions on the cultural plane. In literature, for example, there is relative over-production. From being a reply on a minor scale to the dominating power, the literature produced by natives becomes differentiated and makes itself into a will to particularism. The intelligentsia, which during the period of repression was essentially a consuming public, now themselves become producers. This literature at first chooses to confine itself to the tragic and poetic style; but later on novels, short stories and essays are attempted. It is as if a kind of internal organization or law of expression existed which wills that poetic expression become less frequent in proportion as the objectives and the methods of the struggle for liberation become more precise. Themes are completely altered; in fact, we find less and less of bitter, hopeless recrimination and less also of that violent, resounding, florid writing which on the whole serves to reassure the occupying power. The colonialists have in former times encouraged these modes of expression and made their existence possible. Stinging denunciations, the exposing of distressing conditions and passions which find their outlet in expression are in fact assimilated by the occupying power in a cathartic process. To aid such processes is in a certain sense to avoid their dramatization and to clear the atmosphere.

But such a situation can only be transitory. In fact, the progress of national consciousness among the people modifies and gives precision to the literary utterances of the native intellectual. The continued cohesion of the people constitutes for the intellectual an invitation to go farther than his cry of protest. The lament first makes the indictment; then it makes an appeal. In the period that follows, the words of command are heard. The crystallization of the national consciousness will both disrupt literary styles and themes, and also create a completely new public. While at the beginning the native intellectual used to produce his work to be read exclusively by the oppressor, whether with the intention of charming him or of denouncing him through ethnical or subjectivist means, now the native writer progressively takes on the habit of addressing his own people.

It is only from that moment that we can speak of a national literature. Here there is, at the level of literary creation, the taking up and clarification of themes which are typically nationalist. This may be properly called a literature of combat, in the sense that it calls on the whole people to fight for their existence as a nation. It is a literature of combat, because it moulds the national consciousness, giving it form and contours and flinging open before it new and boundless horizons; it is a literature of combat because it assumes responsibility, and because it is the will to liberty expressed in terms of time and space.

On another level, the oral tradition – stories, epics and songs of the people – which formerly were filed away as set pieces are now beginning to change. The storytellers who used to relate inert episodes now bring them alive and introduce into them modifications which are increasingly fundamental. There is a tendency to bring conflicts up to date and to modernize the kinds of struggle which the stories evoke, together with the names of heroes and the types of weapons. The method of allusion is more and more widely used. The formula 'This all happened long ago' is substituted by that of 'What we are going to speak of happened somewhere else, but it might well have happened here today, and it might happen tomorrow'. The example of Algeria is significant in this context. From 1952–3 on, the storytellers, who were before that time stereotyped and tedious to listen to, completely overturned their traditional methods of storytelling and the contents of their tales. Their public, which was formerly scattered, became compact. The epic, with its typified categories, reappeared; it became an authentic form of entertainment which took on once more a cultural value. Colonialism made no mistake when from 1955 on it proceeded to arrest these storytellers systematically.

The contact of the people with the new movement gives rise to a new rhythm of life and to forgotten muscular tensions, and develops the imagination. Every time the storyteller relates a fresh episode to his public, he presides over a real invocation. The existence of a new type of man is revealed to the public. The present is no longer turned in upon itself but spread out for all to see. The storyteller once more gives free rein to his imagination; he makes innovations and he creates a work of art. It even happens that the characters, which are barely ready for such a transformation – highway robbers or more or less anti-social vagabonds – are taken up and remodelled. The emergence of the imagination and of the creative urge in the songs and epic stories of a colonized country is worth following. The storyteller replies to the expectant people by successive approximations, and makes his way, apparently alone but in fact helped on by his public, towards the seeking out of new patterns, that is to say national patterns. Comedy and farce disappear, or lose their attraction. As for dramatization, it is no longer placed on the plane of the troubled intellectual and his tormented conscience. By losing its characteristics of despair and revolt, the drama becomes part of the common lot of the people and forms part of an action in preparation or already in progress.

Where handicrafts are concerned, the forms of expression which formerly were the dregs of art, surviving as if in a daze, now begin to reach out. Woodwork, for example, which formerly turned out certain faces and attitudes by the million, begins to be differentiated. The inexpressive or overwrought mask comes to life and the arms tend to be raised from the body as if to sketch an action. Compositions containing two, three or five figures appear. The traditional schools are led on to creative efforts by the rising avalanche of amateurs or of critics. This new vigour in this sector of cultural life very often passes unseen; and yet its contribution to the national effort is of capital importance. By carving figures and faces which are full of life, and by taking as his theme a group fixed on the same pedestal, the artist invites participation in an organized movement.

If we study the repercussions of the awakening of national consciousness in the domains of ceramics and pottery-making, the same observations may be drawn. Formalism is abandoned in the craftsman's work. Jugs, jars and trays are modified, at first imperceptibly, then almost savagely. The colours, of which formerly there were but few and which obeyed the traditional rules of harmony, increase in number and are influenced by the repercussion of the rising revolution. Certain ochres and blues, which seemed forbidden to all eternity in a given cultural area, now assert themselves without giving rise to scandal. In the same way the stylization of the human face, which according to sociologists is typical of very clearly defined regions, becomes suddenly completely relative. The specialist coming from the home country and the ethnologist are quick to note these changes. On the whole such changes are condemned in the name of a rigid code of artistic style and of a cultural life which grows up at the heart of the colonial system. The colonialist specialists do not recognize these new forms and rush to the help of the traditions of the indigenous society. It is the colonialists who become the defenders of the native style. We remember perfectly, and the example took on a certain measure of importance since the real nature of colonialism was not involved, the reactions of the white jazz specialists when after the Second World War new styles such as the be-bop took definite shape. The fact is that in their eyes jazz should only be the despairing, broken-down nostalgia of an old Negro who is trapped between five glasses of whisky, the curse of his race, and the racial hatred of the white men. As soon as the Negro comes to an understanding of himself, and understands the rest of the world differently, when he gives birth to hope and forces back the racist universe, it is clear that his trumpet sounds more clearly and his voice less hoarsely. The new fashions in jazz are not simply born of economic competition. We must without any doubt see in them one of the consequences of the defeat, slow but sure, of the southern world of the United States. And it is not utopian to suppose that in fifty years' time the type of jazz howl hiccupped by a poor misfortunate Negro will be upheld only by the whites who believe in it as an expression of nigger-hood, and who are faithful to this arrested image of a type of relationship.

We might in the same way seek and find in dancing, singing, and traditional rites and ceremonies the same upward-springing trend, and make out the same changes and the same impatience in this field. Well before the political or fighting phase of the national movement an attentive spectator can thus feel and see the manifestation of new vigour and feel the approaching conflict. He will note unusual forms of expression and themes which are fresh and imbued with a power which is no longer that of invocation but rather of the assembling of the people, a summoning together for a precise purpose. Everything works together to awaken the native's sensibility and to make unreal and inacceptable the contemplative attitude, or the acceptance of defeat. The native rebuilds his perceptions because he renews the purpose and dynamism of the craftsmen, of dancing and music and of literature and the oral tradition. His world comes to lose its accursed character. The conditions necessary for the inevitable conflict are brought together.

We have noted the appearance of the movement in cultural forms and we have seen that this movement and these new forms are linked to the state of maturity of the national consciousness. Now, this movement tends more and more to express itself objectively, in institutions. From thence comes the need for a national existence, whatever the cost.

A frequent mistake, and one which is moreover hardly justifiable is to try to find cultural expressions for and to give new values to native culture within the framework of colonial domination. This is why we arrive at a proposition which at first sight seems paradoxical: the fact that in a colonized country the most elementary, most savage and the most undifferentiated nationalism is the most fervent and efficient means of defending national culture. For culture is first the expression of a nation, the expression of its preferences, of its taboos and of its patterns. It is at every stage of the whole of society that other taboos, values and patterns are formed. A national culture is the sum total of all these appraisals; it is the result of internal and external extensions exerted over society as a whole and also at every level of that society. In the colonial situation, culture, which is doubly deprived of the support of the nation and of the state, falls away and dies. The condition for its existence is therefore national liberation and the renaissance of the state.

The nation is not only the condition of culture, its fruitfulness, its continuous renewal, and its deepening. It is also a necessity. It is the fight for national existence which sets culture moving and opens to it the doors of creation. Later on it is the nation which will ensure the conditions and framework necessary to culture. The nation gathers together the various indispensable elements necessary for the creation of a culture, those elements which alone can give it credibility, validity, life and creative power. In the same way it is its national character that will make such a culture open to other cultures and which will enable it to influence and permeate other cultures. A non-existent culture can hardly be expected to have bearing on reality, or to influence reality. The first necessity is the re-establishment of the nation in order to give life to national culture in the strictly biological sense of the phrase.

Thus we have followed the break-up of the old strata of culture, a shattering which becomes increasingly fundamental; and we have noticed, on the eve of the decisive conflict for national freedom, the renewing of forms of expression and the rebirth of the imagination. There remains one essential question: what are the relations between the struggle – whether political or military – and culture? Is there a suspension of culture during the conflict? Is the national struggle an expression of a culture? Finally, ought one to say that the battle for freedom, however fertile *a posteriori* with regard to culture, is in itself a negation of culture? In short is the struggle for liberation a cultural phenomenon or not?

We believe that the conscious and organized undertaking by a colonized people to re-establish the sovereignty of that nation constitutes the most complete and obvious cultural manifestation that exists. It is not alone the success of the struggle which afterwards gives validity and vigour to culture; culture is not put into cold storage during the conflict. The struggle itself in its development and in its internal progression sends culture along different paths and traces out entirely new ones for it. The struggle for freedom does not give back to the national culture its former value and shapes; this struggle which aims at a fundamentally different set of relations between men cannot leave intact either the form or the content of the people's culture. After the conflict there is not only the disappearance of colonialism but also the disappearance of the colonized man.

This new humanity cannot do otherwise than define a new humanism both for itself and for others. It is prefigured in the objectives and methods of the conflict. A struggle which mobilizes all classes of the people and which expresses their aims and their impatience, which is not afraid to count almost exclusively on the people's support, will of necessity triumph. The value of this type of conflict is that it supplies the maximum of conditions necessary for the development and aims of culture. After national freedom has been obtained in these conditions, there is no such painful cultural indecision which is found in certain countries which are newly independent, because the nation by its manner of coming into being and in the terms of its existence exerts a fundamental influence over culture. A nation which is born of the people's concerted action and which embodies the real aspirations of the people while changing the state cannot exist save in the expression of exceptionally rich forms of culture.

The natives who are anxious for the culture of their country and who wish to give to it a universal dimension ought not therefore to place their confidence in the single principle of inevitable, undifferentiated independence written into the consciousness of the people in order to achieve their task. The liberation of the nation is one thing; the methods and popular content of the fight are another. It seems to us that the future of national culture and its riches are equally also part and parcel of the values which have ordained the struggle for freedom.

And now it is time to denounce certain pharisees. National claims, it is here and there stated, are a phase that humanity has left behind. It is the day of great concerted actions, and retarded nationalists ought in consequence to set their mistakes aright. We, however, consider that the mistake, which may have very serious consequences, lies in wishing to skip the national period. If culture is the expression of national consciousness, I will not hesitate to affirm that in the case with which we are dealing it is the national consciousness which is the most elaborate form of culture.

The consciousness of self is not the closing of a door to communication. Philosophic thought teaches us, on the contrary, that it is its guarantee. National consciousness, which is not nationalism, is the only thing that will give us an international dimension. This problem of national consciousness and of national culture takes on in Africa a special dimension. The birth of national consciousness in Africa has a strictly contemporaneous connexion with the African consciousness. The responsibility of the African as regards national culture is also a responsibility with regard to African-Negro culture. This joint responsibility is not the fact of a metaphysical principle but the awareness of a simple rule which wills that every independent nation in an Africa where colonialism is still entrenched is an encircled nation, a nation which is fragile and in permanent danger.

If man is known by his acts, then we will say that the most urgent thing today for the intellectual is to build up his nation. If this building up is true, that is to say if it interprets the manifest will of the people and reveals the eager African peoples, then the building of a nation is of necessity accompanied by the discovery and encouragement of universalizing values. Far from keeping aloof from other nations, therefore, it is national liberation which leads the nation to play its part on the stage of history. It is at the heart of national consciousness that international consciousness lives and grows. And this two-fold emerging is ultimately the source of all culture.

Statement made at the Second Congress of Black Artists and Writers, Rome, 1959.

5. Colonial War and Mental Disorders

BUT the war goes on; and we will have to bind up for years to come the many, sometimes ineffaceable, wounds that the colonialist onslaught has inflicted on our people.

That imperialism which today is fighting against a true liberation of mankind leaves in its wake here and there tinctures of decay which we must search out and mercilessly expel from our land and our spirits.

We shall deal here with the problem of mental disorders which arise from the war of national liberation which the Algerian people are carrying on.

Perhaps these notes on psychiatry will be found ill-timed and singularly out of place in such a book; but we can do nothing about that.

We cannot be held responsible that in this war psychiatric phenomena entailing disorders affecting behaviour and thought have taken on importance where those who carry out the 'pacification' are concerned, or that these same disorders are notable among the 'pacified' population. The truth is that colonialism in its essence was already taking on the aspect of a fertile purveyor for psychiatric hospitals. We have since 1954 in various scientific works drawn the attention of both French and international psychiatrists to the difficulties that arise when seeking to 'cure' a native properly, that is to say, when seeking to make him thoroughly a part of a social background of the colonial type.

Because it is a systematic negation of the other person and a furious determination to deny the other person all attributes of humanity, colonialism forces the people it dominates to ask themselves the question constantly: 'In reality, who am I?'

The defensive attitudes created by this violent bringing together of the colonized man and the colonial system form themselves into a structure which then reveals the colonized personality. This 'sensitivity' is easily understood if we simply study and are alive to the number and depth of the injuries inflicted upon a native during a single day spent amidst the colonial regime. It must in any case be remembered that a colonized people is not only simply a dominated people. Under the German occupation the French remained men; under the French occupation, the Germans remained men. In Algeria there is not simply the domination but the decision to the letter not to occupy anything more than the sum total of the land. The Algerians, the veiled women, the palm-trees and the camels make up the landscape, the *natural* background to the human presence of the French.

Hostile nature, obstinate and fundamentally rebellious, is in fact represented in the colonies by the bush, by mosquitoes, natives and fever, and colonization is a success when all this indocile nature has finally been tamed. Railways across the bush, the draining of swamps and a native population which is non-existent politically and economically are in fact one and the same thing.

In the period of colonization when it is not contested by armed resistance, when the sum total of harmful nervous stimuli overstep a certain threshold, the defensive attitudes of the natives give way and they then find themselves crowding the mental hospitals. There is thus during this calm period of successful colonization a regular and important mental pathology which is the direct product of oppression.

Today the war of national liberation which has been carried on by the Algerian people for the last seven years has become a favourable breeding-ground for mental disorders, because so far as the Algerians are concerned it is a total war. We shall mention here some Algerian cases which have been attended by us and who seem to us to be particularly eloquent. We need hardly say that we are not concerned with producing a scientific work. We avoid all arguments over semiology, nosology or therapeutics. The few technical terms used serve merely as references. We must, however, insist on two points. Firstly, as a general rule, clinical psychiatry classifies the different disturbances shown by our patients under the heading 'reactionary psychoses'. In doing this, prominence is given to the event which has given rise to the disorder, although in some cases mention is made of the previous history of the case (the

psychological, affective and biological condition of the patient)
and of the type of background from whence he comes. It seems to
us that in the cases here chosen the events giving rise to the disorder are chiefly the bloodthirsty and pitiless atmosphere, the
generalization of inhuman practices and the firm impression that
people have of being caught up in a veritable Apocalypse.*

Case 2 of Series A is a typical reactionary psychosis, but cases
1, 2, 4 and 5 of Series B give evidence of a much more widely
spread causality although we cannot really speak of one particular
event giving rise to the disorders. These are reactionary psychoses, if we want to use a ready-made label; but here we must
give particular priority to the war: a war which in whole and in
part is a colonial war. After the two great world wars, there is no
lack of publications on the mental pathology of soldiers taking
part in action and civilians who are victims of evacuations and
bombardments. The hitherto unemphasized characteristics of
certain psychiatric descriptions here given confirm, if confirma-
tion were necessary, that this colonial war is singular even in the
pathology that it gives rise to.

Another idea which is strongly held needs in our opinion
to be re-examined; this is the notion of the relative harmless-
ness of these reactional disorders. It is true that others have
described, but always as exceptional cases, certain secondary
psychoses, that is to say cases where the whole of the personality is disrupted definitely. It seems to us that here the rule is

---

* In the unpublished introduction of the first two editions of *Year V of
the Algerian Revolution*, we have already pointed out that a whole generation
of Algerians, steeped in wanton, generalized homicide with all the psycho-
affective consequences that this entails, will be the human legacy of France in
Algeria. Frenchmen who condemn the torture in Algeria constantly adopt a
point of view which is strictly French. We do not reproach them for this; we
merely point it out: they wish to protect the consciences of the actual torturers who today have full power to carry on their work; they wish at the
same time to try to avoid the moral contamination of the young people of
France. As far as we are concerned we are totally in accord with this attitude.
Certain notes here brought together, especially in cases 4 and 5 in Series A,
are sad illustrations and justifications for this obsession which haunts French
believers in democracy. But our purpose is in any case to show that torture,
as might well be expected, upsets most profoundly the personality of the
person who is tortured.

rather the frequent malignancy of these pathological processes. These are disorders which persist for months on end, making a mass attack against the ego, and practically always leaving as their sequel a weakness which is almost visible to the naked eye. According to all available evidence, the future of such patients is mortgaged. An example will best illustrate our point of view.

In one of the African countries which have been independent for several years we had occasion to receive a visit from a patriot who had been in the resistance. This man in his thirties came to ask us for advice and help, for around a certain date each year he suffered from prolonged insomnia, accompanied by anxiety and suicidal obsessions. The critical date was that when on instructions from his organization he had placed a bomb somewhere. Ten people were killed as a result.★

This militant, who never for a single moment thought of repudiating his past action, realized very clearly the manner in which he himself had to pay the price of national independence. It is border-line cases such as his which raise the question of responsibility within the revolutionary framework.

The observations noted here cover the period running from 1954–9. Certain patients were examined in Algeria, either in

★ The circumstances surrounding the appearance of these disorders are interesting for several reasons. Some months after his country's independence was declared, he had made the acquaintance of certain nationals of the former colonial power, and he had found them very likeable. These men and women greeted the new independent state warmly and paid tribute to the courage of the patriots who had fought in the struggle for national freedom. The former militant therefore had what might be called an attack of vertigo. He wondered with a feeling of anguish whether among the victims of the bomb there had been people like his new acquaintances. It was true that the café that it was aimed at was a meeting-place for notorious racists; but there was nothing to prevent a quite ordinary passer-by going in and having a drink. From the first day that he suffered from vertigo the man tried to avoid thinking of these former occurrences. But paradoxically, a few days before the crucial date, the first symptoms made their appearance. Since then, they appeared with great regularity.

In other words, we are for ever pursued by our actions. Their ordering, their circumstances and their motivation may perfectly well come to be profoundly modified *a posteriori*. This is merely one of the snares that history and its various influences sets for us. But can we escape becoming dizzy? And who can affirm that vertigo does not haunt the whole of existence?

hospital centres or as private patients. The others were cared for by the health divisions of the Army of National Liberation.

SERIES A

Five cases are cited here. They are cases of Algerians or Europeans who had very clear symptoms of mental disorders of the reactionary type.

Case 1. Impotence in an Algerian following on the rape of his wife.

B— is a man of twenty-six years old. He came to see us on the advice of the Health Service of the F.L.N. for treatment of insomnia and persistent headaches. A former taxi-driver, he had worked in the nationalist parties since he was eighteen. From 1955 he had been a member of a branch of the F.L.N. He had several times used his taxi for the transport of political pamphlets and also political personnel. When the repression increased in ferocity, the F.L.N. decided to bring the war into the urban centres. B— thus came to have the task of driving commandos to the vicinity of attacking points, and quite often waited for them at those points to bring them back.

One day, however, in the middle of the European part of the town after fairly considerable fighting, a very large number of arrests forced him to abandon his taxi, and the commando unit broke up and scattered. B— who managed to escape through the enemy lines, took refuge at a friend's house. Some days later, without having been able to get back to his home, on the orders of his superiors he joined the nearest band of Maquis.

For several months he was without news of his wife and his little girl of a year and eight months. On the other hand he learned that the police spent several weeks on end searching the town. After two years spent in the Maquis he received a message from his wife in which she asked him to forget her, for she had been dishonoured and he ought not to think of taking up their life together again. He was extremely anxious and asked his commander's leave to go home secretly. This was refused him, but on the other hand measures were taken for a member of the F.L.N. to make contact with B——'s wife and parents.

Two weeks later a detailed report reached the commander of B——'s unit.

His abandoned taxi had been discovered with two machine-gun magazines in it. Immediately afterwards French soldiers accompanied by policemen went to his house. Finding he was absent, they took his wife away and kept her for over a week.

She was questioned about the company her husband kept and beaten fairly brutally for two days. But the third day a French soldier (she was not able to say whether he was an officer) made the others leave the room and then raped her. Some time after a second soldier, this time with others present, raped her saying to her, 'If ever you see your filthy husband again don't forget to tell him what we did to you.' She remained another week without undergoing any fresh questioning. After this she was escorted back to her dwelling. When she told her story to her mother, the latter persuaded her to tell B—— everything. Thus as soon as contact was re-established with her husband, she confessed her dishonour to him.

Once the first shock had passed, and since moreover every minute of his time was filled by activity, B—— was able to overcome his feelings. For several months he had heard many stories of Algerian women who had been raped or tortured, and he had occasion to see the husbands of these violated women; thus his personal misfortunes and his dignity as an injured husband remained in the background.

In 1958, he was entrusted with a mission abroad. When it was time to rejoin his unit, certain fits of absence of mind and sleeplessness made his comrades and superiors anxious about him. His departure was postponed and it was decided he should have a medical examination. This was when we saw him. He seemed at once easy to get to know; a mobile face: perhaps a bit too mobile. Smile slightly exaggerated; surface well-being: 'I'm really very well, very well indeed. I'm feeling better now. Give me a tonic or two, a few vitamins, and I'll build myself up a bit.' A basic anxiety came up to break the surface. He was at once sent to hospital.

From the second day on, the screen of optimism melted

away, and what we saw in front of us was a thoughtful, depressed man, suffering from loss of appetite, who kept to his bed. He avoided political discussion and showed a marked lack of interest in everything to do with the national struggle. He avoided listening to any news which had bearing on the war of liberation. Any approach to his difficulties was extremely long, but at the end of some days we were able to reconstruct his story.

During his stay abroad, he tried to carry through a sexual affair which was unsuccessful. Thinking that this was due to fatigue, a normal result of forced marches and periods of undernourishment, he again tried two weeks later. Fresh failure. Talked about it to a friend who advised him to try vitamin B 12. Took this in form of pills; another attempt, another failure. Moreover, a few seconds before the act, he had an irresistible impulse to tear up a photo of his little girl. Such a symbolic liaison might have caused us to think that unconscious impulsions of an incestuous nature were present. However, several interviews and a dream, in which the patient saw the rapid rotting away of a little cat accompanied by unbearably evil smells, led us to take quite another course. 'That girl,' he said to us one day, speaking of his little daughter, 'has something rotten about her.' From this period on, his insomnia became extremely marked, and in spite of fairly large doses of neuroleptics a state of anxiety excitation was remarked which the Service found rather worrying. Then he spoke to us for the first time about his wife, laughing and saying to us: 'She's tasted the French.' It was at that moment that we reconstructed the whole story. The weaving of events to form a pattern was made explicit. He told us that before every sexual attempt, he thought of his wife. All his confidences appeared to us to be of fundamental interest.

I married this girl although I loved my cousin. But my cousin's parents had arranged a match for their daughter with somebody else. So I accepted the first wife my parents found for me. She was nice, but I didn't love her. I used always to say to myself: 'You're young yet; wait a bit and when you've found the right girl, you'll get a divorce and you'll make a happy marriage.' So you see I wasn't very attached to my wife. And with the troubles, I got further apart than ever. In the end, I used to come and eat my meals and sleep almost without speaking to her.

In the Maquis, when I heard that she'd been raped by the French, I first of all felt angry with the swine. Then I said, 'Oh, well, there's not much harm done; she wasn't killed. She can start her life over again.' And then a few weeks later I came to realize that they'd raped her *because they were looking for me*. In fact, it was to punish her for keeping silence that she'd been violated. She could have very well told them at least the name of one of the chaps in the movement, and from that they could have searched out the whole network, destroyed it, and maybe even arrested me. That wasn't a simple rape, for want of something better to do, or for sadistic reasons like those I've had occasion to see in the villages; it was the rape of an obstinate woman, who was ready to put up with everything rather than sell her husband. And the husband in question, *it was me*. This woman had saved my life and had protected the organization. It was because of me that she had been dishonoured. And yet she didn't say to me: 'Look at all I've had to bear for you.' On the contrary, she said: 'Forget about me; begin your life over again, for I have been dishonoured.'

It was from that moment on that I made my own decision to take back my wife after the war; for it must be said that I've seen peasants drying the tears of their wives after having seen them raped under their very eyes. This left me very much shaken; I must admit moreover that at the beginning I couldn't understand their attitude. But we increasingly came to intervene in such circumstances in order to explain matters to the civilians. I've seen civilians proposing marriage to a girl who was violated by the French soldiers, and who was with child by them. All this led me to reconsider the problem of my wife.

So I decided to take her back; but I didn't know at all how I'd behave when I saw her. And often, while I was looking at the photo of my daughter, I used to think that she too was dishonoured, like as if everything that had to do with my wife was rotten. If they'd tortured her or knocked out all her teeth or broken an arm I wouldn't have minded. But that thing – how can you forget a thing like that? And why did she have to tell me about it all?

He then asked me if his 'sexual failing' was in my opinion caused by his worries.

I replied: 'It is not impossible.'

Then he sat up in bed.

'What would you do if all this had happened to you?'

'I don't know.'

'Would you take back your wife?'

'I think I would. . . .'

'Ah, there you are, you see. You're not quite sure. . . .'

He held his head in his hands and after a few seconds left the room.

From that day on, he was progressively more willing to listen to political discussions and at the same time the headaches and lack of appetite lessened considerably.

After two weeks he went back to his unit. Before he left he told me:

'When independence comes, I'll take my wife back. If it doesn't work out between us, I'll come and see you in Algiers.'

Case 2. Undifferentiated homicidal impulses found in a survivor of a mass murder.

S—, thirty-seven years old, a *fellah*. Comes from a village in the country around Constantine. Never took any part in politics. From the outset of the war, his district was the scene of fierce battles between the Algerian forces and the French army. S— thus had occasion to see dead and wounded. But he continued to keep out of things. From time to time, however, in common with the people as a whole, the peasantry of his village used to come to the aid of Algerian fighting men who were passing through. But one day, early in 1958, a deadly ambush was laid not far from the village. After this the enemy forces went into operation and besieged the village, which in fact had no soldiers in it. All the inhabitants were summoned and questioned; nobody replied. A few hours after, a French officer arrived by helicopter and said: 'There's been too much talk about this village. Destroy it.' The soldiers began to set fire to the houses while the women who were trying to get a few clothes together or save some provisions were driven away by blows with rifle-butts. Some peasants took advantage of the general confusion to run away. The officer gave the order to bring together the men who remained and had them brought out to near a water-course where the killing began. Twenty-nine men were shot at point-blank range. S— was wounded by two bullets which went through his right thigh and his left arm respectively; the arm injury gave rise to a fracture of the humerus.

S— fainted and came to to find himself in the midst of a group of A.L.N. He was treated by the Health Service and evacuated as soon as it was possible to move him. While on the way, his behaviour became more and more abnormal, and worried his escort continually. He demanded a gun, although he was helpless and a civilian, and refused to walk in front of anybody, no matter who they were. He refused to have anyone behind him. One night he got hold of a soldier's gun and awkwardly tried to fire on the sleeping soldiers. He was disarmed rather roughly. From then on they tied his hands together, and it was thus that he arrived at the Centre.

He began by telling us that he wasn't dead yet and that he had played a good trick on the others. Bit by bit, we managed to reconstruct his story of the assassination he had attempted. S— was not anxious, he was rather in fact over-excited, with violent phases of agitation, accompanied by screaming. He did not break anything much, but tired everybody out by his incessant chatter, and the whole Service was permanently on the alert on account of his declared intention of 'killing everybody'. During his stay in hospital he attacked about eight patients with make-shift weapons. Nurses and doctors were not spared either. We almost wondered whether we were not witnessing one of those masked forms of epilepsy which is characterized by a wholesale aggressivity which is nearly always present.

Deep sleep treatment was then tried. From the third day on, a daily interview made it possible for us to understand better the moving force of the pathological process. The patient's intellectual confusion progressively toned down. Here are some extracts from his statements:

God is with me ... but he certainly isn't with those who are dead ... I've had hellish good luck. .... In life you've got to kill so as not to be killed. .... When I think that I know nothing at all about all that business. .... There are Frenchmen in our midst. They disguise themselves as Arabs. They've all got to be killed. Give me a machine-gun. All these so-called Algerians are really Frenchmen ... and they won't leave me alone. As soon as I want to go to sleep they come into my room. But now I know all about them. Everyone wants to kill me. But I'll

defend myself. I'll kill them all, every single one of them. I'll cut their
throats one after the other, and yours with them. You all want to kill
me but you should set about it differently. I'd kill you all as soon as
look at you, big ones and little ones, women, children, dogs, birds,
donkeys . . . everyone will be dead. And afterwards I'll be able to
sleep in peace. . . .

All this was said in jerks; the patient's attitude remained
hostile, suspicious and aloof.

After three weeks, his state of excitement had disappeared,
but a certain reticence and a tendency to seek solitude gave us
grounds for fearing a more serious development of his disorder.
However, after a month he asked to be let out in order to learn
a trade that would be compatible with his disability. He was
then entrusted to the care of the Social Service of the F.L.N.
We saw him six months after, and he was going on well.

*Case 3. Marked anxiety psychosis of the depersonalization type
after the murder of a woman while temporarily insane.*

Dj—, a former student, a soldier in the A.L.N., nineteen years
old. His illness already dated from some months back by the
time he came to the Centre. His appearance was characteristic:
he seemed very depressed, his hands were constantly moist
and his lips were dry; his chest was lifted by continual sighs.
Pernicious insomnia; two attempts at suicide since the trouble
started. During the conversation, he struck hallucinatory attitudes while listening. Sometimes his glance fixed itself for a
few seconds on a point in space, while his face lit up, giving
the impression to observers that the patient was witnessing a
play. Thoughts woolly. Certain phenomena known in psychiatry
by the name of blocking: a gesture or phrase is begun and then
suddenly interrupted without apparent reason. But in particular
one element aroused our attention: the patient talked of his
blood being spilt, of his arteries which were being emptied and
of his heart which kept missing a beat. He implored us to stop
the haemorrhage and not to let him be 'sucked by a vampire'
within the very precincts of the hospital. Sometimes he could not
speak any more, and asked us for a pencil. Wrote: 'I have lost
my voice; my whole life is ebbing away.' This living depersonali-

zation gave us reason to believe that the illness had reached a serious stage of development.

Several times during the course of our conversations, the patient spoke to us of a woman who when night fell came to persecute him. Having learnt beforehand that his mother whom he had been very fond of was dead, and that nothing had been able to console him for her loss (his voice had considerably sunk as he spoke of her, and he shed some tears), I directed the investigation towards the maternal image. When I asked him to describe the woman who obsessed him, I might even say persecuted him, he declared that she was not an unknown person, that he knew her very well and that it was he that had killed her. It was thus a matter of finding out whether we had to deal with an unconscious guilt complex following on the death of the mother, as Freud has described in *Mourning and Melancholia*. We asked the patient to talk to us about this woman in greater detail, since he had known her so well, and since also it was he who had killed her. Thus we were able to reconstruct the following story:

I left the town where I had been a student to join the Maquis. After some months, I had news of my people. I learnt that my mother had been killed point-blank by a French soldier and two of my sisters had been taken to the soldiers' quarters. Up to now, I have no news of what happened to them. I was terribly shaken by the death of my mother. Since my father had died some years before, I was the only man in the family, and my sole ambition had always been to manage to do something to make life easier for my mother and my sisters. One day we went to an estate belonging to settlers, where the agent, who was an active colonist, had already killed two Algerian civilians. We came to his house, at night, but he wasn't there. Only his wife was at home. When she saw us, she started to cry and implored us not to kill her: 'I know you've come for my husband,' she said, 'but he isn't here. I've told him again and again not to have anything to do with politics.' We decided to wait for her husband. But as far as I was concerned, when I looked at that woman I thought of my mother. She was sitting in an armchair and her thoughts seemed to be elsewhere. I wondered why we didn't kill her; then all of a sudden she noticed I was looking at her. She flung herself upon me screaming 'Please don't kill me . . . I have children.' A moment after she was dead; I'd killed her with my knife. My commander disarmed me and ordered me to leave. I was questioned by the platoon commander a few days later. I thought I was going to be shot, but I didn't give a damn.* And then I started vomiting after every meal, and I slept badly. After that this woman started coming every night and asking for my blood. But my mother's blood – where's that?

At nightfall that evening, as soon as the patient went to bed, the room was 'invaded by women' in spite of everything. It was a manifold repetition of the same woman. Every one of them had an open wound in her stomach. They were bloodless, pale and terribly thin. They tormented the young patient and insisted that he should give them back their spilt blood. At this moment the sound of running water filled the room and grew so loud that it seemed like a thundering waterfall, and the young patient saw the parquet of his room drenched with blood – his blood – while the women slowly got their colour back, and their wounds began to close up. The patient awoke, bathed with sweat and in deep distress, and remained in a state of nervous excitement until the dawn.

The young patient was treated for several weeks, after which time the oneiroid symptoms (nightmares) had practically disappeared. However, a serious deficiency remained in his personality. When he started thinking of his mother, the disembowelled woman rose up before him in redoubled horror. Though it may appear unscientific, in our opinion time alone can bring some improvement to the disrupted personality of this young man.

Case 4. A European policeman in a depressed state meets while under hospital treatment one of his victims, an Algerian patriot who is suffering from stupor.

A—, twenty-eight years old, no children. We learnt that for several years both he and his wife underwent treatment, unfortunately with no success, in order to have children. He was sent to us by his superiors because he had behaviour disturbances.

Immediate contact seemed fairly good. The patient spoke

* After considering the medico-legal experts' report which emphasized the pathological character of the action, the legal proceedings which had been set in motion by the General Staff were closed.

to us spontaneously about his difficulties. Satisfactory relations with his wife and parents-in-law. His trouble was that at night he heard screams which prevented him from sleeping. In fact, he told us that for the last few weeks before going to bed he shut the shutters and stopped up all the windows (it was summer) to the complete despair of his wife who was stifled by the heat. Moreover, he stuffed his ears with cottonwool in order to make the screams seem less piercing. He sometimes even in the middle of the night turned on the wireless or put on some music in order not to hear his nocturnal uproar. He consequently explained to us at full length the whole story that was troubling him.

A few months before, he had been transferred to an anti-F.L.N. brigade. At the beginning, he was entrusted with surveying certain shops or cafés; but after some weeks he used to work almost exclusively at the police headquarters. Here he came to deal with interrogations; and these never occurred without some 'knocking about'. 'The thing was that they never would own up to anything.'

Sometimes we almost wanted to tell them that if they had a bit of consideration for us they'd speak out without forcing us to spend hours tearing information word by word out of them. But you might as well talk to the wall. To all the questions we asked they'd only say 'I don't know.' Even when we asked them what their name was. If we asked them where they lived, they'd say 'I don't know.' So of course, we have to go through with it. But they scream too much. At the beginning that made me laugh. But afterwards I was a bit shaken. Nowadays as soon as I hear someone shouting I can tell you exactly at what stage of the questioning we've got to. The chap who's had two blows of the fist and a belt of the baton behind his ear has a certain way of speaking, of shouting and of saying he's innocent. After he's been left two hours strung up by the wrists he has another kind of voice. After the bath, still another. And so on. But above all it's after the electricity that it becomes really too much. You'd say that the chap was going to die any minute. Of course there are some that don't scream; those are the tough ones. But they think they're going to be killed right away. But we're not interested in killing them. What we want is information. When we're dealing with those tough ones, the first thing we do is to make them squeal; and sooner or later we manage it. That's already a victory. Afterwards we go on. Mind you, we'd like to avoid that. But they don't make things easy for us. Now I've come so as I hear their screams even when I'm at home. Especially the screams of the ones who died at the police headquarters. Doctor, I'm fed up with this job. And if you manage to cure me, I'll ask to be transferred to France. If they refuse, I'll resign.

Faced with such a picture, I prescribed sick leave. As the patient in question refused to go to hospital, I treated him privately. One day, shortly before the therapeutic treatment was due to begin, I had an urgent call from my department. When A— reached my house, my wife asked him to wait for me, but he preferred to go for a walk in the hospital grounds, and then come back to meet me. A few minutes later as I was going home I passed him on the way. He was leaning against a tree, looking overcome, trembling and drenched with sweat: in fact having an anxiety crisis. I took him into my car and drove him to my house. Once lying on the sofa, he told me he had met in the hospital one of my patients who had been questioned in the police barracks (he was an Algerian patriot) and who was under treatment for 'disorders of a stuporous nature following on shock'. I then learnt that the policeman had taken an active part in inflicting torture on my patient. I administered some sedatives which calmed A—'s anxiety. After he had gone, I went to the house in the hospital where the patriot was being cared for. The personnel had noticed nothing; but the patient could not be found. Finally we managed to discover him in a toilet where he was trying to commit suicide: he on his side had recognized the policeman and thought that he had come to look for him and take him back again to the barracks.

Afterwards, A— came back to see me several times, and after a very definite improvement in his condition, managed to get back to France on account of his health. As for the Algerian patriot, the personnel spent a long time convincing him that the whole thing was an illusion, that policemen were not allowed inside the hospital, that he was very tired, that he was there to be looked after, etc.

Case 5. A European police inspector who tortured his wife and children.

R—, thirty years old. Came of his own accord to consult us. He was a police inspector and stated that for several weeks 'things weren't working out'. Married, had three children. He smoked a lot: five packets of cigarettes a day. He had lost his appetite and his sleep was frequently disturbed by nightmares. These nightmares had no special distinguishing features. What bothered him most were what he called 'fits of madness'. In the first place, he disliked being contradicted:

Can you give me an explanation for this, doctor: as soon as someone goes against me I want to hit him. Even outside my job, I feel I want to settle the fellows who get in my way, even for nothing at all. Look here, for example, suppose I go to the kiosk to buy papers. There's a lot of people. Of course you have to wait. I hold out my hand (the chap who keeps the kiosk is a pal of mine) to take my papers. Someone in the queue gives me a challenging look and says 'Wait your turn.' Well, I feel I want to beat him up and I say to myself, 'If I had you for a few hours my fine fellow you wouldn't look so clever afterwards.'

The patient dislikes noise. At home he wants to hit everybody all the time. In fact, he does hit his children, even the baby of twenty months, with unaccustomed savagery.

But what really frightened him was one evening when his wife had criticized him particularly for hitting his children too much. (She had even said to him 'My word, anyone'd think you were going mad.') He threw himself upon her, beat her and tied her to a chair, saying to himself 'I'll teach her once and for all that I'm master in this house.'

Fortunately his children began roaring and crying. He then realized the full gravity of his behaviour, untied his wife and the next day decided to consult a doctor, 'a nerve specialist'. He stated that 'before, he wasn't like that'; he said that he very rarely punished his children and at all events never fought with his wife. The present phenomena had appeared 'since the troubles'. 'The fact is,' he said, 'nowadays we have to work like troopers. Last week, for example, we operated like as if we belonged to the army. Those gentlemen in the government say there's no war in Algeria and that the arm of the law, that's to say the police, ought to restore order. But there *is* a war going on in Algeria, and when they wake up to it it'll be too late. The thing that kills me most is the torture. You don't know what that is, do you? Sometimes I torture people for ten hours at a stretch . . .'

'What happens to you when you are torturing?'

You may not realize, but it's very tiring. . . . It's true we take it in turns, but the question is to know when to let the next chap have a go. Each one thinks he's going to get the information at any minute and takes good care not to let the bird go to the next chap after he's softened him up nicely, when of course the other chap would get the honour and glory of it. So sometimes we let them go; and sometimes we don't.

Sometimes we even offer the chap money, money out of our own pockets, to try to get him to talk. Our problem is as follows: are you able to make this fellow talk? It's a question of personal success. You see, you're competing with the others. In the end your fists are ruined. So you call in the Senegalese. But either they hit too hard and destroy the creature or else they don't hit hard enough and it's no good. In fact, you have to be intelligent to make a success of that sort of work. You have to know when to lay it on and when to lay it off. You have to have a flair for it. When the chap is softened up, it's not worth your while going on hitting him. That's why you have to do the work yourself; you can judge better how you're getting on. I'm against the ones that have the chap dealt with by others and simply come to see every hour or so what state he's in. Above all, what you mustn't do is to give the chap the impression that he won't get away alive from you. Because then he wonders what's the use of talking if that won't save his life. In that case you'll have no chance at all of getting anything out of him. He must go on hoping; hope's the thing that'll make him talk.

But the thing that worries me most is this affair with my wife. It's certain that there's something wrong with me. You've got to cure me, doctor.

His superiors refused to give him sick leave, and since moreover the patient did not wish to have a psychiatrist's certificate, we tried to give him treatment 'while working full-time'. The weaknesses of such a procedure may easily be imagined. This man knew perfectly well that his disorders were directly caused by the kind of activity that went on inside the rooms where interrogations were carried out, even though he tried to throw the responsibility totally upon 'present troubles'. As he could not see his way to stopping torturing people (that made nonsense to him for in that case he would have to resign) he asked me without beating about the bush to help him to go on torturing Algerian patriots without any prickings of conscience, without any behaviour problems and with complete equanimity.*

SERIES B

We have here brought together certain cases or groups of cases in which the event giving rise to the illness is in the first place the atmosphere of total war which reigns in Algeria.

Case 1. The murder by two young Algerians thirteen and fourteen years old respectively of their European playmate.

We had been asked to give expert medical advice in a legal matter. Two young Algerians thirteen and fourteen years old, pupils in a primary school, were accused of having killed one of their European schoolmates. They admitted having done it. The crime was reconstructed, and photos were added to the record. Here one of the children could be seen holding the victim while the other struck at him with a knife. The little defendants did not go back on their declarations. We had long conversations with them. We here reproduce the most characteristic of their remarks:

(*a*) The boy thirteen years old:

'We weren't a bit cross with him. Every Thursday we used to go and play with catapults together, on the hill above the village. He was a good friend of ours. He usen't to go to school any more because he wanted to be a mason like his father. One day we decided to kill him, because the Europeans want to kill all the Arabs. We can't kill big people. But we could

---

* With these observations we find ourselves in the presence of a coherent system which leaves nothing intact. The executioner who loves birds and enjoys the peace of listening to a symphony or a sonata is simply one stage in the process. Farther on in it we may well find a whole existence which enters into complete and absolute sadism.

kill ones like him, because he was the same age as us. We didn't know how to kill him. We wanted to throw him into a ditch, but he'd only have been hurt. So we got the knife at home and we killed him.'

'But why did you pick on him?'

'Because he used to play with us. Another boy wouldn't have gone up the hill with us.'

'And yet you were pals?'

'Well then, why do they want to kill us? His father is in the militia and he said we ought to have our throats cut.'

'But he didn't say anything to you?'

'Him? No.'

'You know he is dead now.'

'Yes.'

'What does being dead mean?'

'When it's all finished, you go to heaven.'

'Was it you that killed him?'

'Yes.'

'Does having killed somebody worry you?'

'No, since they want to kill us, so . . .'

'Do you mind being in prison?'

'No.'

(b) The boy fourteen years old.

This young defendant was in marked contrast with his school-fellow. He was already almost a man, and an adult in his muscular control, his appearance and the content of his replies. He did not deny having killed either. Why had he killed? He did not reply to the question but asked me had I ever seen a European in prison. Had there ever been a European arrested and sent to prison after the murder of an Algerian? I replied that in fact I had never seen any Europeans in prison.

'And yet there are Algerians killed every day, aren't there?'

'Yes.'

'So why are only Algerians found in the prisons? Can you explain that to me?'

'No. But tell me why you killed this boy who was your friend.'

'I'll tell you why. You've heard tell of the Rivet business?'*

'Yes.'

'Two of my family were killed then. At home, they said that the French had sworn to kill us all, one after the other. And did they arrest a single Frenchman for all those Algerians who were killed?'

'I don't know.'

'Well, nobody at all was arrested. I wanted to take to the mountains, but I was too young. So X— and I said we'd kill a European.'

'Why?'

'In your opinion, what should we have done?'

'I don't know. But you are a child and what is happening concerns grown-up people.'

'But they kill children too. . . .'

'That is no reason for killing your friend.'

'Well, kill him I did. Now you can do what you like.'

'Had your friend done anything to harm you?'

'Not a thing.'

'Well?'

'Well, there you are. . . .'

Case 2. Accusatory delirium and suicidal conduct disguised as 'terrorist activity' in a young Algerian twenty-two years old.

This patient was sent to our hospital by the French judicial authorities. This measure was taken after medical and legal advice given by French psychiatrists practising in Algeria.

The patient was an emaciated man in a complete state of aberration. His body was covered with bruises and two fractures of the jaw made all absorption of nourishment impossible. Thus for more than two weeks the patient was fed by various injections.

After two weeks, the blank in his thoughts receded; we

* Rivet is a village which since a certain day in the year 1956 has become celebrated in the region around Algiers. For on that evening the village was invaded by the militia who dragged forty men from their beds and afterwards murdered them.

were able to establish contact and we managed to reconstruct the dramatic history of this young man.

During his youth he went in for scouting with unusual enthusiasm. He became one of the main leaders of the Moslem Scout Movement. But at nineteen years old he dropped scouting completely in order to have no preoccupation other than his profession. He was a multicopying-machine maker; he studied hard and dreamt of becoming a great specialist in his profession. The first of November 1954 found him absorbed by strictly professional problems. At the time he showed no interest at all in the national struggle. Already he no longer frequented the company of his former companions. He himself defined himself at that time as 'completely bent on increasing his technical capacity'.

However, about the middle of 1955, when spending the evening with his family, he suddenly had the impression that his parents considered him as a traitor. After a few days this fleeting impression became blunted but at the back of his mind a certain misgiving persisted, a sort of uneasiness that he did not understand.

On account of this, he decided to eat his meals quickly, shrinking from the family circle, and shut himself into his room, He avoided all contacts. It was in these conditions that catas-trophe intervened. One day, in the middle of the street at about half past twelve he distinctly heard a voice calling him a coward. He turned round, but saw nobody. He quickened his pace, and decided that from henceforward he would not go to work. He stayed in his room and did not eat any dinner. During the night the crisis came on. For three hours he heard all sorts of insults coming from out of the night and resounding in his head: 'Traitor, traitor, coward . . . all your brothers who are dying . . . traitor, traitor. . . .'

He was seized with indescribable anxiety: 'For eighteen hours my heart beat at the rhythm of 130 pulsations to the minute. I thought I was going to die.'

From that time on, the patient could no longer swallow a bite. He wasted away almost visibly; he shut himself up in complete darkness, and refused to open the door to his parents. Around the third day he took refuge in prayer. He stayed kneeling, he told me, from seventeen to eighteen hours on end each day. On the fourth day, acting on impulse 'like a madman', with 'a beard that was also enough to make him be taken for a madman', wearing neither coat nor tie, he went out into the town. Once in the street, he did not know where to go; but he started walking, and at the end of some time he found himself in the European town. His physical appearance (he looked like a European) seemed then to safeguard him against being stopped and questioned by the police patrols.

As a contrast to this, beside him Algerian men and women were arrested, maltreated, insulted and searched. Paradoxically, he had no papers on him. This uncalled-for consideration towards him on the part of the enemy patrols confirmed his delusion that 'everybody knew he was with the French. Even the soldiers had their orders; they left him alone.'

In addition, the glances of the arrested Algerians, who were waiting to be searched with their hands behind their necks, seemed to him to be full of contempt. The prey of overwhelming agitation, he moved away, striding rapidly. It was at this moment that he happened to walk in front of the building which was the French Staff Headquarters. In the gateway stood several soldiers armed with machine-guns. He went towards the soldiers, threw himself upon one of them and tried to snatch his machine-gun shouting 'I am an Algerian.'

He was quickly overcome and was brought to the police where they insisted on making him confess the names of his 'superiors' and the different members of the network to which he (supposedly) belonged. After some days the police and the soldiers realized that they were dealing with a sick man. An expert opinion was sought which concluded that he was suffering from mental disorders and that he should be sent to hospital. 'All I wanted to do,' he said, 'was to die. Even at the police barracks I thought and hoped that after they'd tortured me they would kill me. I was glad to be struck, for that showed me that they considered that I too was their enemy. I could no longer go on hearing those accusing voices without doing something. I am not a coward. I am not a woman. I am not a traitor.' *

* During the year 1955, cases of this type were very numerous in Algeria. Unfortunately not all the patients had the good fortune to be sent to hospital.

Case 3. Neurotic attitude of a young Frenchwoman whose father, a highly placed civil servant, was killed in an ambush.

This girl, twenty-one years old, a student, came to consult me about certain minor symptoms of anxiety complex which interfered with her studies and with her social relationships. Her hands were constantly moist and at times presented very worrying symptoms when sweat 'flowed all over her hands'. Constrictions of the chest accompanied by nocturnal headaches. Bit her nails. But the thing that was most apparent was above all the over-easy contact, obviously too rapid, while a severe anxiety could be clearly sensed underlying the facile approach. The death of her father, though judging from the date fairly recent, was mentioned by the patient with such lightheartedness that we quickly directed our investigations towards her relations with her father. The account which she gave us was clear, completely lucid, with a lucidity which touched on insensibility and later revealed, precisely by its rationalism, this girl's uneasiness and the nature and origin of her conflict.

My father was highly placed in the civil service. He was responsible for a very large rural area. As soon as the troubles started, he threw himself into the Algerian man-hunt with frenzied rage. Sometimes it happened that he would eat nothing at all, and not even sleep, he was in such a state of excitement over putting down the rebellion. I saw without being able to do anything about it the slow metamorphosis of my father. Finally, I decided not to go to see him any more and to stay in town. The fact was that every time I went home I spent entire nights awake, for screams used to rise up in my room from down below; in the cellar and in the unused rooms of the house Algerians were being tortured so as to obtain information. You have no idea how terrible it is to hear screaming all night like that. Sometimes I used to wonder how it was that a human being was able to bear hearing those screams of pain – quite apart from the actual torture. And so it went on. Finally, I didn't ever go home. The rare times that my father came to see me in town I wasn't able to look him in the face without being terribly frightened and embarrassed. I found it increasingly difficult to force myself to kiss him.

For you must understand that I had lived a long time in the village. I knew almost all the families that lived there. The Algerian boys of my age and I had played together when we were small. Every time I went home my father told me that fresh people had been arrested. In the end I didn't dare walk in the street any more. I was so sure of meeting hatred everywhere. In my heart I knew that those Algerians were right. If I were an Algerian girl, I'd be in the Maquis.

One day, however, she received a telegram which announced that her father was seriously injured. She went to the hospital and found her father in a coma. Shortly afterwards he died. He had been wounded while on a reconnoitring expedition with a military detachment; the patrol fell into an ambush laid by the Algerian National Army.

The funeral sickened me [she said]. All those officials who came to weep over the death of my father whose 'high moral qualities conquered the native population' disgusted me. Everyone knew that it was false. There wasn't a single person who didn't know that my father had the whip-hand of all the interrogation centres in the whole region. Everyone knew that the number of deaths under torture reached ten a day, and there they came to tell their lies about my father's devotion, his self-sacrifice, his love for his country, and so on. I ought to say that now such words have no meaning for me, or at any rate hardly any. I went back to the town directly afterwards, and I avoided all the authorities. They offered me an allowance but I refused it. I don't want their money. It is the price of the blood spilt by my father. I don't want any of it. I am going to work.

Case 4. Behaviour disturbances in young Algerians of under ten.

These children were refugees, the children of fighting men or of civilians killed by the French. They were sent to various different centres in Tunisia and Morocco. These children were sent to school, and games and outings were organized for them. They were examined regularly by doctors; that is how we came to have occasion to see some of them.

(*a*) In each of these different children there exists a very marked love for parental images. Everything which resembles a father or a mother is sought out with the greatest tenacity and jealously guarded.

(*b*) Generally speaking, they all have a noise phobia which is very noticeable. These children are very much affected when they are scolded. They have a great thirst for peace and for affection.

(*c*) Many of them suffer from sleeplessness and also from sleep-walking.

(*d*) Periodical enuresis.

(*e*) Sadistic tendencies. A game that is often played is to stretch a sheet of paper and feverishly poke holes in it. All their pencils are chewed and their nails bitten with distressing regularity. They quarrel frequently among themselves despite a deep fundamental affection.

Case 5. Puerperal psychoses among the refugees.

The name *puerperal psychoses* is given to mental disorders which occur in women around childbirth. Such disorders may appear immediately before or some weeks after giving birth. The determinism of such illnesses is very complex; but it is considered that the principal causes are the upsetting of the functioning of the endocrine glands and the existence of an 'affective shock'. The latter heading, though vague, covers what most people refer to as 'violent emotion'.

On the Moroccan and Tunisian frontiers there are to be found something like 300,000 refugees since the decision of the French government to practise their burnt-earth policy over hundreds of kilometres. The destitution in which they exist is well known. International Red Cross committees have repeatedly paid visits to these places and after having observed the extreme poverty and precariousness of living conditions there have recommended increased aid to these refugees from international organizations. It was thus only to be expected, considering the under-nourishment which is rife in these camps, that pregnant women there should show particular propensities for the development of puerperal psychoses.

The atmosphere of permanent insecurity in which the refugees exist is kept up by frequent invasions of French troops applying 'the right of following and pursuit', bombardments from the air, machine-gunnings – it is well known that no further attention is now paid to bombardments of Moroccan and Tunisian territories by the French army, of which Sakiet-Sidi-Youssef, the martyred village in Tunisia, was the most appalling – together with the break-up of homes which is a consequence of the conditions of the evacuation. To tell the truth there are very few Algerian women who give birth in such conditions who do not suffer from mental disorders.

These disorders take various forms. Sometimes they are visible as states of agitation which sometimes turn into rages; sometimes deep depressions and tonic immobility with many attempted suicides; or sometimes finally anxiety states with tears, lamentations and appeals for mercy. In the same way the form which the delusions take are many and diverse. We may find a delusion of persecution against the French who want to kill the new-born infant or the child not yet born; or else the mother may have the impression of imminent death, in which the mothers implore invisible executioners to spare their child.

Here once more we must point out that the fundamental nature of these problems is not cleared up by the regression and soothing of the disorders. The circumstances of the cured patients maintains and feeds these pathological kinks.

SERIES C

Affective-intellectual modifications and mental disorders after torture

In this series we will group together patients in a fairly serious condition whose disorders appeared immediately after or during the tortures. We shall describe various different groups in this category, because we realize that the characteristic morbidity groups correspond to different methods of torture employed, quite independently of its evil effects, whether glaring or hidden, upon the personality.

Category 1. After so-called preventive tortures of an indiscriminate nature

We here refer to brutal methods which are directed towards getting prisoners to speak rather than to actual torture. The principle that over and above a certain threshold pain becomes intolerable takes on here singular importance. The aim is to arrive as quickly as possible at that threshold. There is no finicking about. There is a mass attack taking several forms: several policemen striking the prisoner at the same time; four policemen standing around the prisoner and hitting him backwards and forwards to each other, while another burns his chest with a cigarette and still another hits the soles of his feet with a stick. Certain methods of torture used in Algeria seemed to us to be particularly atrocious; the confidences of those who had been tortured are our reference.

(*a*) Injection of water by the mouth accompanied by an enema of soapy water given at high pressure.*

(*b*) Introduction of a bottle into the anus.

Two forms of torture called 'motionless torture':

(*c*) The prisoner is placed on his knees, with his arms parallel to the ground, the palms of his hands turned upwards, his torso and head straight. No movement is allowed. Behind the prisoner a policeman sitting on a chair keeps him motionless by blows of his truncheon.

(*d*) The prisoner is placed standing with his face to the wall, his arms lifted and his hands against the wall. Here too if he makes the slightest movement or shows the slightest sign of relaxing the blows rain down.

We must now point out that there are two categories of people who undergo torture:

(*a*) Those who know something.

(*b*) Those who know nothing.

(*a*) Those who know something are very rarely seen in hospital-centres. Evidently, it may be common knowledge that such-and-such a patriot has been tortured in the French prisons, but you never meet him as a patient.†

(*b*) On the contrary, those who know nothing come very frequently to consult us. We are not here speaking of Algerians taken prisoner during a general arrestation or a round-up: they

---

* This type of torture is the cause of a very large number of deaths. After these enemas given at high pressure, the mucous membrane of the intestine becomes in fact the seat of numerous lesions which provoke minute perforations of the intestine. Gaseous embolisms and cases of peritonitis are thus very frequently caused.

† We are here speaking of course of those Algerians who, knowing something, have not confessed under torture; for it is well known that an Algerian who confesses is killed immediately afterwards.

do not come to see us as patients either. We are speaking expressly of those Algerians who do not belong to any organization, who are arrested and brought to police quarters or to farms used as centres of interrogation in order to be tortured there.

SYMPTOMS OF PSYCHIATRIC CASES ENCOUNTERED.
(*a*) Agitated nervous depressions: four cases.

These are patients who are sad, without really being anxious. They are depressed and spend most of their time in bed; they shun contact, and are liable suddenly to show signs of very violent agitation the significance of which is always difficult to grasp.

(*b*) Loss of appetite arising from mental causes: five cases.

These patients present serious problems, for every mental anorexia is accompanied by a phobia against all physical contact with another. The nurse who comes near the patient and tries to touch him, to take his hand, for example, is at once pushed stiffly away. It is not possible to carry out artificial feeding or to administer medicine.*

(*c*) Motor instability: eleven cases.

Here we have to deal with patients who will not keep still. They insist on being alone and it is difficult to get them to allow themselves to be shut up with the doctor in his consulting-room.

Two feelings seemed to us to be frequent in the first category of tortured people:

First that of suffering *injustice*. Being tortured night and day for nothing seemed to have broken something in these men. One of these sufferers had a particularly painful experience. After some days of useless torturing, the police came to realize that they were dealing with a peaceable man who knew nothing whatever about anybody in an F.L.N. network. In spite of being convinced of this, a police inspector had said: 'Don't let him go like that. Give him a bit more, so that when he gets out he'll keep quiet.'†

---

* The medical attendants are obliged to sit by the patient night and day working to explain matters to him. We can understand that the formula of 'treating him a bit rough' is of no possible value here.

† This preventive torture becomes in certain districts 'preventive repression'. Thus at Rivet, though peace reigned, the settlers did not want to be

Secondly, there was *indifference to all moral arguments*. For these patients, there is no just cause. A cause which entrains torture is a weak cause. Therefore the fighting strength of the cause must at all costs be increased; its justness must not be questioned. Force is the only thing that counts.

Category 2. After tortures by electricity.

In this category we have placed the Algerian patriots who were mainly tortured by electricity. In fact, although before electricity was used as one of the general methods of torture, from September 1956 on certain questionings were carried on exclusively by electricity.

DESCRIPTIONS OF PSYCHIATRIC CASES ENCOUNTERED.
(*a*) Localized or generalized cenesthopathies: three cases.

These patients felt 'pins and needles' throughout their bodies; their hands seemed to be torn off, their heads seemed to be bursting, and their tongues felt as if they were being swallowed.

(*b*) Apathy, aboulia, and lack of interest: seven cases.

These are patients who are inert, who cannot make plans, who have no resources, who live from day to day.

(*c*) Electricity phobia.

Fear of touching a switch, of turning on the radio, fear of the telephone. Completely impossible for the doctor to even mention the eventual possibility of electric shock treatment.

Category 3. After the 'truth serum'.

The basic principles of this treatment are well known. When dealing with a patient who seems to suffer from an unconscious inner conflict which consultations do not manage to exteriorize, the doctor has recourse to chemical methods of exploration. Pentothal, given by intra-venous injections, is the most common

---

taken unawares (the neighbouring districts were beginning to stir) and decided purely and simply to do away with all potential members of the F.L.N. Over forty Algerians were killed in a single day.

serum used to liberate the patient of a conflict which seems to go beyond his powers of adaptation. The doctor intervenes in order to liberate the patient from this 'foreign body'.*

It has been generally observed that it is difficult to control the progressive disintegration of psychical processes when using this method. Very often a spectacular worsening of the illness was observed, or new and quite inexplicable symptoms appeared. Thus, generally speaking, this technique has been more or less abandoned.

In Algeria, military doctors and psychiatrists have found a wide field for experiment in police quarters. For if in cases of neurosis pentothal sweeps away the barriers which bar the way to bringing to light an interior conflict, it ought equally in the case of Algerian patriots to serve to break down the political barrier and make confession easier for the prisoner without having recourse to electricity; medical tradition lays down that suffering should be avoided. This is the medical form that 'subversive war' takes.

The scenario is as follows. First, 'I am a doctor, I am not a policeman. I am here to help you.' In this way after a few days the confidence of the prisoner is won.†

After that, 'I'm going to give you a few injections, for you're badly shaken'. For a few days, treatment of any kind at all is given – vitamins, treatment for heart disease, sugar serums. On the fourth or fifth day the intra-venous injection of pentothal is given. The interrogation begins.

---

* In fact, it is not 'foreign' at all. A conflict is only the result of the dynamic evolution of the personality, and here there can be no 'foreign body'. We ought rather to say that the problem is one of a 'badly integrated body'.

† We can cite in the same way the case of psychiatrists who were prime movers in '*Présence française*' who when they were told off to give an expert opinion on a prisoner had the habit from the very first of proclaiming their great friendship with the defending lawyer, and of assuring the prisoner that the two of them (the barrister and the psychiatrist) would get him out of there. All the prisoners who had the benefit of expert opinions were guillotined. These psychiatrists boasted in front of us of their elegant method of over-coming 'resistance'.

PSYCHIATRIC SYMPTOMS.

(*a*) Verbal stereotypy:

The patient continually repeats sentences of the type of 'I didn't tell them anything. You must believe me; I didn't talk.' Such stereotypies are accompanied by a permanent anxiety state. In fact the patient does not even know whether he has given any information away. The sense of culpability towards the cause he was fighting for and his brothers in arms whose names and addresses he may have given here weighs so heavily as to be dramatic. No assurance can bring peace to these broken consciences.

(*b*) Intellectual or sensory perception clouded.

The patient cannot affirm the existence of a given visible object. Reasoning is assimilated but in undifferentiated fashion. There is a fundamental inability to distinguish between true and false. Everything is true and everything is false at the same time.

(*c*) Fear amounting to phobia of all private conversations.

This fear is derived from the acute impression that at any moment a fresh interrogation may take place.

(*d*) Inhibition.

The patient is on his guard; he registers each word of the question that is put to him and elaborates every word of his projected reply. From this comes the impression of a quasi-inhibition, with psychical slowing down, interrupted sentences, repetition and faltering, etc.

It is obvious that these patients obstinately refuse all intravenous injections.

Category 4. After brain-washing

Much has been said recently about 'psychological action' in Algeria. We do not wish to proceed to a critical study of these methods. We are content to bring to mind here their psychiatric consequences. There are two categories of centres where torture by brain-washing is carried on in Algeria.

I. FOR INTELLECTUALS.

The principle here is to lead the prisoner on to play a part. We can see that this is a throw-back to a particular school of psycho-sociology.*

(*a*) Playing the game of collaboration.

The intellectual is invited to collaborate and at the same time reasons for collaboration are brought forward. He is thus obliged to lead a double life: he is a man well-known for his patriotism who is imprisoned for preventive reasons. The task undertaken is to attack from the inside those elements which constitute national consciousness. Not only is the intellectual in question expected to collaborate, but he is given orders to discuss matters 'freely' with those opposed to his viewpoint or those who hold back, and to convince them. This is an elegant way of bringing him to focus attention on other patriots, and thus to serve as informer. If by chance he says that he cannot find any opponents, these latter are pointed out to him, or else he is told to behave as if he was dealing with such.

(*b*) Making public statements on the value of the French heritage and on the merits of colonization.

In order to carry out this task as well as possible, the intellectual is surrounded by 'political advisers': officers for Native Affairs, or better still psychologists, social psychiatrists, sociologists, etc.

(*c*) Taking the arguments for the Algerian Revolution and overthrowing them one by one.

Algeria is not a nation; it has never been a nation; it will never be a nation.

* We know that in the United States of America a trend towards psycho-sociology has developed. Supporters of this school think that the tragedy of the contemporary individual is contained in the fact that he has no longer any part to play, and that present-day social conditions force him to exist only as a cog in the machine. From this comes the proposal of a therapeutic which will allow a man to take various roles in a veritable game of activity. Anyone can play any role; it even happens that in a single day a person's role may be changed; symbolically you may put yourself in the place of anyone you please. The factory psychiatrists in the United States are, it seems, making huge strides in group psychotherapy among workers. The latter are in fact enabled to identify themselves with heroes. Strained relations between employers and workers are considerably diminished.

There is no such thing as the 'Algerian people'.

Algerian patriotism is nonsense.

The *fellaghas* are ambitious peasants, criminals and poor mistaken creatures.

Taking each theme in turn, the intellectual is expected to make a reasoned statement on it, and the statement must be convincing. Marks (the well-known 'rewards') are given and counted up at the end of every month. They serve as a means of deciding whether or not the intellectual will be allowed out.

(*d*) Leading a totally pathological communal life.

To be alone is an act of rebellion: so the intellectual is always with somebody. Silence is also forbidden; thinking must be done aloud.

Evidence of brain-washing. The case was that of a person with a university education who was interned and subjected to brain-washing which lasted for months on end. One day the camp officials congratulated him on the progress he had made and announced that he would soon be set free.

He knew about the enemy's manoeuvres, and took care not to take this news too seriously. Their technique is in fact to announce to the prisoners that they are going to be freed, and then a few days before the date fixed to organize a meeting at which collective criticisms are made. At the end of the meeting the decision is often taken to postpone setting the prisoner free, since he does not seem to present all the signs of a definitive cure. The meeting, say those psychologists who were present at it, has served to draw attention to the nationalistic virus.

However this time there was no subterfuge. The prisoner was freed for good and all. Once outside, in his own town and with his own family, the former prisoner congratulated himself on having played his part so well. He rejoiced that he was able to take his place once again in the national conflict and already began to establish contact with his leaders. It was at that moment that a terrible, burning doubt flashed through his mind. Perhaps he had never deceived anybody – neither his jailors, nor his fellow-prisoners, nor even himself.

Where would the game end?

Here once again we had to reassure the patient, and to free him from the burden of guilt.

Psychiatric Symptoms Encountered. (*a*) Phobia of all collective discussion. As soon as three or four people came together, the inhibition made its appearance again, and mistrust and reticence weighed heavily upon those present.

(*b*) The impossibility of explaining and defending any given position. Thought proceeds by antithetic couplings. Everything that is affirmed can, at the same instant, be denied with the same force. This is certainly the most painful sequel that we encountered in this war. An obsessional personality is the fruit of the 'psychological action' used in the service of colonialism in Algeria.

II. FOR NON-INTELLECTUALS.

In such centres as that of Berrouaghia, subjectivity is not taken as the starting-point for modifying the attitude of the individual. On the contrary, the body is dealt with: it is broken in the hope that national consciousness will thus be demolished. It is a thorough breaking-in. 'Rewards' are taken to mean the absence of torture or the possibility of getting food to eat.

(*a*) You must declare that you do not belong to the F.L.N. You must shout this out in groups. You must repeat it for hours on end.

(*b*) After that, you must recognize that you were once in the F.L.N. and that you have come to realize that it was a bad thing. Thus, down with the F.L.N.

After this stage, we come to another: the future of Algeria is French; it can be no other than French.

Without France, Algeria will go back to the Middle Ages.

Finally, you are French. Long live France.

Here, the disorders met with are not serious. It is the painful, suffering body that calls for rest and peace.

Psycho-somatic disorders

A marked increase in mental disorders and the creation of conditions favourable to the development of specific morbid phenomena are not the only consequences of the colonial war in Algeria. Quite apart from the pathology of torture there flourishes in Algeria a pathology of atmosphere, a state which leads medical practitioners to say when confronted with a case which they cannot understand: 'This'll all be cleared up when this damned war is over.'

We propose to group together in this fourth series the illnesses met with among Algerians, some of whom were interned in concentration camps. The main characteristic of these illnesses is that they are of the psycho-somatic type.

The name 'psycho-somatic pathology' is given to the general body of organic disorders the development of which is favoured by a conflicting situation.*

The name psycho-somatic is used because the determinism is psychic in origin. This pathology is considered as a means whereby the organism responds to, in other words adapts itself to the conflict it is faced with, the disorder being at the same time a symptom and a cure. More precisely, it is generally conceded that the organism (once again we are speaking of the cortico-visceral unity, the psycho-somatic unity of former times) resolves the conflict by unsatisfactory, but on the whole economical means. The organism in fact chooses the lesser evil in order to avoid catastrophe.

On the whole, this pathology is very well known today, although the different therapeutic methods proposed (relaxation and suggestion, for example) seem to us very uncertain. In the Second World War in England during the air-raids and in the Soviet Union among the besieged populations of towns, notably in Stalingrad, there was a great increase in reports of the occur-

* This nomenclature which expresses an idealist conception is less and less frequently used. In fact the terminology 'cortico-visceral' inherited from Soviet research work – especially that of Pavlov – has at least the advantage that it puts the brain back in its place, that is to say it considers the brain as the matrix where, precisely, the psychism is elaborated.

rence of such disorders. Today, we know very well that it is not necessary to be wounded by a bullet in order to suffer from the fact of war in body as well as in mind. Like all other wars, the Algerian war has created its contingent of cortico-visceral illnesses. With the exception of Group G described below, all the disorders met with in Algeria have already been described during the course of 'traditional' wars. Group G seems to us to be specific to the colonial war in Algeria. This particular form of pathology (a generalized muscular contraction) had already called forth attention before the Revolution began. But the doctors described it by portraying it as a congenital stigma of the native, an 'original' part of his nervous system where, it was stated, it was possible to find the proof of a pre-dominance of the extra-pyramidal system in the native.* This contracture is in fact simply the postural accompaniment to the native's reticence, the expression in muscular form of his rigidity and his refusal with regard to colonial authority.

PSYCHIATRIC SYMPTOMS ENCOUNTERED.

(*a*) Stomach ulcers. Very numerous. The pains are felt pre-dominantly at night, with considerable vomiting, loss of weight, sadness and moroseness, and irritability in exceptional cases. It should be noted that the majority of these patients are very young: from eighteen to twenty-five years old. As a general rule, we never advise surgical intervention. A gastrectomy was per-formed on two occasions, and in these two same cases a second intervention was necessary in the same year as the first.

(*b*) Nephritic colic.

Here again we find pains which came on intensely at night. Obviously, stones are hardly ever present. These colics may occur, though rarely, in patients of fourteen to sixteen years old.

(*c*) Menstruation trouble in women.

This pathology is very well known, and we shall not spend much time on it. Either the women affected remain three or four months without menstruation, or else considerable pain accompanies it, which has repercussions on character and conduct.

* The higher a person is on the neurological plane, the less he is extra-pyramidal. As we see, everything tallies.

(*d*) Intense sleeplessness caused by idiopathic tremors.

The patients are young adults, to whom all rest is denied because of a generalized slight shaking, reminiscent of a total case of Parkinson's disease. Here, too, 'scientific thinkers' could invoke an extra-pyramidal determinism.

(*e*) Hair turning white early.

Among the survivors of the interrogation centres, the hair often turns white suddenly, either in patches, in certain areas, or totally. Very often this is accompanied by serious debility and sexual impotence.

(*f*) Paroxysmal tachycardias.

The cardiac rhythm accelerates abruptly: 120, 130 or 140 per minute. These tachycardias are accompanied by anxiety, and by an impression of imminent death; the end of the crisis is marked by a heavy sweating fit.

(*g*) Generalized contraction with muscular stiffness.

These symptoms are found in patients of the masculine sex who find it increasingly difficult (in two cases the appearance of the symptoms was abrupt) to execute certain movements: going upstairs, walking quickly or running. The cause of this difficulty lies in a characteristic rigidity which inevitably reminds us of the impairing of certain regions of the brain (central grey nuclei). It is an extended rigidity and walking is performed with small steps. The passive flexion of the lower limbs is almost impossible. No relaxation can be achieved. The patient seems to be made all of a piece, subjected as he is to a sudden contraction and incapable of the slightest voluntary relaxation. The face is rigid but expresses a marked degree of bewilderment.

The patient does not seem able to 'release his nervous tension'. He is constantly tense, waiting between life and death. Thus one of such patients said to us: 'You see, I'm already stiff like a dead man.' *

Criminal impulses found in North Africans which have their origin in the National War of Liberation.

It is not only necessary to fight for the liberty of your people. You must also teach that people once again, and first learn

* It is hardly necessary to add that there is no question here of hysterical contraction.

once again yourself, what is the full stature of a man; and this you must do for as long as the fight lasts. You must go back into history, that history of men damned by other men; and you must bring about and render possible the meeting of your people and other men.

In reality, the soldier who is engaged in armed combat in a national war deliberately measures from day to day the sum of all degradation inflicted upon many by colonial oppression. The man of action has sometimes the exhausting impression that he must restore the whole of his people, that he must bring every one of them up out of the pit and out of the shadows. He very often sees that his task is not only to hunt down the enemy forces but also to overcome the kernel of despair which has hardened in the native's being. The period of oppression is painful; but the conflict, by reinstating the down-trodden, sets on foot a process of reintegration which is fertile and decisive in the extreme. A people's victorious fight not only consecrates the triumph of its rights; it also gives to that people consistence, coherence and homogeneity. For colonialism has not simply depersonalized the individual it has colonized; this depersonalization is equally felt in the collective sphere, on the level of social structures. The colonized people find that they are reduced to a body of individuals who only find cohesion when in the presence of the colonizing nation.

The fight carried on by a people for its liberation leads it, according to circumstances, either to refuse or else to explode the so-called truths which have been established in its consciousness by the colonial civil administration, by the military occupation, and by economic exploitation. Armed conflict alone can really drive out these falsehoods created in man which force into inferiority the most lively minds among us and which, literally, mutilate us.

How many times – in Paris, in Aix, in Algiers, or in Basse-Terre – have we not heard men from the colonized countries violently protesting against the pretended laziness of the black man, of the Algerian and of the Vietnamese? And yet is it not the simple truth that under the colonial regime a *fellah* who is keen on his work or a Negro who refuses to rest are nothing but pathological cases? The native's laziness is the conscious sabotage of the colonial machine; on the biological plane it is a remarkable system of auto-protection; and in any case it is a sure brake upon the seizure of the whole country by the occupying power.

The resistance that forests and swamps present to foreign penetration is the natural ally of the native. His point of view must be understood; it is time to stop remonstrating and declaring that the nigger is a great worker and that the Arab is first-rate at clearing ground. Under the colonial regime, what is true for the Arab and for the Negro is that they should not lift their little finger nor in the slightest degree help the oppressor to sink his claws deeper into his prey. The duty of the native who has not yet reached maturity in political consciousness and decided to hurl back oppression is literally to make it so that the slightest gesture has to be torn out of him. This is a very concrete manifestation of non-cooperation, or at least of minimum cooperation.

These observations which concern the relations between the native and his work could equally be applied to the respect the native has for the oppressor's laws, to the regular payment of rates and taxes and to the relations which the native has with the colonial system. Under the colonial regime, gratitude, sincerity and honour are empty words. During the last few years I have had occasion to verify a very classical fundamental idea: that honour, dignity and respect for the given word can only manifest themselves in the framework of national and international homogeneity. From the moment that you and your like are liquidated like so many dogs, you have no other resource but to use all and every means to regain your importance as a man. You must therefore weigh as heavily as you can upon the body of your torturer in order that his soul, lost in some by-way, may finally find once more its universal dimension. During these last years I have had occasion to see that in war-time Algeria honour, self-sacrifice, love of life and scorn of death have taken on no ordinary forms. There is no question of singing the praises of those who are fighting. We are concerned here with a very ordinary statement which even the most rabid colonialists have not failed to make: the fighting Algerian has an unusual manner of fighting and dying, and no reference to Islam or to Paradise can explain that generous dedication of self when there is question of defending his people or shielding his brothers. And then there is that overwhelming silence – but of course the body cries out – that silence that overwhelms the torturer. Let us admit that here we find again that very ancient law which forbids any element whatsoever to remain unmoved when the nation has begun to march, when man affirms and claims at the same time his limitless humanity.

Among the characteristics of the Algerian people as observed by colonialism we will particularly notice their appalling criminality. Before 1954 magistrates, policemen, barristers, journalists and legal doctors agreed unanimously that criminality in Algeria was a problem. It was affirmed that the Algerian was a born criminal. A theory was elaborated and scientific proofs were found to support it. This theory was taught in the universities for over twenty years. Algerian medical students received this education and imperceptibly, after accommodating themselves to colonialism, the *élite* came also to accommodate themselves to the inherent stigma of the Algerian people: they were born slackers, born liars, born robbers and born criminals.

We propose here to repeat this official theory, and to recall to mind the concrete bases and the scientific arguments used to create it. Later on we shall go over the facts and try to reinterpret them.

The Algerian frequently kills other men. It is a fact, the magistrates will tell you, that four-fifths of cases brought to court deal with blows and woundings. The proportion of criminality in Algeria is one of the heaviest and largest in the world, or so they affirm. There are no minor delinquencies. When the Algerian, and this applies equally to all North Africans, puts himself outside the law, it is always outside to the maximum.

The Algerian kills savagely. First, the favourite weapon is the knife. The magistrates 'who know the country' have created a minor philosophy on this subject. The Kabyles for example prefer a pistol or a gun. The Arabs of the plain have a preference for the knife. Certain magistrates wonder if the Algerian has not an inner need for the sight of blood. The Algerian, you are told, needs to feel warm blood, and to bathe in the blood of his victim. These magistrates, policemen and doctors hold serious dissertations on the relationship between the Moslem soul and blood.*

A certain number of magistrates go so far as to say that the reason why an Algerian kills a man is primarily and above all in order to slit his throat. The savagery of the Algerian shows itself especially in the number of wounds he inflicts, some of these being unnecessary once the victim has been killed. Autopsies establish one fact incontestably: the murderer gives the impression, by inflicting many wounds of equal deadliness, that he wished to kill an incalculable number of times.

The Algerian kills for no reason. Very frequently magistrates and policemen are nonplussed by the motives of a murder; it may arise out of a gesture, an illusion, an ambiguous statement, a quarrel over an olive-tree which is possessed in common, or an animal which has strayed by an eighth of an acre. Confronted by such a murder, sometimes by a double or triple murder, the looked-for cause and the expected motive which would justify or give grounds for these murders is finally found to be of disappointing triviality. From thence springs the frequent impression that the social group is hiding the real motives.

Finally, robbery as practised by an Algerian is always coupled with house-breaking whether accompanied or not by manslaughter, and in any case with aggression against the owner.

All these elements which cluster around Algerian criminality have appeared to specify its nature sufficiently clearly to enable a tentative systematization to be built up.

Similar though somewhat less weighty observations were made in Tunisia and Morocco; and thus the question shifted more and more on to the ground of North African criminality. For over thirty years, under the constant direction of Professor Porot, professor of psychiatry at the faculty of Algiers, several teams worked with the aim of specifying the forms of expression of this criminality and to establish a sociological, functional and anatomical interpretation for them.

We shall here quote the main works on this subject by the

---

* In fact we know that Islam forbids its followers to eat meat unless they are sure that the animal has been drained of its blood. This is why the animals' throats are cut.

psychiatric school of the faculty of Algiers. The conclusions of the researches carried on for over twenty years were, let us recall to mind, the subject of authoritative lectures from the Chair of Psychiatry.

It is thus that Algerian doctors who are graduates of the faculty of Algiers are obliged to hear and learn that the Algerian is a born criminal. Moreover, I remember certain among us who in all sincerity upheld and developed these theories that they had learned. They even added 'It's a hard pill to swallow, but it's been scientifically established.'

The North African is a criminal; his predatory instinct is well known; his intense aggressivity is visible to the naked eye. The North African likes extremes, so we can never entirely trust him. Today he is the best of friends, tomorrow the worst of enemies. He is insensible to shades of meaning, and Cartesianism is fundamentally foreign to him; the sense of balance, the weighing and pondering of an opinion or action clashes with his most intimate nature. The North African is a violent person, of a hereditary violence. We find him incapable of self-discipline, or of canalizing his impulses. Yes, the Algerian is a congenital impulsive.

But we must be precise. This impulsiveness is largely aggressive and generally homicidal. It is in this fashion that we come to explain the unorthodox behaviour of the Algerian who is a prey to melancholia. The French psychiatrists in Algeria found themselves faced with a difficult problem. They were accustomed when dealing with a patient subject to melancholia to fear that he would commit suicide. Now the melancholic Algerian takes to killing. This illness of the moral consciousness, which is always accompanied by auto-accusation and auto-destructive tendencies, took on in the case of Algerians hetero-destructive forms. The melancholic Algerian does not commit suicide. He kills. This is the homicidal melancholia which has been thoroughly studied by Professor Porot in the thesis of his pupil Monserrat.

How did the Algerian school deal with such an anomaly? First, said the school of Algiers, killing oneself is a turning into and against oneself; it implies looking at oneself; it means practising introspection. Now the Algerian is not given to an inner life. There is no inner life where the North African is concerned. On the contrary, the North African gets rid of his worries by throwing himself on the people who surrounded him. He does not analyse. Since by definition melancholia is an illness of the moral conscience it is clear that the Algerian can only develop pseudo-melancholia, since the precariousness of his conscience and the feebleness of his moral sense are well known. This incapacity on the part of the Algerian to analyse a situation and to organize a mental panorama are perfectly understandable if we refer to the two classes of causality set forth by French writers.

First we must notice intellectual aptitudes. The Algerian is strongly marked by mental debility. If we are to really understand this datum we must go back to the semiology established by the Algerian school of psychiatry. The native, it is stated by them, presents the following characteristics:

Complete or almost complete lack of emotivity.

Credulous and susceptible in the extreme.

Persistent obstinacy.

Mental puerility, without the spirit of curiosity found in the Western child.

Tendency to accidents and pithiatic reactions.*

The Algerian does not see the whole of a question. The questions he asks himself always concern the details and exclude all synthesis. He is a pointillist, clinging to objects, lost in details, insensible to ideas and impervious to concepts. Verbal expression is reduced to a minimum. His actions are always impulsive and aggressive. He is incapable of grasping detail when looking at the whole, and he absolutizes the element and takes the part for the whole. Thus, he will have total reactions when confronted with particular incitements and with insignificant causes such as a fig-tree, a gesture, or a sheep on his land. His congenital aggressivity finds ways of expressing itself on the slightest pretext. It is a state of aggressivity in its purest form.†

---

* Professor A. Porot, *Medico-psychological Annals*, 1918.

† In the mouth of the Doyen of the judges of a court of Algeria, this aggressivity on the part of the Algerian is expressed by his love of the 'fantastic'. 'We are wrong', he stated in 1955, 'in believing this whole revolt to

Leaving the descriptive stage, the Algiers school begins on that of explanation. It was in 1935 at the Congress of Mental Specialists and Neurologists that Professor Porot defined the scientific bases of his theory. In the discussion that followed the report by Baruk on hysteria, he pointed out that 'the native of North Africa, whose superior and cortical activities are only slightly developed, is a primitive creature whose life, essentially vegetative and instinctive, is above all regulated by his diencephalon'.

In order to estimate the importance of this discovery of Professor Porot's, we should remember that the characteristic of the human species when compared to other vertebrates is that it is corticalized. The diencephalon is one of the most primitive parts of the brain and man is above all the vertebrate in which the cortex dominates.

For Professor Porot, the life of the native of North Africa is dominated by diencephalic urges. It is as much as to say that in a way the native North African is deprived of a cortex. Professor Porot does not shrink from this contradiction and in April 1939 in the *Southern Medical and Surgical Gazette* he states precisely, in collaboration with his pupil Sutter who is at present professor of psychiatry in Algiers: 'Primitivism is not a lack of maturity nor a marked stoppage in the development of the intellectual psychism. It is a social condition which has reached the limit of its evolution; it is logically adopted to a life different from ours.'

This primitivism is not merely a way of living which is the result of a special upbringing; it has much deeper roots. We even consider that it must have its substratum in a particular predisposition of the architectonic structure, or at least in the dynamic hierarchization of the nervous centres. We are in the presence of a coherent body of comportment and of a coherent life which can be explained scientifically. The Algerian has no cortex: or, more precisely, he is dominated, like the inferior vertebrates, by the diencephalon. The cortical functions,

---

be political. From time to time that love of a scrimmage that they have has to come out!' For the ethnologist, the establishment of a series of tests and projective games which would have canalized the global aggressive instincts of the native would have had in 1955–6 the power to bring the revolution in Aurès to an end.

if they exist at all, are very feeble, and are practically unintegrated into the dynamic of existence.

There is thus neither mystery nor paradox. The hesitation of the colonist in giving responsibility to the native is not racism nor paternalism, but quite simply a scientific appreciation of the biologically limited possibilities of the native.

Let us end this review by seeking for a summing-up which takes the whole of Africa for its field from Dr A. Carothers, an expert from the World Health Organization. This international expert brought together the essentials of his observations in a book which was published in 1954.*

Dr Carothers's work was carried on in Central and East Africa, but his conclusions form a group with those of the North-African school. For in fact the international expert states: 'The African makes very little use of his frontal lobes. All the particularities of African psychiatry can be put down to frontal laziness.'†

In order to make his point clearer, Dr Carothers establishes a lively comparison. He puts forward the idea that the normal African is a 'lobotomized European'. We know that the Anglo-Saxon school believed that they had found a radical cure for certain serious forms of mental illness by practising the section of an important part of the brain. Since then, however, the establishment of the fact that this method seriously impaired the personality has led to its being abandoned. According to Dr Carothers, the likeness existing between the normal African native and the lobotomized European is striking.

Dr Carothers, having studied the works of different authors working in Africa, offers us a conclusion which is the basis of a uniform conception of the African. He writes: 'Such are the given facts of the case which do not concern European categories. They have been gathered in different regions of East, West and South Africa, and on the whole each author had little or no knowledge of the work of the others. The essential similarity of these researches is therefore quite remarkable.'‡

We should point out before concluding that Dr Carothers

* Carothers: *Normal and Pathological Psychology of the African. Ethno-psychiatric Studies.* Ed. Masson.

† Op. cit., p. 176.   ‡ Op. cit., p. 178.

defined the Mau-Mau revolt as the expression of an unconscious frustration complex whose re-occurrence could be scientifically avoided by spectaclar psychological adaptations.

So it was that unusual behaviour – the African's frequent criminality, the triviality of his motives, the murderous and always very bloody nature of brawls – raised a problem in observers' minds. The proposed explanation, which has come to be taught as a subject in the universities, seems in the last analysis to be the following: the lay-out of the cerebral structures of the North African are responsible both for the native's laziness, for his intellectual and social inaptitude and for his almost animal impulsivity. The criminal impulses of the North African are the transcription into the nature of his behaviour of a given arrangement of the nervous system. It is a reaction which is neurologically understandable and written into the nature of things, of *the thing* which is biologically organized. The lack of integration of the frontal lobes in the cerebral dynamic is the explanation of the African's laziness, of his crimes, his robberies, his rapes and his lies. It was a sub-prefect who has now become a prefect who voiced the conclusion to me: 'We must counter these natural creatures,' he said, 'who obey the laws of their nature blindly, with a strict, relentless ruling class. We must tame nature, not convince it.' Discipline, training, mastering and today pacifying are the words most frequently used by the colonialists in occupied territories.

If we have spent a long time in going over the theories held by colonialist scientists, it was less with the intention of showing their poverty and absurdity than of raising a very important theoretical and practical problem. In fact, Algerian criminality only represented a sub-section of the questions which were raised by the Revolution, which could be reasoned out on the level of political discussion and de-mystification. But it so happens that the talks which formed the subject of this theme were so fruitful that they allowed us to understand and discern more deeply the idea of social and individual liberation. When in revolutionary practice the question of Algerian criminality is raised in the presence of leaders and militants, when the average figures of crimes, misdemeanours and robberies are cited for the period before the Revolution, when it is explained that the nature of a crime or the frequency of offences depend on the relations which exist between men and women and between persons and the state, and when everybody understands this; when we see before us the breaking-up of the idea of the Algerian or the North African who is a criminal by vocation, an idea which was equally implanted into the consciousness of the Algerian because after all 'we're a quick-tempered, rowdy, bad lot; that's the way it is': then it can be said for sure that the Revolution is making progress.

The important theoretical problem is that it is necessary at all times and in all places to make explicit, to demystify, and to harry the insult to mankind that exists in oneself. There must be no waiting until the nation has produced new men; there must be no waiting until men are imperceptibly transformed by revolutionary processes in perpetual renewal. It is quite true that these two processes are essential, but consciousness must be helped. The application of revolutionary theory, if it is to be completely liberating and particularly fruitful, exacts that nothing unusual should exist. One feels with particular force the necessity to totalize the event, to draw everything after one, to settle everything, to be responsible for everything. Now conscience no longer boggles at going back into the past, or at marking time if it is necessary. This is why in the progress made by a fighting unit over a piece of ground the end of an ambush does not mean rest, but rather is the signal for consciousness to take another step forward, for everything ought to keep pace together.

Yes, the Algerian of his own accord accepts the verdict of the magistrates and the policemen.* So we had to take this Algerian criminality which was experienced on the narcissistic level as a manifestation of authentic virility, and place the problem on the level of colonial history. For example, we had to show that the criminal tendencies of Algerians in France differed

* It is moreover clear that this identification with the image picture produced by the European was very ambivalent. In fact the European seemed to be paying homage – an equally ambivalent homage – to the violent, passionate, brutal, jealous, proud, arrogant Algerian who stakes his life on a detail or on a word. We should point out in passing that in their dealings with the French of France, the Europeans of Algeria tend to identify themselves more and more with this image of the Algerian in opposition to the French.

fundamentally from those of the Algerians who were submitted to exploitation which was directly colonial.

A second thing ought to be noticed: in Algeria, Algerian criminality takes place in practice inside a closed circle. The Algerians rob each other, cut each other up and kill each other. In Algeria, the Algerian rarely attacks Frenchmen, and avoids brawls with the French. In France, on the other hand, the emigrant creates an intersocial and intergroup criminality.

In France, Algerian criminality is diminishing. It is directed especially at the French, and its motives are radically new. A certain paradox has helped us considerably in demystifying the militants: it has been established that since 1954 crimes in common law have almost disappeared. There are no more disputes and no longer any insignificant details which entail the death of a man. There are no longer explosive outbursts of rage because my wife's forehead or her left shoulder were seen by my neighbour. The national conflict seems to have canalized all anger, and nationalized all affective or emotional movements. The French judges and barristers had already observed this; but the militant had to be made conscious of it; he had to be brought to understand the reasons for it.

It remains for us to give the explanation.

Should it be said that war, that privileged expression of an aggressivity which is at last made social, canalizes in the direction of the occupying power all congenitally murderous acts? It is a commonplace that great social upheavals lessen the frequency of delinquency and mental disorders. This regression of Algerian criminality can thus be perfectly explained by the existence of a war which broke Algeria in two, and threw on to the side of the enemy the judicial and administrative machine.

But in the countries of the Magrab which have already been liberated this same phenomenon which was noticed during the conflicts for liberation continues to exist and even becomes more marked once independence is proclaimed. It would therefore seem that the colonial context is sufficiently original to give grounds for a reinterpretation of the causes of criminality. This is what we did for those on active service. Today every one of us knows that criminality is not the consequence of the hereditary character of the Algerian, nor of the organization of his

nervous system. The Algerian war, like all wars of national
liberation bring to the fore the true protagonists. In the colonial
context, as we have already pointed out, the natives fight
among themselves. They tend to use each other as a screen,
and each hides from his neighbour the national enemy. When,
tired out after a hard sixteen-hour day the native sinks down to
rest on his mat, and a child on the other side of the canvas
partition starts crying and prevents him from sleeping, it so
happens that it is a little Algerian. When he goes to beg for a
little semolina or a drop of oil from the grocer, to whom he
already owes some hundreds of francs, and when he sees that
he is refused, an immense feeling of hatred and an overpowering
desire to kill rises within him: and the grocer is an Algerian.
When, after having kept out of his way for weeks he finds himself one day cornered by the *caid* who demands that he should
pay 'his taxes', he cannot even enjoy the luxury of hating a
European administrator; there before him is the *caid* who is the
object of his hatred – and the *caid* is an Algerian.

The Algerian, exposed to temptations to commit murder
every day – famine, eviction from his room because he has
not paid the rent, the mother's dried-up breasts, children like
skeletons, the building-yard which has closed down, the unemployed that hang about the foreman like crows – the native
comes to see his neighbour as a relentless enemy. If he strikes
his bare foot against a big stone in the middle of the path,
it is a native who has placed it there; and the few olives that
he was going to pick, X—'s children have gone and eaten in
the night. For during the colonial period in Algeria and elsewhere many things may be done for a couple of pounds of
semolina. Several people may be killed over it. You need to
use your imagination to understand that: your imagination,
or your memory. In the concentration camps men killed each
other for a bit of bread. I remember one horrible scene. It was
in Oran in 1944. From the camp where we were waiting to
embark, soldiers were throwing bits of bread to little Algerian
children who fought for them among themselves with anger and
hate. Veterinary doctors can throw light on such problems by
reminding us of the well-known 'pecking order' which has been
observed in farmyards. The corn which is thrown to the hens is

in fact the object of relentless competition. Certain birds, the strongest, gobble up all the grains while others who are less aggressive grow visibly thinner. Every colony tends to turn into a huge farmyard, where the only law is that of the knife.

In Algeria since the beginning of the war of National Liberation, everything has changed. The whole foodstocks of a family or a *mechta*** may in a single evening be given to a passing company. The family's only donkey may be lent to transport a wounded fighter; and when a few days later the owner learns of the death of his animal which has been machine-gunned by an aeroplane, he will not begin threatening and swearing. He will not question the death of his donkey, but he will ask anxiously if the wounded man is safe and sound.

Under the colonial regime, anything may be done for a loaf of bread or a miserable sheep. The relations of man with matter, within the world outside and with history are in the colonial period simply relations with food. For a colonized man, in a contest of oppression like that of Algeria, living does not mean embodying moral values or taking his place in the coherent and fruitful development of the world. To live means to keep on existing. Every date is a victory: not the result of work, but a victory felt as a triumph for life. Thus to steal dates or to allow one's sheep to eat the neighbour's grass is not a question of the negation of the property of others, nor the transgression of a law, nor lack of respect. These are attempts at murder. In order to understand that a robbery is not an illegal or an unfriendly action, but an attempt at murder, one must have seen in Kabylia men and women for weeks at a time going to get earth at the bottom of the valley and bringing it up in little baskets. The fact is that the only perspective is that belly which is more and more sunken, which is certainly less and less demanding, but which must be contented all the same. Who is going to take the punishment? The French are down in the plain with the police, the army and the tanks. On the mountain there are only Algerians. Up above there is Heaven with the promise of a world beyond the grave; down below there are the French with their very concrete promises of prison, beatings-up and executions. You are forced to come up

* Mountain village in Algeria (*translator*).

against yourself. Here we discover the kernel of that hatred of self which is characteristic of racial conflicts in segregated societies.

The Algerian's criminality, his impulsivity and the violence of his murders are therefore not the consequence of the organization of his nervous system nor of a peculiar trait in his character, but the direct product of the colonial situation. The fact that the soldiers of Algeria have discussed this problem; that they are not afraid of questioning the beliefs fostered among themselves by colonialism; that they understand that each man formed the screen for his neighbour and that in reality each man committed suicide when he went for his neighbour: all these things should have primordial importance in the revolutionary conscience. Once again, the objective of the native who fights against himself is to bring about the end of domination. But he ought equally to pay attention to the liquidation of all untruths implanted in his being by oppression. Under a colonial regime such as existed in Algeria, the ideas put forward by colonialism not only influenced the European minority, but also the Algerians. Total liberation is that which concerns all sectors of the personality. The ambush or the attack, the torture or the massacre of his brothers plants more deeply the determination to win, wakes up the unwary and feeds the imagination. When the nation stirs as a whole, the new man is not an *a posteriori* product of that nation; rather, he coexists with it and triumphs with it. This dialectic requirement explains the reticence with which adaptations of colonization and reforms of the façade are met. Independence is not a word which can be used as an exorcism, but an indispensable condition for the existence of men and women who are truly liberated, in other words who are truly masters of all the material means which make possible the radical transformation of society.

6. Conclusion

COME, then, comrades; it would be as well to decide at once to change our ways. We must shake off the heavy darkness in which we were plunged, and leave it behind. The new day which is already at hand must find us firm, prudent and resolute.

We must leave our dreams and abandon our old beliefs and friendships of the time before life began. Let us waste no time in sterile litanies and nauseating mimicry. Leave this Europe where they are never done talking of Man, yet murder men everywhere they find them, at the corner of every one of their own streets, in all the corners of the globe. For centuries they have stifled almost the whole of humanity in the name of a so-called spiritual experience. Look at them today swaying between atomic and spiritual disintegration.

And yet it may be said that Europe has been successful in as much as everything that she has attempted has succeeded.

Europe undertook the leadership of the world with ardour, cynicism and violence. Look at how the shadow of her palaces stretches out ever farther! Every one of her movements has burst the bounds of space and thought. Europe has declined all humility and all modesty; but she has also set her face against all solicitude and all tenderness.

She has only shown herself parsimonious and niggardly where men are concerned; it is only men that she has killed and devoured.

So, my brothers, how is it that we do not understand that we have better things to do than to follow that same Europe?

That same Europe where they were never done talking of Man, and where they never stopped proclaiming that they were only anxious for the welfare of Man: today we know with what sufferings humanity has paid for every one of their triumphs of the mind.

Come, then, comrades, the European game has finally ended; we must find something different. We today can do everything, so long as we do not imitate Europe, so long as we are not obsessed by the desire to catch up with Europe.

Europe now lives at such a mad, reckless pace that she has shaken off all guidance and all reason, and she is running head-long into the abyss; we would do well to avoid it with all possible speed.

Yet it is very true that we need a model, and that we want blueprints and examples. For many among us the European model is the most inspiring. We have therefore seen in the preceding pages to what mortifying set-backs such an imitation has led us. European achievements, European techniques and the European style ought no longer to tempt us and to throw us off our balance.

When I search for Man in the technique and the style of Europe, I see only a succession of negations of man, and an avalanche of murders.

The human condition, plans for mankind and collaboration between men in those tasks which increase the sum total of humanity are new problems, which demand true inventions.

Let us decide not to imitate Europe; let us combine our muscles and our brains in a new direction. Let us try to create the whole man, whom Europe has been incapable of bringing to triumphant birth.

Two centuries ago, a former European colony decided to catch up with Europe. It succeeded so well that the United States of America became a monster, in which the taints, the sickness and the inhumanity of Europe have grown to appalling dimensions.

Comrades, have we not other work to do than to create a third Europe? The West saw itself as a spiritual adventure. It is in the name of the spirit, in the name of the spirit of Europe, that Europe has made her encroachments, that she has justified her crimes and legitimized the slavery in which she holds four-fifths of humanity.

Yes, the European spirit has strange roots. All European thought has unfolded in places which were increasingly more deserted and more encircled by precipices; and thus it was that the custom grew up in those places of very seldom meeting man.

A permanent dialogue with oneself and an increasingly obscene narcissism never ceased to prepare the way for a half delirious state, where intellectual work became suffering and the reality was not at all that of a living man, working and creating himself, but rather words, different combinations of words, and the tensions springing from the meanings contained in words. Yet some Europeans were found to urge the European workers to shatter this narcissism and to break with this unreality.

But in general the workers of Europe have not replied to these calls; for the workers believe, too, that they are part of the prodigious adventure of the European spirit.

All the elements of a solution to the great problems of humanity have, at different times, existed in European thought. But Europeans have not carried out in practice the mission which fell to them, which consisted of bringing their whole weight to bear violently upon these elements, of modifying their arrangement and their nature, of changing them and, finally, of bringing the problem of mankind to an infinitely higher plane.

Today, we are present at the stasis of Europe. Comrades, let us flee from this motionless movement where gradually dialectic is changing into the logic of equilibrium. Let us reconsider the question of mankind. Let us reconsider the question of cerebral reality and of the cerebral mass of all humanity, whose connexions must be increased, whose channels must be diversified and whose messages must be re-humanized.

Come, brothers, we have far too much work to do for us to play the game of rear-guard. Europe has done what she set out to do and on the whole she has done it well; let us stop blaming her, but let us say to her firmly that she should not make such a song and dance about it. We have no more to fear; so let us stop envying her.

The Third World today faces Europe like a colossal mass whose aim should be to try to resolve the problems to which Europe has not been able to find the answers.

But let us be clear: what matters is to stop talking about output, and intensification, and the rhythm of work.

No, there is no question of a return to Nature. It is simply a very concrete question of not dragging men towards mutilation, of not imposing upon the brain rhythms which very quickly obliterate it and wreck it. The pretext of catching up must not be used to push man around, to tear him away from himself or from his privacy, to break and kill him.

No, we do not want to catch up with anyone. What we want to do is to go forward all the time, night and day, in the company of Man, in the company of all men. The caravan should not be stretched out, for in that case each line will hardly see those who precede it; and men who no longer recognize each other meet less and less together, and talk to each other less and less.

It is a question of the Third World starting a new history of Man, a history which will have regard to the sometimes prodigious theses which Europe has put forward, but which will also not forget Europe's crimes, of which the most horrible was committed in the heart of man, and consisted of the pathological tearing apart of his functions and the crumbling away of his unity. And in the framework of the collectivity there were the differentiations, the stratification and the bloodthirsty tensions fed by classes; and finally, on the immense scale of humanity, there were racial hatreds, slavery, exploitation and above all the bloodless genocide which consisted in the setting aside of fifteen thousand millions of men.

So, comrades, let us not pay tribute to Europe by creating states, institutions and societies which draw their inspiration from her.

Humanity is waiting for something other from us than such an imitation, which would be almost an obscene caricature.

If we want to turn Africa into a new Europe, and America into a new Europe, then let us leave the destiny of our countries to Europeans. They will know how to do it better than the most gifted among us.

But if we want humanity to advance a step farther, if we want to bring it up to a different level than that which Europe has shown it, then we must invent and we must make discoveries.

If we wish to live up to our peoples' expectations, we must seek the response elsewhere than in Europe.

Moreover, if we wish to reply to the expectations of the people of Europe, it is no good sending them back a reflection, even an ideal reflection, of their society and their thought with which from time to time they feel immeasurably sickened.

For Europe, for ourselves and for humanity, comrades, we must turn over a new leaf, we must work out new concepts, and try to set afoot a new man.